10 Best College Majors for Your Personality

Part of JIST's Best Jobs® Series

Laurence Shatkin, Ph.D., and The Editors @ JIST

Also in JIST's *Best Jobs*® Series

- *Best Jobs for the 21st Century*
- *200 Best Jobs for College Graduates*
- *300 Best Jobs Without a Four-Year Degree*
- *250 Best Jobs Through Apprenticeships*
- *50 Best Jobs for Your Personality*
- *40 Best Fields for Your Career*
- *225 Best Jobs for Baby Boomers*

- *250 Best-Paying Jobs*
- *175 Best Jobs Not Behind a Desk*
- *150 Best Jobs for Your Skills*
- *150 Best Jobs Through Military Training*
- *150 Best Jobs for a Better World*
- *200 Best Jobs for Introverts*
- *150 Best Low-Stress Jobs*

JIST Works
America's Career Publisher®

10 Best College Majors for Your Personality

© 2008 by JIST Publishing

Published by JIST Works, an imprint of JIST Publishing
7321 Shadeland Station, Suite 200
Indianapolis, IN 46256-3923

Phone: 800-648-JIST   Fax: 877-454-7839
E-mail: info@jist.com   Web site: www.jist.com

Some Other Books by the Authors

The Editors at JIST

EZ Occupational Outlook Handbook
Salary Facts Handbook
Enhanced Occupational Outlook Handbook
Health-Care CareerVision Book and DVD
Business CareerVision Book and DVD
Guide to America's Federal Jobs

Laurence Shatkin

90-Minute College Major Matcher
Best Jobs series
Today's Hot Job Targets

Quantity discounts are available for JIST products. Have future editions of JIST books automatically delivered to you on publication through our convenient standing order program. Please call 800-648-JIST or visit www.jist.com for a free catalog and more information.

Visit www.jist.com for information on JIST, free job search information, tables of contents and sample pages, and ordering information on our many products.

Acquisitions Editor: Susan Pines
Development Editor: Stephanie Koutek
Cover and Interior Designer: Aleata Halbig
Cover Image: Todd Davidson, Stock Illustration Source, Getty Images
Interior Layout: Aleata Halbig
Proofreaders: Linda Seifert, Jeanne Clark
Indexer: Marilyn Augst

Printed in the United States of America

13 12 11 10 09 08   9 8 7 6 5 4 3 2 1

Library of Congress Cataloging-in-Publication Data

10 best college majors for your personality / the Editors at JIST and Laurence Shatkin.
    p. cm.
Includes index.
ISBN 978-1-59357-547-2 (alk. paper)
1. College majors--United States. 2. Vocational guidance--United States. I. Shatkin, Laurence. II. JIST Works, Inc.
III. Title: Ten best college majors for your personality.
LB2361.5.A13 2008
378.2'41--dc22

2008000846

ISBN 978-1-59357-547-2

This Is a Big Book, But It Is Very Easy to Use

Psychologists often use the concept of *personality* as a convenient way of summarizing many characteristics of a person. It can be especially useful when you're making decisions about your education and your career.

What kind of personality do *you* have? Forget about common labels such as "happy-go-lucky," "dependable," "even-tempered," "friendly," or "funny." These might help you get a date on Saturday night, but they're not much help in choosing a college major.

That's where this book can help. Learn about the personality types that many psychologists and guidance practitioners use to describe people, college majors, and careers. Take a quick assessment to help you clarify your dominant personality type. Then dig into a gold mine of facts about the college majors that are the best fit for your personality type—and that are the best for other reasons, such as their potential for income and job openings. Lists of "best majors" will suggest promising majors that you may never have considered. Turn to the descriptive profiles of the majors to learn what courses to expect, what specializations you may choose from, and what jobs may be open to you when you graduate. Get detailed facts about these jobs, based on the latest government data.

You're probably expecting college to improve your earning potential. So why not find a major that suits your personality *and* has outstanding economic potential? This book can show you the way.

Some Things You Can Do with This Book

- ◎ Explore and select a college major that relates to a career objective that suits your personality.
- ◎ Learn about college majors that previously were unfamiliar to you.
- ◎ Understand what majors are good preparation for a career you already have in mind.
- ◎ Learn key facts about jobs that may be a good fit for your personality.

These are a few of the many ways you can use this book. We hope you find it as interesting to browse as we did to put together. We have tried to make it easy to use and as interesting as possible.

When you are done with this book, pass it along or tell someone else about it. We wish you well in your education, in your career, and in your life.

Credits and Acknowledgments: While the authors created this book, it is based on the work of many others. The occupational information is based on data obtained from the U.S. Department of Labor and the U.S. Census Bureau. These sources provide the most authoritative occupational information available. The noneconomic job-related information is from the O*NET database, which was developed by researchers and developers under the direction of the U.S. Department of Labor. They, in turn, were assisted by thousands of employers who provided details on the nature of work in the many thousands of job samplings used in the database's development. We used the most recent version of the O*NET database, release 12. We appreciate and thank the staff of the U.S. Department of Labor for their efforts and expertise in providing such a rich source of data. The taxonomy of college majors (the Classification of Instructional Programs) is from the U.S. Department of Education.

Table of Contents

Summary of Major Sections

Introduction. A short overview to help you better understand and use the book. *Starts on page 1.*

Part I. Your Personality and Your Major. Provides an overview of personality and of personality types. This section also explores the relationship between personality and college majors. *Starts on page 13.*

Part II. What's Your Personality Type? Take An Assessment. Helps you discover your personality type with a short, easy-to-complete assessment. *Starts on page 17.*

Part III. The Best Majors Lists. Very useful for exploring college majors! Lists are arranged into easy-to-use groups based on personality types. The first group of lists presents the 10 best majors for each personality type. Other lists identify, for each personality type, majors linked to jobs with the highest earnings, the fastest job growth, and the most job openings. More-specialized lists follow, ranking majors related to jobs by education level, majors linked to best jobs by worker demographics, and majors that prepare for jobs requiring either high or low math and verbal skills. The column starting at right presents all the list titles. *Starts on page 27.*

Part IV. Descriptions of the Best College Majors for Your Personality. Provides complete descriptions of the majors that appear on the lists in Part III, plus five related majors. Each description contains information on specializations and college and high school courses, plus definitions and key facts for related jobs. *Starts on page 79.*

Appendix A. Resources for Further Exploration. *Starts on page 269.*

Appendix B. Majors Sorted by Three-Letter Personality Code. *Starts on page 271.*

Appendix C. The GOE Interest Areas and Work Groups. *Starts on page 273.*

Appendix D. Definitions of Skills Used in Descriptions of Majors. *Starts on page 279.*

Appendix E. Definitions of Values Used in Descriptions of Majors. *Starts on page 283.*

Detailed Table of Contents

Introduction

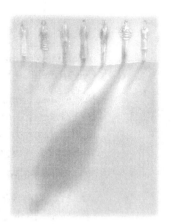

Choosing a major can be scary. It's not a simple either/or decision, like choosing a car with either stick shift or automatic. It means a commitment of several years and, in most cases, a great amount of money. Although it's a personal decision, your friends and relatives will probably feel free to second-guess it. How can you sort out all of the possible choices and pick one that's right for you?

This book can help. It won't *tell* you what to do, but it will guide you to the information you need to make an intelligent choice—information about yourself, about majors, and about careers.

Many successful careers begin with an associate (two-year) degree, but workers with a bachelor's have 33 percent higher earnings and 30 percent less unemployment, so this book focuses on majors that require four or more years of education beyond high school.

Factors to Consider When You Choose a Major

When you're trying to choose a major, a good place to start is to think about why you're going to college at all. Some people have trivial reasons for going to college, and choosing a major is easy for them. For example, if you're going to college because all of your friends are going, then choose the same major that your best friends chose. If you're going because you think that's where the really cool social scene is, study whatever's easiest for you so your coursework won't interfere with your social life.

But most people who go to college have a more important reason: making themselves more employable in the future. They view college as an investment of time and money that will pay off through future employment opportunities. Whether they are planning for a specific job goal or a general area of employment, they expect that a college degree will result in higher earnings and less time spent unemployed. And they're right about this. In fact, the economic value of a college education continues to grow.

Therefore, an important factor to consider when you choose a college major is the **potential economic rewards of the major**. Different majors promise different earnings and job opportunities. This book can help with your decision because it ranks majors in terms of their

1

potential economic rewards, based on the latest information available from the U.S. Department of Labor.

But money alone can't buy happiness. It would not be wise to decide on how to invest the time, money, and energy you're devoting to college simply by selling them to the highest bidder. Instead, you should consider the following additional factors when you think about choosing a college major:

- What majors are **interesting** to you?
- What majors are consistent with your **skills**?
- What majors match your preferences for **styles and locations of learning**?

This is a lot to consider, but fortunately there is a shortcut that can summarize these various noneconomic factors: **personality**. Career professionals and academic advisors often use an analysis of personality that focuses on six major types, referred to by the six-letter abbreviation RIASEC. Developed by occupational researcher John Holland, RIASEC stands for the personality types that he identified: Realistic, Investigative, Artistic, Social, Enterprising, and Conventional. (Part I discusses this scheme in detail.) Once you identify your personality type and match it to college majors, as this book will help you do, you can identify majors that suit your interests, your skills, and how and where you enjoy learning.

How to Use This Book

This is a book that you can dive right into:

- **If you don't know much about what personality types are,** you'll want to read Part I, which is an overview of the theory behind using personality types as a way of making choices about college majors and careers. You'll also see definitions of the six personality types that are used in this book.

- **If you want to understand your own personality type,** you'll want to do the assessment in Part II. It takes only 20 or 30 minutes to complete and can guide you to majors that suit you.

- **If you like lists and want an easy way to compare majors,** you should turn to Part III. Here you can browse lists showing the 10 majors for each personality type that are linked to jobs with the best pay, the fastest growth, and the most job openings. You can see these "best majors" broken down in various ways, such as by amount of education required.

- **For detailed information about majors,** turn to Part IV and read the profiles of the majors. We include 46 majors and itemize their specializations, their course requirements, characteristics of related jobs, and other facts that go beyond what you can learn from the lists in Part III. Because the descriptions are organized by personality type, you may find it helpful to browse within a section that fits you and become acquainted with unfamiliar majors that may deserve consideration. The information about related jobs may also open your eyes to options that are new to you.

On the other hand, if you like to do things in a methodical way, you may want to read the sections in order:

- ☉ Part I will give you useful background on **how personality type can be a guide** in choosing a major and career.

- ☉ The assessment in Part II will help you **identify your dominant personality type.**

- ☉ With a clearer understanding of your personality type, you can **browse the appropriate lists of "best majors"** in Part III and take notes on the majors that have the greatest appeal for you. If you find yourself bordering between two personality types, as many people do (for example, Investigative and Artistic), you may look at the lists for both types or turn to Appendix B for a complete list of majors by three-letter (primary and secondary) codes.

- ☉ Then you can **look up the descriptions of these majors** in Part IV and narrow down your list. Ask yourself, Do the required courses interest me? Do the related jobs look rewarding? Can I handle the amount of education that these jobs will require?

Of course, no single book can tell you everything you need to know about college majors and careers. That's why you will probably want to confirm your tentative choices by using some of the resources listed in Appendix A. Other appendixes will help you understand some of the terms used in the Part IV descriptions.

Where the Information Came From

Because this book is about both college majors and the jobs they are related to, it uses information from a variety of sources.

The Classification of Instructional Programs, developed by the U.S. Department of Education, provided a standard title and definition for each major.

The information for the "Typical Sequence of College Courses" is derived from research in actual college catalogs. The courses are those that appeared in several catalogs and were commonly required for the majors. The number of courses listed often varies. Some majors have fairly standard requirements that can be listed in detail; in some cases, a professional association mandates that certain courses be included. For other majors, notably the interdisciplinary subjects (such as Humanities or American Studies, which straddle several departments), requirements are either so minimal or so varied that it is difficult to list more than a handful of typical courses.

The "Typical Sequence of High School Courses" sections are based on a general understanding of which high school courses are considered prerequisites for the college-level courses required by the major.

You should be aware that course requirements and prerequisites for majors vary widely from one college to another. The descriptions outline average requirements, but before you declare a major you need to be aware of *all* the courses that your college (or your intended college) requires. For example, most colleges do not require a course in thermodynamics as part of their bachelor's degree program in electrical engineering. However, Georgia Tech does, and so do some other colleges. Some colleges require *all* students to take certain core courses in writing, public speaking, math, or religion, and these core courses often are not reflected in this book's descriptions of majors.

The job-related information came from databases and books created by the U.S. Department of Labor and the U.S. Census Bureau. The definition, work tasks, personality (RIASEC) types, skills (including verbal and math), values, and work conditions are derived from the Department of Labor's O*NET (Occupational Information Network) database, which is now the primary source of detailed information on occupations. The Labor Department updates the O*NET on a regular basis, and we used the most recent one available—O*NET release 12.

The information about earnings; growth; number of openings; and workers who are part-time, self-employed, male, and female is based on figures from the U.S. Bureau of Labor Statistics (BLS) and the U.S. Census Bureau.

As you look at the economic and demographic figures, keep in mind that they are estimates. They give you a general idea about the number of workers employed, annual earnings, rate of job growth, annual job openings, and composition of the workforce.

When you see these figures, you may sometimes wonder how to interpret them: Is $60,000 a good yearly salary? Is 15 percent job growth considered slow or fast? What number of job openings represents a good job market? It helps to compare these figures for any one occupation to the national averages. For all workers in all occupations, the median earnings (half earned more and half less) were $30,400 in May 2006. For the 88 occupations linked to the majors included in this book, the average earnings were about $70,000. (This is a weighted average of the median earnings for the jobs, which means that jobs with bigger workforces were given greater weight. It is also not precise, because we lack accurate earnings figures for Actors, whose income is irregular, and for certain highly paid jobs, such as Anesthesiologists, whose income is reported only as "more than $145,600.") The average projected job growth for all jobs over the 10-year period ending 2014 is 13.0 percent, but for the 88 occupations in this book, the average is 22.8 percent.

For the 762 occupations for which job-opening figures are available from the Bureau of Labor Statistics, the average number of job openings each year is about 69,000, whereas for the 88 occupations in this book, the average is about 28,000. If that difference surprises you, think about what you find when you read the help-wanted advertisements. Most of the jobs require considerably less than a bachelor's degree, but most of them also are not as rewarding or fulfilling as you want; that's why you're reading this book.

When you see figures in this book describing jobs, remember that they always describe an average and therefore have limitations. Just as there is no precisely average person, there is no such thing as a statistically average example of a particular job. We say this because data, while helpful, can also be misleading.

Take, for example, the yearly earnings information about related jobs in this book. This is highly reliable data obtained from a very large U.S. working population sample by the Bureau of Labor Statistics. It tells us the median annual pay received in May 2006 by people in various job titles.

This sounds great, except that half of all people in that occupation earned less than that amount. For example, people who are new to the occupation or with only a few years of work experience often earn much less than the median amount. People who live in rural areas or who work for smaller employers typically earn less than those who do similar work in cities (where the cost of living is higher) or for bigger employers. People in certain areas of the country earn less than those in others. Other factors also influence how much you are likely to earn in a given job in your area. For example, dentists in the New York metropolitan area earn an average of $125,880 per year, whereas dentists in four metropolitan areas in North Carolina earn an average of more than $137,050 per year. Although the cost of living tends to be higher in the New York area, North Carolina has only one dentistry school, and therefore dentists there experience less competition for patients and can command higher fees. So you can see that many factors can cause earnings to vary widely.

Also keep in mind that the figures for job growth and number of openings are projections by labor economists—their best guesses about what we can expect between now and 2014. They are not guarantees. A major economic downturn, war, or technological breakthrough could change the actual outcome.

Finally, don't forget that the job market consists of both job openings and job seekers. The figures on job growth and openings don't tell you how many people will be competing with you to be hired. The Department of Labor does not publish figures on the supply of job candidates, so we are unable to tell you about the level of competition you can expect. Competition is an important issue that you should research for any tentative career goal. In some cases the _Occupational Outlook Handbook_ provides informative statements. You should speak to people who educate or train tomorrow's workers; they probably have a good idea of how many of their graduates find rewarding employment and how quickly. People in the workforce also can provide insights into this issue. Use your critical thinking skills to evaluate what people tell you. For example, recruiters for training programs are highly motivated to get you to sign up, whereas people in the workforce may be trying to discourage you from competing. Get a variety of opinions to balance out possible biases.

So, in reviewing the information in this book, please understand the limitations of the data. You need to use common sense in making decisions about education and careers as in most other things in life. We hope that, using that approach, you find the information helpful and interesting.

How the Majors in This Book Were Selected

Study the catalog or Web site of any large university and you'll find dozens of majors listed. We wanted to save you time by identifying the best commonly offered majors associated with each personality type.

Here is the procedure we followed to select the 41 majors (10 for each personality type, with some appearing on multiple lists) that we included in the lists in this book:

1. We began with the descriptions of 120 college majors that were developed for an earlier book, *90-Minute College Major Matcher* (JIST Publishing). These covered the most commonly offered programs. We matched these 120 majors to O*NET occupations by using the recommended matches made by the National Center for O*NET Development, with one slight modification: We removed the postsecondary teaching jobs. Theoretically, students in any major can go on to teach the subject in college—for example, some Electrical Engineering majors aspire to do what their professors are doing rather than work in the industry—but this number is difficult to determine and usually quite small, so it made more sense to create the pseudo-major "Graduate Study for College Teaching" as an option for those who want to use their education for that career goal. Another problem with the match-ups made by the National Center for O*NET Development is the abundance of postsecondary teaching jobs. O*NET includes 36 postsecondary teaching jobs, but job-outlook information is available only for a single job that combines them all (Postsecondary Teachers). Therefore, the job we linked to "Graduate Study for College Teaching" is the combined occupation Postsecondary Teachers.

2. O*NET provides two kinds of information on RIASEC personality types: It identifies the dominant RIASEC type or types for every job and it gives every job a numerical rating on all six RIASEC types. When a major was linked to a single job, we used the dominant RIASEC type or types that O*NET assigned to the related job. When a major was linked to more than one job, we averaged the numerical ratings of each of the six RIASEC types for all of the related jobs. (We determined a weighted average, which means that jobs with bigger workforces were given greater weight in the calculations.) Our rules were that if the second-highest-rated RIASEC type was rated at more than 70 percent of the highest, we used both highest-rated types, and if the second-highest type passed this test *and* the third-highest type was rated at more than 75 percent of the highest, we used the three highest-rated types. These rules approximated the approach used by O*NET to identify the top RIASEC type(s) for occupations.

3. We used the first one or two types to create preliminary lists of majors for ranking. For example, Industrial Design is rated as Artistic and was put on the list of Artistic majors. Public Administration has two top-rated personality types, Enterprising and

Conventional, and therefore was put on two lists. Human Resources Management is described by three personality types—Enterprising, Social, and Conventional—but it appears on the lists of majors for only its two highest-rated types, Enterprising and Social.

4. To be able to sort these preliminary lists, we computed the economic potential of each major by assembling economic information about the jobs related to majors: the annual earnings, the job growth projected for a 10-year period ending in 2014, and the number of job openings expected annually during that same time span. When more than one job was linked to a major, we computed a weighted average for earnings and job growth in related jobs and computed the *total* number of annual openings in related jobs.

5. We ranked the majors in each of the six lists in three different ways: by earning potential, by potential job growth, and by potential job openings. We then added the numerical ranks for each major in each list to produce an overall score. To emphasize majors leading to jobs with the best economic rewards, we selected the 10 majors from each list with the best numerical scores. These majors are the focus of this book. Because some majors appeared on two lists, the total number of unique majors was 41 rather than 60.

For example, International Business is the Conventional major with the best combined score for earnings, growth, and number of job openings—based on the two related jobs Chief Executives and General and Operations Managers. Therefore, International Business is listed first in our "10 Best Conventional Majors" list even though it is not the Conventional major with the best earning potential (which is International Relations), the best potential for job growth (which is Pharmacy), or the best potential for job openings (which is Business Management).

All 41 of these majors appear not only on the lists in Part III of this book but also in the descriptions in Part IV. Five additional majors are described in Part IV but could not be included in the Part III lists because they are not linked to any particular job except college teaching, which is already represented in the lists by the pseudo-major Graduate Study for College Teaching. For example, American Studies is one such major that appears in Part IV but not in Part III. People with a degree in this subject sometimes go on to careers in law, marketing, or politics, but this major is not the obvious one to link to these jobs, so it would be a mistake to calculate the economic rewards of the major on the basis of these or any other jobs. On the other hand, American Studies is a popular major and could be combined with postgraduate study in law, social work, library science, or several other fields covered by this book, so we decided that this major and four others—African-American Studies, Area Studies, Humanities, and Women's Studies—should be included in the Part IV descriptions. Thus a total of 46 majors are described in this book.

A Sample Description of a Major

The 46 descriptions of majors in this book all have the same data elements. Following is a sample, together with explanations of how to interpret the information.

Title ⟶ ## Drama/Theater Arts

Personality Type ⟶ **Personality Type:** Artistic–Enterprising–Social

Useful Facts About the Major ⟶ ### Useful Facts About the Major

Focuses on the general study of dramatic works and their performance.

Related CIP Program ⟶ **Related CIP Program:** 50.0501 Drama and Dramatics/Theatre Arts, General

Specializations in the Major ⟶ **Specializations in the Major:** Acting; design and technology; directing.

Typical Sequence of College Courses ⟶ **Typical Sequence of College Courses:** English composition, foreign language, history of theater, acting technique, dramatic literature, performance techniques, theater technology (e.g., set/costume/lighting), theater practicum.

Typical Sequence of High School Courses ⟶ **Typical Sequence of High School Courses:** English, foreign language, literature, public speaking.

Career Snapshot ⟶ ### Career Snapshot

Drama is one of the most ancient art forms and continues to entertain audiences today. As in all performing arts, there are better opportunities for teachers than for performers. Teaching at the postsecondary level usually requires a master's degree. The technical aspects of theater—set design, lighting, costume design, and makeup—also offer jobs for nonperformers. The academic program includes many opportunities to learn through student performances.

Useful Averages for the Related Jobs ⟶ ### Useful Averages for the Related Jobs

- **Annual Earnings:** $56,310
- **Growth:** 16.4%
- **Self-Emp~ ~ ~:** 30.4%

- **Part-Time:** 23.3%
- **Verbal Skill Rating:** 66.0
- **Math Skill Rating:** 35.9

Other Details About the Related Jobs

Total Annual Job Openings: 22,000

Interest Area: 03 Arts and Communication ⟵ Interest Area

Skills—Management of personnel resources; ⟵ Skills
speaking; time management; monitoring; active listening; social perceptiveness. **Values**— ⟵ Values
Authority; creativity; ability utilization; autonomy; recognition; responsibility. **Work** ⟵ Work Conditions
Conditions—Indoors, environmentally controlled; sitting.

Related Jobs ⟵ Related Jobs

1. Actors

Personality Type: Artistic–Enterprising–Social

Earnings: No data available
Growth: 16.1%
Annual Openings: 11,000

Most Common Education/Training Level: Long-term on-the-job training

Play parts in stage, television, radio, video, or motion picture productions for entertainment, information, or instruction. Interpret serious or comic role by speech, gesture, and body movement to entertain or inform audience. May dance and sing. Study and rehearse roles from scripts to interpret, learn, and memorize lines, stunts, and cues as directed. Work closely with directors, other actors, and playwrights to find the interpretation most suited to the role. Learn about characters in scripts and their relationships to each other to develop role interpre-
~~~~ Collaborate with other ~cto~ ~ as p~ ~ of

Here are some details on each of the major parts of the descriptions you will find in Part IV:

- ◎ Title—This is a commonly used title for the major. Sometimes the major may also be known under other names. For example, Humanities is sometimes called Liberal Arts.

- ◎ Personality Type—This consists of the one, two, or three RIASEC types that describe this major, based on the jobs linked to the major. If more than one type is listed, they appear in descending order of importance. Only the first one or two types are used to assign the major to the lists in Part III.

- ◎ Useful Facts About the Major—This section begins with a definition of the major derived from the Classification of Instructional Programs (CIP), a database created by the U.S. Department of Education.

- ◎ Related CIP Program—This is the title of the CIP program that provided the definition used in the previous data element.

- ◎ Specializations in the Major—These are the most commonly available concentrations that may be offered in the major. In some cases, these are job specializations rather than educational pathways.

- ◎ Typical Sequence of College Courses—These courses are ordered roughly as they might be taken to complete the major. Survey courses and introductory courses, especially in supporting disciplines (for example, a writing course within a science major) are usually ordered near the beginning, whereas specialized and advanced courses are usually ordered near the end. Some of these titles may represent multiple-semester courses or even separate courses with different names collapsed into one title.

- ◎ Typical Sequence of High School Courses—These are the courses that are most commonly expected to provide secondary-level preparation for the college major. Additional courses are required by almost all high schools and are expected for college admission.

- ◎ Career Snapshot—This is an overview of the jobs that the major leads to. It usually indicates the level of education the employers expect for new hires, as well as the job outlook.

- ◎ Useful Averages for the Related Jobs—The economic information here, as well as the Total Annual Job Openings figure, comes from various U.S. Department of Labor and Census databases for this occupation, as explained elsewhere in this introduction. The figures for verbal and math skills are derived from the O*NET database, as explained in Part III (where you'll find lists of majors that require high and low levels of these skills). Note that these skill ratings are based on the *requirements of the related jobs* and may not indicate the level of achievement necessary for admission to the major or the level of ability required for completion of the courses.

- ◎ Interest Area—This information cross-references the Guide for Occupational Exploration (the GOE), a system developed by the U.S. Department of Labor that organizes jobs based on interests. We use the groups from the *New Guide for Occupational Exploration,* as published by JIST. This book uses a set of interest areas based on the 16 career clusters developed by the U.S. Department of Education and used in a variety of career information systems. You can find the full outline of the GOE interest areas in Appendix C. Because the GOE classification of interests is more detailed than the six RIASEC personality types, it may help you identify majors that relate to your specific interests.

◉ Skills—The O*NET database provides data on many skills; we decided to list only those that were most important for the jobs related to the major rather than list pages of unhelpful details. For each major, we computed the weighted average skill ratings for all related jobs. We then identified any skill that is rated at a level higher than the average rating for that skill for all jobs and that also is not rated as an unimportant skill. If there are more than eight, we include only the eight with the highest ratings, and we present them from highest to lowest score (that is, in terms of by how much its score exceeds the average score). We include up to 10 skills if scores were tied for eighth place. If no skill has a rating higher than the average for all jobs, we say "None met the criteria." If the names of the skills are not clear to you, you can find definitions in Appendix D. Note that the skills are based on the requirements of the jobs and may not correspond exactly to the skills needed for academic success in the major.

◉ Values—These are various characteristics of jobs that many people view as beneficial. They are derived from the O*NET database and are defined in Appendix E. To identify the most important values for the jobs related to the major, we used the same method as we used for skills. Also like the skills, the values are based on the related jobs and may not be completely relevant to the experience of being in the major. For example, although a job may offer many opportunities for authority, students are seldom in positions of authority.

◉ Work Conditions—This entry, also derived from O*NET data about the related jobs, mentions aspects of the work settings that some people may want to avoid, such as exposure to loud noises or the necessity of standing for long periods of time. We determined the dominant work conditions by using the same method as we used for skills, except that the ordering of these environmental factors is not significant. Like the other work-related characteristics, the work conditions may not accurately describe the environment where the major is studied, unless the major involves a lot of workplace learning (for example, clinical practice in health-care majors).

◉ Related Jobs—The jobs described here are linked to the major according to matches made by the O*NET Development Center, with modifications as noted earlier in this introduction. The information on earnings, growth, job openings, and most common level of education or training is derived from the U.S. Department of Labor. Note that in some cases an occupation may require less education than a college degree, but graduates of the major are commonly hired into this job. For example, the job linked to Advertising is Advertising Sales Agents, which can be learned through moderate-term on-the-job training. Nevertheless, some employers prefer applicants with a college degree, particularly for sales positions that require meeting with clients, and in fact slightly over half the Advertising Sales Agents currently employed have a bachelor's degree or higher, so this is a logical career choice to link to the Advertising major. The occupations that are linked to the majors are derived from the taxonomy called Standard Occupational Classification (SOC), and usually each SOC occupation is the exact equivalent of an O*NET occupation. In those few cases where a SOC occupation corresponds to two or more O*NET occupations, the facts for the multiple O*NET occupations are listed under the heading "Job Specializations." Where necessary, statements of work tasks are edited to avoid exceeding 2,200 characters.

PART I

Your Personality and Your Major

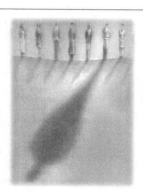

People often use the term "personality" to refer to various aspects of people they know. When describing their friends, their classmates, or even themselves, they may refer to aspects of personality such as sense of humor, optimism, ambition, irritability, or decisiveness.

Many such concepts of personality are interesting to know about a person but not very useful in helping someone decide on a college major. Fortunately, psychologists have found other aspects of personality that can be valuable to consider when making educational and career plans. In this part of the book, you'll learn about the relationship between personality and college majors, and you will gain a working understanding of the most commonly used scheme for describing personality types in this context.

Why Personality Is Useful for Choosing a Major

Personality theorists believe that people with similar personality types naturally tend to associate with one another in the workplace, the classroom, and other places. As they do so, they create an environment that is hospitable to their personality type. For example, a workplace or classroom with a lot of Artistic types tends to reward creative thinking and behavior. Therefore your personality type not only predicts how well your skills will match the demands of the tasks in a particular major or job; it also predicts how well you will fit in with the culture of the classroom or work site as shaped by the people who will surround you and interact with you. Your personality type thus is a key to career choice because it affects your satisfaction with the job, your productivity in it, and the likelihood that you will persist in this type of work. Likewise, your personality indicates which majors might be good choices for you because most college students choose their major to help advance their careers.

One of the advantages of using personality as a key to choosing a major and a career is that it is economical—it provides a tidy summary of many aspects of people, majors, and careers. Consider how knotty the decision about a major could get if you were to consider each related job and reflect on how well you might fit into each specific component of the work environment. For example, you could focus on the skills required and your ability to meet them. Next you could analyze the kinds of knowledge that are used on the job and decide how much you enjoy working with those topics. Then you could consider a broad array of satisfactions, such as variety, creativity, and independence; for each one, you would evaluate its importance to you and then determine the potential of various majors to lead to career options that could satisfy this need. You can see that, when looked at under a microscope like this, the choice of a major gets extremely complex.

But the personality-based approach allows you to view the alternatives from 40,000 feet. When you compare yourself or a major to certain basic personality types, you encounter much less complexity. With fewer ideas and facts to sort through and consider, the task of deciding becomes much easier.

The RIASEC Personality Types

During the 1950s, the career guidance researcher John Holland was trying to find a meaningful new way to arrange the output of an interest inventory and relate it to college majors, based on the relationship between the majors and the jobs they prepare for. He devised a set of six personality types that would differentiate well between different majors and different people and would have neutral connotations, neither positive nor negative. He called his six types Realistic, Investigative, Artistic, Social, Enterprising, and Conventional. (The acronym *RIASEC* is a convenient way to remember them.)

The following table shows how these labels apply to both people and work:

Personality Type	How It Applies to People	How It Applies to Work
Realistic	Realistic personalities like work activities that include practical, hands-on problems and solutions. They enjoy dealing with plants; animals; and real-world materials such as wood, tools, and machinery. They enjoy outside work. Often they do not like occupations that mainly involve doing paperwork or working closely with others.	Realistic occupations frequently involve work activities that include practical, hands-on problems and solutions. They often deal with plants; animals; and real-world materials such as wood, tools, and machinery. Many of the occupations require working outside and do not involve a lot of paperwork or working closely with others.
Investigative	Investigative personalities like work activities that have to do with ideas and thinking more than with physical activity. They like to search for facts and figure out problems mentally rather than to persuade or lead people.	Investigative occupations frequently involve working with ideas and require an extensive amount of thinking. These occupations can involve searching for facts and figuring out problems mentally.

Personality Type	How It Applies to People	How It Applies to Work
Artistic	Artistic personalities like work activities that deal with the artistic side of things, such as forms, designs, and patterns. They like self-expression in their work. They prefer settings where work can be done without following a clear set of rules.	Artistic occupations frequently involve working with forms, designs, and patterns. They often require self-expression and the work can be done without following a clear set of rules.
Social	Social personalities like work activities that assist others and promote learning and personal development. They prefer to communicate more than to work with objects, machines, or data. They like to teach, to give advice, to help, or otherwise to be of service to people.	Social occupations frequently involve working with, communicating with, and teaching people. These occupations often involve helping or providing service to others.
Enterprising	Enterprising personalities like work activities having to do with starting up and carrying out projects, especially business ventures. They like persuading and leading people and making decisions. They like taking risks for profit. These personalities prefer action rather than thought.	Enterprising occupations frequently involve starting up and carrying out projects. These occupations can involve leading people and making many decisions. They sometimes require risk taking and often deal with business.
Conventional	Conventional personalities like work activities that follow set procedures and routines. They prefer working with data and details rather than with ideas. They prefer work in which there are precise standards rather than work in which you have to judge things by yourself. These personalities like working where the lines of authority are clear.	Conventional occupations frequently involve following set procedures and routines. These occupations can include working with data and details more than with ideas. Usually there is a clear line of authority to follow.

Holland went further by arranging these six personality types on a hexagon:

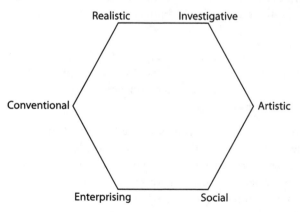

Figure 1: Holland's hexagon of personality types. (After Holland, A Theory of Vocational Choice, 1959.)

He used this diagram to explain that people tend to resemble one type primarily, but they may also have aspects of one or more adjacent types. Each personality type tends to have little in common with the types on the opposite side of the hexagon. Therefore, for example, a person might be primarily Enterprising, with an additional but smaller resemblance to the Conventional type. Such a person would be described by the two-letter code EC and might be well suited to work in the jobs linked to the college majors Public Administration and Finance (both coded EC). This person would have much less in common with Investigative or Artistic personality types and likely would not be very happy or productive in the physician jobs linked to the Medicine major (coded I) or in jobs related to the Art major. But this person could get along well with both Enterprising and Conventional personalities and, to a lesser extent, possibly with Realistic or Social personalities.

The Holland hexagon can be a little misleading in its neat symmetrical shape, especially when you look at jobs for which a college education is appropriate preparation. Most people prepare for Realistic and Conventional jobs by getting on-the-job training rather than a college degree. College is more suited for preparing people for jobs located at the other points on the hexagon, and graduate school is especially designed to teach Investigative skills. It's no accident that of the 46 majors described in this book, only one has Realistic as its first personality code and only two have Conventional in that position.

But that doesn't mean that people who have Realistic or Conventional personalities should forget about pursuing a college-level career. A large number of college-level jobs have Realistic or Conventional as their *second* personality type, meaning that the jobs have a significant representation of work tasks and situations that these personality types will find suitable. In assembling the lists of best majors for each personality type, we used both the first and second personality types and therefore were able to identify 10 outstanding majors for each of the six types.

Very few of the majors included in this book represent only one personality type, so when you read the description of a major, be sure to look at the full personality type, which may cover two or even three RIASEC types. For each related job, look at the personality types, the work tasks, and the skills and decide whether the job is a good fit for your personality.

Since Holland did his pioneering work, a number of career decision-making assessments have been developed to help people determine what personality type best describes them (and perhaps an additional adjacent type or types that are also important). You can find one such assessment in Part II of this book. Others are available online or in the offices of career professionals, sometimes for a fee.

Keep in mind that although all of these assessments produce outputs with RIASEC codes and some of them also link these codes to college majors, they will not necessarily produce the exact same output. Assessment of personality is not as exact a science as, say, chemistry. Neither is the task of linking personalities to majors.

You should not regard the output of any personality assessment as the final word on what college major or career will suit you best. Use a variety of approaches to decide what kind of person you are and narrow down the kinds of learning and work you enjoy. Actual work experience is probably the best way to test a tentative career choice, and experience in introductory college courses can often give a good indication of how well a related major would satisfy you.

PART II

What's Your Personality Type? Take an Assessment

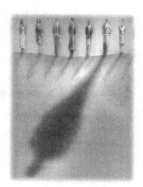

In this section, you can take a Personality Type Inventory that will help you determine your primary RIASEC personality type and perhaps one or two secondary RIASEC personality types. It asks if you like or dislike various activities and then lets you score your responses. You can use your scores in the following sections of the book to identify specific highly rewarding majors to explore.

It's easy to use the Personality Type Inventory—just turn the page and follow the directions beginning with Step 1. This is not a test, so there are no right or wrong answers. There is also no time limit for completing this inventory.

If someone else will be using this book, you should photocopy the inventory pages and mark your responses on the photocopy. This inventory is for your personal use. Any other use, including reproduction or distribution, is prohibited by U.S. copyright law.

Note: This inventory is based on the O*NET Interest Profiler, Version 3.0, developed by the U.S. Department of Labor (DOL). The DOL's edition consists of several components, including the Interest Profiler Instrument, Interest Profiler Score Report, and Interest Profiler O*NET Occupations Master List. The DOL provides a separate Interest Profiler User's Guide with information on the profiler's development and validity as well as tips for professionals using it in career counseling and academic advisement. Additional information on these items is available at www.onetcenter.org, which is maintained by the DOL. This Personality Type Inventory is a version of the DOL's O*NET Interest Profiler that uses its work activity items and scoring system but has shorter directions, format changes, and additional content.

Restrictions for use: This and any other form of the O*NET Interest Profiler should be used for career exploration, career planning, and vocational counseling purposes only, and no other use has been authorized or is valid. Results should not be used for employment or hiring decisions or for applicant screening for jobs or training programs. Please see the DOL's separate "O*NET User's Agreement" at www.onetcenter.org/agree/tools for additional details on restrictions and use. The word "O*NET" is a trademark of the U.S. Department of Labor, Employment and Training Administration.

JIST Publishing offers a color foldout version of this assessment. It is called the *O*NET Career Interests Inventory*, and it is sold in packages of 25.

Step 1: Respond to the Statements

Carefully read each work activity (items 1 through 180). For each item, fill in just one of the three circles as follows:

If you think you would LIKE the activity, fill in the circle containing the L, like this:

$$\text{(L)} \qquad \text{(?)} \qquad \text{(D)}$$

If you think you would DISLIKE the activity, fill in the circle containing the D, like this:

$$\text{(L)} \qquad \text{(?)} \qquad \text{(D)}$$

If you are UNSURE whether you would like the activity, fill in the circle with the ?, like this:

$$\text{(L)} \qquad \text{(?)} \qquad \text{(D)}$$

As you respond to each activity, don't consider whether you have the education or training needed for it or how much money you might earn if it were part of your job. Simply fill in the circle based on whether you would like, would dislike, or aren't sure about the activity.

After you respond to all 180 activities, you'll score your responses in Step 2.

Would you LIKE the activity or DISLIKE the activity, or are you UNSURE?

1. Build kitchen cabinets   Ⓛ   ⍰   Ⓓ
2. Guard money in an armored car   Ⓛ   ⍰   Ⓓ
3. Operate a dairy farm   Ⓛ   ⍰   Ⓓ
4. Lay brick or tile   Ⓛ   ⍰   Ⓓ
5. Monitor a machine on an assembly line   Ⓛ   ⍰   Ⓓ
6. Repair household appliances   Ⓛ   ⍰   Ⓓ
7. Drive a taxicab   Ⓛ   ⍰   Ⓓ
8. Install flooring in houses   Ⓛ   ⍰   Ⓓ
9. Raise fish in a fish hatchery   Ⓛ   ⍰   Ⓓ
10. Build a brick walkway   Ⓛ   ⍰   Ⓓ
11. Assemble electronic parts   Ⓛ   ⍰   Ⓓ
12. Drive a truck to deliver packages to offices and homes   Ⓛ   ⍰   Ⓓ
13. Paint houses   Ⓛ   ⍰   Ⓓ
14. Enforce fish and game laws   Ⓛ   ⍰   Ⓓ
15. Operate a grinding machine in a factory   Ⓛ   ⍰   Ⓓ
16. Work on an offshore oil-drilling rig   Ⓛ   ⍰   Ⓓ
17. Perform lawn care services   Ⓛ   ⍰   Ⓓ
18. Assemble products in a factory   Ⓛ   ⍰   Ⓓ
19. Catch fish as a member of a fishing crew   Ⓛ   ⍰   Ⓓ
20. Refinish furniture   Ⓛ   ⍰   Ⓓ
21. Fix a broken faucet   Ⓛ   ⍰   Ⓓ
22. Do cleaning or maintenance work   Ⓛ   ⍰   Ⓓ
23. Maintain the grounds of a park   Ⓛ   ⍰   Ⓓ
24. Operate a machine on a production line   Ⓛ   ⍰   Ⓓ
25. Spray trees to prevent the spread of harmful insects   Ⓛ   ⍰   Ⓓ
26. Test the quality of parts before shipment   Ⓛ   ⍰   Ⓓ
27. Operate a motorboat to carry passengers   Ⓛ   ⍰   Ⓓ
28. Repair and install locks   Ⓛ   ⍰   Ⓓ
29. Set up and operate machines to make products   Ⓛ   ⍰   Ⓓ
30. Put out forest fires   Ⓛ   ⍰   Ⓓ

____ **Page Score for R**

Would you LIKE the activity or DISLIKE the activity, or are you UNSURE?

31. Study space travel   (L)   (?)   (D)
32. Make a map of the bottom of an ocean   (L)   (?)   (D)
33. Study the history of past civilizations   (L)   (?)   (D)
34. Study animal behavior   (L)   (?)   (D)
35. Develop a new medicine   (L)   (?)   (D)
36. Plan a research study   (L)   (?)   (D)
37. Study ways to reduce water pollution   (L)   (?)   (D)
38. Develop a new medical treatment or procedure   (L)   (?)   (D)
39. Determine the infection rate of a new disease   (L)   (?)   (D)
40. Study rocks and minerals   (L)   (?)   (D)
41. Diagnose and treat sick animals   (L)   (?)   (D)
42. Study the personalities of world leaders   (L)   (?)   (D)
43. Conduct chemical experiments   (L)   (?)   (D)
44. Conduct biological research   (L)   (?)   (D)
45. Study the population growth of a city   (L)   (?)   (D)
46. Study whales and other types of marine life   (L)   (?)   (D)
47. Investigate crimes   (L)   (?)   (D)
48. Study the movement of planets   (L)   (?)   (D)
49. Examine blood samples using a microscope   (L)   (?)   (D)
50. Investigate the cause of a fire   (L)   (?)   (D)
51. Study the structure of the human body   (L)   (?)   (D)
52. Develop psychological profiles of criminals   (L)   (?)   (D)
53. Develop a new way to better predict the weather   (L)   (?)   (D)
54. Work in a biology lab   (L)   (?)   (D)
55. Invent a replacement for sugar   (L)   (?)   (D)
56. Study genetics   (L)   (?)   (D)
57. Study the governments of different countries   (L)   (?)   (D)
58. Do research on plants or animals   (L)   (?)   (D)
59. Do laboratory tests to identify diseases   (L)   (?)   (D)
60. Study weather conditions   (L)   (?)   (D)

____ **Page Score for I**

Would you LIKE the activity or DISLIKE the activity, or are you UNSURE?

61. Conduct a symphony orchestra   (L)   (?)   (D)
62. Write stories or articles for magazines   (L)   (?)   (D)
63. Direct a play   (L)   (?)   (D)
64. Create dance routines for a show   (L)   (?)   (D)
65. Write books or plays   (L)   (?)   (D)
66. Play a musical instrument   (L)   (?)   (D)
67. Perform comedy routines in front of an audience   (L)   (?)   (D)
68. Perform as an extra in movies, plays, or television shows   (L)   (?)   (D)
69. Write reviews of books or plays   (L)   (?)   (D)
70. Compose or arrange music   (L)   (?)   (D)
71. Act in a movie   (L)   (?)   (D)
72. Dance in a Broadway show   (L)   (?)   (D)
73. Draw pictures   (L)   (?)   (D)
74. Sing professionally   (L)   (?)   (D)
75. Perform stunts for a movie or television show   (L)   (?)   (D)
76. Create special effects for movies   (L)   (?)   (D)
77. Conduct a musical choir   (L)   (?)   (D)
78. Act in a play   (L)   (?)   (D)
79. Paint sets for plays   (L)   (?)   (D)
80. Audition singers and musicians for a musical show   (L)   (?)   (D)
81. Design sets for plays   (L)   (?)   (D)
82. Announce a radio show   (L)   (?)   (D)
83. Write scripts for movies or television shows   (L)   (?)   (D)
84. Write a song   (L)   (?)   (D)
85. Perform jazz or tap dance   (L)   (?)   (D)
86. Direct a movie   (L)   (?)   (D)
87. Sing in a band   (L)   (?)   (D)
88. Design artwork for magazines   (L)   (?)   (D)
89. Edit movies   (L)   (?)   (D)
90. Pose for a photographer   (L)   (?)   (D)

____ **Page Score for A**

Would you LIKE the activity or DISLIKE the activity, or are you UNSURE?

91. Teach an individual an exercise routine   Ⓛ   ⑦   Ⓓ
92. Perform nursing duties in a hospital   Ⓛ   ⑦   Ⓓ
93. Give CPR to someone who has stopped breathing   Ⓛ   ⑦   Ⓓ
94. Help people with personal or emotional problems   Ⓛ   ⑦   Ⓓ
95. Teach children how to read   Ⓛ   ⑦   Ⓓ
96. Work with mentally disabled children   Ⓛ   ⑦   Ⓓ
97. Teach an elementary school class   Ⓛ   ⑦   Ⓓ
98. Give career guidance to people   Ⓛ   ⑦   Ⓓ
99. Supervise the activities of children at a camp   Ⓛ   ⑦   Ⓓ
100. Help people with family-related problems   Ⓛ   ⑦   Ⓓ
101. Perform rehabilitation therapy   Ⓛ   ⑦   Ⓓ
102. Do volunteer work at a nonprofit organization   Ⓛ   ⑦   Ⓓ
103. Help elderly people with their daily activities   Ⓛ   ⑦   Ⓓ
104. Teach children how to play sports   Ⓛ   ⑦   Ⓓ
105. Help disabled people improve their daily living skills   Ⓛ   ⑦   Ⓓ
106. Teach sign language to people with hearing disabilities   Ⓛ   ⑦   Ⓓ
107. Help people who have problems with drugs or alcohol   Ⓛ   ⑦   Ⓓ
108. Help conduct a group therapy session   Ⓛ   ⑦   Ⓓ
109. Help families care for ill relatives   Ⓛ   ⑦   Ⓓ
110. Provide massage therapy to people   Ⓛ   ⑦   Ⓓ
111. Plan exercises for disabled students   Ⓛ   ⑦   Ⓓ
112. Counsel people who have a life-threatening illness   Ⓛ   ⑦   Ⓓ
113. Teach disabled people work and living skills   Ⓛ   ⑦   Ⓓ
114. Organize activities at a recreational facility   Ⓛ   ⑦   Ⓓ
115. Take care of children at a day-care center   Ⓛ   ⑦   Ⓓ
116. Organize field trips for disabled people   Ⓛ   ⑦   Ⓓ
117. Assist doctors in treating patients   Ⓛ   ⑦   Ⓓ
118. Work with juveniles on probation   Ⓛ   ⑦   Ⓓ
119. Provide physical therapy to people recovering from an injury   Ⓛ   ⑦   Ⓓ
120. Teach a high school class   Ⓛ   ⑦   Ⓓ

___ **Page Score for S**

Would you LIKE the activity or DISLIKE the activity, or are you UNSURE?

121. Buy and sell stocks and bonds   Ⓛ   ⑦   Ⓓ
122. Manage a retail store   Ⓛ   ⑦   Ⓓ
123. Sell telephone and other communication equipment   Ⓛ   ⑦   Ⓓ
124. Operate a beauty salon or barbershop   Ⓛ   ⑦   Ⓓ
125. Sell merchandise over the telephone   Ⓛ   ⑦   Ⓓ
126. Run a stand that sells newspapers and magazines   Ⓛ   ⑦   Ⓓ
127. Give a presentation about a product you are selling   Ⓛ   ⑦   Ⓓ
128. Buy and sell land   Ⓛ   ⑦   Ⓓ
129. Sell compact discs at a music store   Ⓛ   ⑦   Ⓓ
130. Run a toy store   Ⓛ   ⑦   Ⓓ
131. Manage the operations of a hotel   Ⓛ   ⑦   Ⓓ
132. Sell houses   Ⓛ   ⑦   Ⓓ
133. Sell candy and popcorn at sports events   Ⓛ   ⑦   Ⓓ
134. Manage a supermarket   Ⓛ   ⑦   Ⓓ
135. Manage a department within a large company   Ⓛ   ⑦   Ⓓ
136. Sell a soft drink product line to stores and restaurants   Ⓛ   ⑦   Ⓓ
137. Sell refreshments at a movie theater   Ⓛ   ⑦   Ⓓ
138. Sell hair-care products to stores and salons   Ⓛ   ⑦   Ⓓ
139. Start your own business   Ⓛ   ⑦   Ⓓ
140. Negotiate business contracts   Ⓛ   ⑦   Ⓓ
141. Represent a client in a lawsuit   Ⓛ   ⑦   Ⓓ
142. Negotiate contracts for professional athletes   Ⓛ   ⑦   Ⓓ
143. Be responsible for the operation of a company   Ⓛ   ⑦   Ⓓ
144. Market a new line of clothing   Ⓛ   ⑦   Ⓓ
145. Sell newspaper advertisements   Ⓛ   ⑦   Ⓓ
146. Sell merchandise at a department store   Ⓛ   ⑦   Ⓓ
147. Sell automobiles   Ⓛ   ⑦   Ⓓ
148. Manage a clothing store   Ⓛ   ⑦   Ⓓ
149. Sell restaurant franchises to individuals   Ⓛ   ⑦   Ⓓ
150. Sell computer equipment in a store   Ⓛ   ⑦   Ⓓ

____ **Page Score for E**

Would you LIKE the activity or DISLIKE the activity, or are you UNSURE?

		L	?	D
151.	Develop a spreadsheet using computer software	L	?	D
152.	Proofread records or forms	L	?	D
153.	Use a computer program to generate customer bills	L	?	D
154.	Schedule conferences for an organization	L	?	D
155.	Keep accounts payable/receivable for an office	L	?	D
156.	Load computer software into a large computer network	L	?	D
157.	Transfer funds between banks using a computer	L	?	D
158.	Organize and schedule office meetings	L	?	D
159.	Use a word processor to edit and format documents	L	?	D
160.	Operate a calculator	L	?	D
161.	Direct or transfer phone calls for a large organization	L	?	D
162.	Perform office filing tasks	L	?	D
163.	Compute and record statistical and other numerical data	L	?	D
164.	Generate the monthly payroll checks for an office	L	?	D
165.	Take notes during a meeting	L	?	D
166.	Keep shipping and receiving records	L	?	D
167.	Calculate the wages of employees	L	?	D
168.	Assist senior-level accountants in performing bookkeeping tasks	L	?	D
169.	Type labels for envelopes and packages	L	?	D
170.	Inventory supplies using a hand-held computer	L	?	D
171.	Develop an office filing system	L	?	D
172.	Keep records of financial transactions for an organization	L	?	D
173.	Record information from customers applying for charge accounts	L	?	D
174.	Photocopy letters and reports	L	?	D
175.	Record rent payments	L	?	D
176.	Enter information into a database	L	?	D
177.	Keep inventory records	L	?	D
178.	Maintain employee records	L	?	D
179.	Stamp, sort, and distribute mail for an organization	L	?	D
180.	Handle customers' bank transactions	L	?	D

____ **Page Score for C**

Step 2: Score Your Responses

Do the following to score your responses:

1. **Score the responses on each page.** On each page of responses, go from top to bottom and add the number of "L"s you filled in. Then write that number in the "Page Score" box at the bottom of the page. Go on to the next page and do the same there.

2. **Determine your primary interest area.** Which Page Score has your highest score: **R, I, A, S, E,** or **C**? Enter the letter for that personality type in the box below.

   My Primary Personality Type: ___

   You will use your Primary Personality Type *first* to explore college majors. (If two Page Scores are tied for the highest scores or are within 5 points of each other, use both of them for your Primary Personality Type. You are equally divided between two types.)

   - R = Realistic
   - I = Investigative
   - A = Artistic
   - S = Social
   - E = Enterprising
   - C = Conventional

3. **Determine your secondary interest areas.** Which Page Score has your next highest score? Which has your third highest score? Enter the letters for those areas in the box below.

   My Secondary Personality Types: ___ ___

   (If you do not find many interesting majors that you like using your Primary Personality Type, you can use your Secondary Personality Types to look at more educational options.)

Step 3: Find College Majors that Suit Your Personality Type

Start with your Primary Personality Type. Turn to Part III and look at the Best Majors lists for your type. Find lists that suit your particular priorities and see what majors appear there. Don't rule out a major just because the title is not familiar to you.

When you find majors that interest you or that you want to learn more about, turn to Part IV. The descriptions of majors there are grouped by Primary Personality Types and are listed alphabetically within each type. Of course, you can also look at majors that are linked to one of your Secondary Personality Types.

If you want to find majors that *combine* your Primary Personality Type and a Secondary Personality Type, turn to Appendix B. All 46 majors in this book are listed there by their one-, two-, or three-letter RIASEC codes. For example, if your Primary Personality Type is Social and your Secondary Personality Type is Investigative, you would look in Appendix B for the letter S and then for majors coded SI, such as American Studies, Nursing (R.N. Training), and Graduate Study for College Teaching.

You may discover that you can't find an appealing major in your Primary Personality Type that *also* is coded for one of your Secondary Personality Types. That is not necessarily a problem. John Holland himself has remarked, "You cannot expect a single job to satisfy all aspects of your personality." This is also true for majors. While you're in college, use elective courses to explore interests related to your Secondary Personality Types. Later, when you're in the workforce, use recreational time for the same purpose. At any age, volunteer work can be another outlet for these interests and abilities.

PART III

The Best Majors Lists

This part contains a lot of interesting lists, and it's a good place for you to start using the book. Here are some suggestions for using the lists to explore college majors that may suit your personality type:

- The table of contents at the beginning of this book presents a complete listing of the list titles in this section. You can browse the lists or use the table of contents to find those that interest you most.

- We gave the lists clear titles, so most require little explanation. We provide comments for each group of lists.

- As you review the lists of majors, one or more of the majors may appeal to you enough that you want to seek additional information. As this happens, mark that major (or, if someone else will be using this book, write it on a separate sheet of paper) so that you can look up the description of the major and its related jobs in Part IV.

- Keep in mind that all majors in these lists meet our basic criteria for being included in this book, as explained in the introduction. All lists consist of majors that are offered at many colleges and universities, with emphasis on majors leading to jobs with high pay, high growth, or large numbers of openings. These measures are easily quantified and are often presented in lists of best jobs in the newspapers and other media, so we decided they would be useful for evaluating college majors. While earnings, growth, and openings are important, there are other factors to consider in your educational and career planning. Obviously you are considering the personality types that characterize college majors; that's why you're reading this book. Other examples of factors to consider are availability of the major at a nearby college, your qualifications to enter the major (some have high entry requirements), and your comfort level with specific course requirements for the major. Many other factors that may help define the ideal major for you are difficult or impossible to quantify and thus are not used in this book, so you will need to consider the importance of these issues yourself.

◎ All data used to create these lists comes from the U.S. Department of Labor and the Census Bureau. The earnings figures are based on the average annual pay received by full-time workers in jobs related to the major. Because the earnings represent the national averages, actual pay rates can vary greatly by location, amount of previous work experience, and other factors. Projected job-growth rates are also national averages but can vary by location and industry. Many of the majors can lead to more than one career, and in some cases one career option may have much higher average pay or faster job growth than another option. In these lists we use the average pay and average job growth for *all* the related jobs, using a formula that gives extra weight to the jobs with the largest workforces. We also computed the *total* number of annual job openings for all related jobs. The descriptions of majors in Part IV list the average figures for earnings, job growth, and job openings for *each* related job.

Some Details on the Lists

The sources of the information we used in constructing these lists are presented in this book's introduction. Here are some additional details on how we created the lists:

◎ Some majors have the same scores for one or more data elements. For example, among the Enterprising majors, Accounting and Marketing are linked to jobs (five for Accounting, three for Marketing) that are expected to grow at the same rate, an average of 16.4 percent. Therefore, in the list of majors with the best job-growth potential we ordered these two majors alphabetically, and their order has no other significance. There was no way to avoid these ties, so simply understand that the difference of a few positions on a list may not mean as much as it seems.

◎ One of the majors listed here in Part III, Graduate Study for College Teaching, represents a wide variety of subject areas. In reality, *all* of the majors listed here can be studied at the graduate level as preparation for a postsecondary teaching career. For example, you might get a bachelor's degree in Civil Engineering and then get a master's and perhaps a doctorate in the same field in order to land a job teaching the subject in college. However, only a very small fraction of people who major in Civil Engineering have college teaching as their career goal. Therefore, when we matched college majors with the jobs they prepare for, we decided it would be misleading to match *every* major to a postsecondary teaching career. Instead, we created a generic major called Graduate Study for College Teaching and linked it to the job Postsecondary Teachers. In Part IV you can see a description of this major and its related job, and you'll also find cross-references to five majors (such as Humanities) that are not included in the Part III lists because they often are studied with the goal of postgraduate study—either in the same field as preparation for college teaching or in another field, such as Medicine or Law, as preparation for a profession.

Here is a reminder of the personality type that each code letter represents: R=Realistic, I=Investigative, A=Artistic, S=Social, E=Enterprising, C=Conventional.

Best Majors Overall for Each Personality Type: Majors Related to Jobs with the Highest Pay, Fastest Growth, and Most Openings

The four sets of lists that follow are the most important lists in this book. The first set of lists presents, for each personality type, the majors related to jobs with the highest combined scores for pay, growth, and number of openings. These are very appealing lists because they represent majors that prepare for jobs with the very highest quantifiable measures from our labor market. The 41 majors in these six lists, plus 5 related majors, are the ones that are described in detail in Part IV.

The three additional sets of lists present, for each personality type, majors linked to jobs with the highest scores in each of three measures: annual earnings, projected percentage growth, and largest number of openings.

The 10 Best Majors for Each Personality Type

These are the lists that most people want to see first. For each personality type, you can see the majors that prepare for jobs with the highest overall combined ratings for earnings, projected growth, and number of openings. (The section in the introduction called "How the Majors in This Book Were Selected" explains in detail how we linked majors to jobs and rated the majors so we could assemble this list.)

Although each list covers one personality type, you'll notice a wide variety of majors on the list. For example, among the top 10 Investigative majors are some in the fields of computer technology, health care, and engineering. Among the top 10 Artistic majors are some in business, education, communications, and (naturally) the arts. Part of the reason for the variety in these lists is that the majors on the list for a personality type may have that type as their **first or second** RIASEC code. For example, the fourth-ranked major on the Artistic list, Advertising, is coded EA, which means that Artistic is actually its secondary type; Enterprising is its primary type. (As the introduction explains, we used this approach because otherwise some lists would contain only one or two majors.)

A look at one list will clarify how we ordered the majors—take the Realistic list as an example. Computer Science was linked to four occupations with outstanding figures for income, growth, and job openings: Computer and Information Systems Managers; Computer Software Engineers, Applications; Computer Software Engineers, Systems Software; and Database Administrators. These highly promising linked jobs caused Computer Science to be the major with the best total score, and it is at the top of the list. The other majors follow in descending order based on their total scores. Several majors had tied scores and are simply listed one after another, so there are often only very small or even no differences between the scores of majors that are near each other on the list. All the other majors lists in this book use these majors as their source list. You can find descriptions for each of these majors in Part IV, beginning on page 79.

Remember that the figures for earnings, growth, and job openings are based on specific related jobs that are entered by many graduates of these majors; however, some graduates enter nontraditional jobs (for example, an English major who goes into advertising), so the figures do not indicate the economic rewards of *all* graduates of these majors. Figures on earnings in related jobs are sometimes limited; see the comments that precede the next set of lists.

The 10 Best Realistic Majors

Major	Annual Earnings of Related Jobs	Percent Growth of Related Jobs	Annual Openings of Related Jobs	Personality Types
1. Computer Science	$82,718	38.0%	142,000	IRC
2. Computer Engineering	$83,960	35.3%	126,000	IRC
3. Architecture	$90,798	14.7%	22,000	ERI
4. Biochemistry	$74,650	26.2%	21,000	IR
5. Microbiology	$72,437	26.4%	21,000	IR
6. Civil Engineering	$84,707	15.0%	34,000	RIE
7. Landscape Architecture	$100,030	14.0%	16,000	ERI
8. Petroleum Engineering	$104,897	12.1%	16,000	ERI
9. Aeronautical/Aerospace Engineering	$99,721	11.7%	21,000	IRE
10. Electrical Engineering	$89,095	11.7%	38,000	IRE

The 10 Best Investigative Majors

Major	Annual Earnings of Related Jobs	Percent Growth of Related Jobs	Annual Openings of Related Jobs	Personality Types
1. Medicine	$144,916	24.0%	287,000	I
2. Computer Engineering	$83,960	35.3%	126,000	IRC
3. Computer Science	$82,718	38.0%	142,000	IRC
4. Pharmacy	$94,520	24.8%	16,000	ICR
5. Graduate Study for College Teaching	$57,770	32.2%	329,000	SI
6. Biochemistry	$74,650	26.2%	21,000	IR
7. Microbiology	$72,437	26.4%	21,000	IR
8. Nursing (R.N. Training)	$57,280	29.4%	229,000	SI
9. Physician Assisting	$74,980	50.0%	10,000	IS
10. Industrial Engineering	$86,333	14.4%	28,000	EIR

The 10 Best Artistic Majors

Major	Annual Earnings of Related Jobs	Percent Growth of Related Jobs	Annual Openings of Related Jobs	Personality Types
1. Public Relations	$55,966	21.9%	52,000	EAS
2. Communications Studies/Speech	$48,357	20.2%	62,000	AE
3. Drama/Theater Arts	$56,310	16.9%	11,000	AES
4. Advertising	$48,594	17.4%	33,000	EA
5. Early Childhood Education	$29,250	30.1%	105,000	SA
6. Film/Cinema Studies	$51,199	16.8%	18,000	AES
7. Art	$55,182	12.5%	29,000	A
8. English	$43,702	14.5%	34,000	A
9. Journalism and Mass Communications	$43,942	14.2%	38,000	A
10. Industrial Design	$42,091	14.4%	42,000	A

The 10 Best Social Majors

Major	Annual Earnings of Related Jobs	Percent Growth of Related Jobs	Annual Openings of Related Jobs	Personality Types
1. Graduate Study for College Teaching	$57,770	32.2%	329,000	SI
2. Nursing (R.N. Training)	$57,280	29.4%	229,000	SI
3. Physician Assisting	$74,980	50.0%	10,000	IS
4. Physical Therapy	$66,200	36.8%	13,000	SRI
5. Health Information Systems Administration	$73,340	23.0%	33,000	ES
6. Hospital/Health Facilities Administration	$73,340	23.0%	33,000	ES
7. Human Resources Management	$50,296	24.0%	84,000	ESC
8. Occupational Therapy	$60,470	33.7%	7,000	SR
9. Industrial and Labor Relations	$49,299	25.7%	49,000	ESC
10. Early Childhood Education	$29,250	30.1%	105,000	SA

The 10 Best Enterprising Majors

Major	Annual Earnings of Related Jobs	Percent Growth of Related Jobs	Annual Openings of Related Jobs	Personality Types
1. International Business	$94,442	16.6%	246,000	EC
2. Marketing	$92,429	20.0%	72,000	EC
3. Public Administration	$86,701	16.4%	310,000	EC
4. Business Management	$83,211	16.4%	481,000	EC
5. Transportation and Logistics Management	$101,203	15.2%	85,000	EC
6. International Relations	$144,875	14.7%	38,000	EC
7. Accounting	$54,500	20.0%	173,000	CE
8. Health Information Systems Administration	$73,340	23.0%	33,000	ES
9. Hospital/Health Facilities Administration	$73,340	23.0%	33,000	ES
10. Human Resources Management	$50,296	24.0%	84,000	ESC

The 10 Best Conventional Majors

Major	Annual Earnings of Related Jobs	Percent Growth of Related Jobs	Annual Openings of Related Jobs	Personality Types
1. International Business	$94,442	16.6%	246,000	EC
2. Business Management	$83,211	16.4%	481,000	EC
3. Public Administration	$86,701	16.4%	310,000	EC
4. Pharmacy	$94,520	24.8%	16,000	ICR
5. Marketing	$92,429	20.0%	72,000	EC
6. Transportation and Logistics Management	$101,203	15.2%	85,000	EC
7. Accounting	$54,500	20.0%	173,000	CE
8. International Relations	$144,875	14.7%	38,000	EC
9. Actuarial Science	$82,800	22.2%	3,000	CI
10. Finance	$70,359	14.4%	155,000	EC

The 5 Majors with the Best Income Potential for Each Personality Type

On the following six lists you'll find, for each personality type, the five majors meeting our criteria for this book that have the best income potential. These are appealing lists, for obvious reasons.

If you compare these six lists, you may notice that some personality types have better income possibilities than others. For example, the five Enterprising majors listed here are linked to jobs that command much higher incomes than those linked to the five Artistic majors listed here. Keep in mind that these figures are only averages; there are a few graduates of Drama/Theater Arts programs (for example, think of famous movie directors) who are earning more than graduates of a Medical program, whereas other Drama/Theater Arts grads are barely scraping by. In several cases (indicated by notes) the average earnings are probably *higher* than the figures given here, because one or more linked jobs have earnings that the Department of Labor reports as "more than $145,600." We had to use the figure of $145,600 to compute the averages, but for some of these linked jobs (for example, Anesthesiologists) the actual earnings are probably considerably higher. On the other hand, the average earnings figure of $56,310 for Drama/Theater Arts is probably *too high*. This income figure is based on the earnings of only one linked job, Producers and Directors, but this major is also linked to a second job, Actors, that is notorious for its low pay for most workers. Unfortunately, income for Actors is so irregular that the Department of Labor publishes no annual earnings figures for them, which means that we could not factor Actors' pay into the average.

In conclusion, if a major interests you, look at its description in Part IV and note the earnings figures for the related jobs, paying special attention to those jobs you'd *actually consider* as career goals. Also remember what we said earlier about how earnings can vary by region of the country, by amount of experience, and because of many other factors.

The 5 Realistic Majors with the Best Income Potential

Major	Annual Earnings of Related Jobs	Personality Types
1. Petroleum Engineering	$104,897	ERI
2. Landscape Architecture	$100,030	ERI
3. Aeronautical/Aerospace Engineering	$99,721	IRE
4. Architecture	$90,798	ERI
5. Electrical Engineering	$89,095	IRE

The 5 Investigative Majors with the Best Income Potential

Major	Annual Earnings of Related Jobs	Personality Types
1. Medicine	$144,916	I
2. Pharmacy	$94,520	ICR
3. Industrial Engineering	$86,333	EIR
4. Computer Engineering	$83,960	IRC
5. Computer Science	$82,718	IRC

Earnings for Job 1 are based on limited data about related occupations and are probably too low.

The 5 Artistic Majors with the Best Income Potential

Major	Annual Earnings of Related Jobs	Personality Types
1. Drama/Theater Arts	$56,310	AES
2. Public Relations	$55,966	EAS
3. Art	$55,182	A
4. Film/Cinema Studies	$51,199	AES
5. Advertising	$48,594	EA

Earnings for Job 1 are based on limited data about related occupations and are probably too high.

The 5 Social Majors with the Best Income Potential

Major	Annual Earnings of Related Jobs	Personality Types
1. Physician Assisting	$74,980	IS
2. Health Information Systems Administration	$73,340	ES
3. Hospital/Health Facilities Administration	$73,340	ES
4. Physical Therapy	$66,200	SRI
5. Occupational Therapy	$60,470	SR

The 5 Enterprising Majors with the Best Income Potential

Major	Annual Earnings of Related Jobs	Personality Types
1. International Relations	$144,875	EC
2. Transportation and Logistics Management	$101,203	EC
3. International Business	$94,442	EC
4. Marketing	$92,429	EC
5. Public Administration	$86,701	EC

Earnings for Jobs 2, 3, and 5 are based on limited data about related occupations and are probably too low.

The 5 Conventional Majors with the Best Income Potential

Major	Annual Earnings of Related Jobs	Personality Types
1. International Relations	$144,875	EC
2. Transportation and Logistics Management	$101,203	EC
3. Pharmacy	$94,520	ICR
4. International Business	$94,442	EC
5. Marketing	$92,429	EC

Earnings for Jobs 2 and 4 are based on limited data about related occupations and are probably too low.

The 5 Majors with the Best Job-Growth Potential for Each Personality Type

From the six lists of 10 majors that met our criteria for this book, these six lists show the five majors for each personality type that are linked to jobs projected to have the highest percentage increase in the numbers of people employed through 2014.

You will notice that just as income opportunities vary among the lists of majors for various personality types, job opportunities also vary. The jobs linked to the top Investigative and Social majors have better opportunities than do the jobs linked to the top majors in the other groups. This is partly because an aging population with greater need for medical and personal care is going to need many workers trained in Investigative and Social subjects. In addition, the kind of work done in Investigative and Social occupations typically cannot be done by computers or by overseas workers.

The 5 Realistic Majors with the Best Job-Growth Potential

Major	Percent Growth of Related Jobs	Personality Types
1. Computer Science	38.0%	IRC
2. Computer Engineering	35.3%	IRC
3. Microbiology	26.4%	IR
4. Biochemistry	26.2%	IR
5. Civil Engineering	15.0%	RIE

The 5 Investigative Majors with the Best Job-Growth Potential

Major	Percent Growth of Related Jobs	Personality Types
1. Physician Assisting	50.0%	IS
2. Computer Science	38.0%	IRC
3. Computer Engineering	35.3%	IRC
4. Graduate Study for College Teaching	32.2%	SI
5. Nursing (R.N. Training)	29.4%	SI

The 5 Artistic Majors with the Best Job-Growth Potential

Major	Percent Growth of Related Jobs	Personality Types
1. Early Childhood Education	30.1%	SA
2. Public Relations	21.9%	EAS
3. Communications Studies/Speech	20.2%	AE
4. Advertising	17.4%	EA
5. Drama/Theater Arts	16.9%	AES

The 5 Social Majors with the Best Job-Growth Potential

Major	Percent Growth of Related Jobs	Personality Types
1. Physician Assisting	50.0%	IS
2. Physical Therapy	36.8%	SRI
3. Occupational Therapy	33.7%	SR
4. Graduate Study for College Teaching	32.2%	SI
5. Early Childhood Education	30.1%	SA

The 5 Enterprising Majors with the Best Job-Growth Potential

Major	Percent Growth of Related Jobs	Personality Types
1. Human Resources Management	24.0%	ESC
2. Health Information Systems Administration	23.0%	ES
3. Hospital/Health Facilities Administration	23.0%	ES
4. Accounting	20.0%	CE
5. Marketing	20.0%	EC

The 5 Conventional Majors with the Best Job-Growth Potential

Major	Percent Growth of Related Jobs	Personality Types
1. Pharmacy	24.8%	ICR
2. Actuarial Science	22.2%	CI
3. Accounting	20.0%	CE
4. Marketing	20.0%	EC
5. International Business	16.6%	EC

The 5 Majors with the Best Job-Opening Potential for Each Personality Type

From the six lists of 10 majors that met our criteria for this book, this list shows the five majors for each personality type whose related occupations are projected to have the largest number of job openings per year through 2014.

Majors linked to jobs with many openings present several advantages that may be attractive to you. Because there are many openings, these jobs can be easier to obtain, particularly when you first enter the job market after completing your major. These majors may also create more opportunities for you to move from one employer to another with relative ease. Though a few of the majors lead to jobs with unimpressive pay, most lead to jobs that pay quite well and can provide good long-term career opportunities or the ability to move up to more responsible roles.

It is interesting that the top majors in the Artistic list are linked to jobs in education and applied arts. Those fields are where the most Artistic job openings will be, rather than in the fine or performing arts, where keen competition for jobs is the rule. The two personality types with the highest figures for job openings are Conventional and Enterprising, reflecting the many job opportunities in the business world.

The 5 Realistic Majors with the Best Job-Opening Potential

Major	Total Annual Openings of Related Jobs	Personality Types
1. Computer Science	142,000	IRC
2. Computer Engineering	126,000	IRC
3. Electrical Engineering	38,000	IRE
4. Civil Engineering	34,000	RIE
5. Architecture	22,000	ERI

The 5 Investigative Majors with the Best Job-Opening Potential

Major	Total Annual Openings of Related Jobs	Personality Types
1. Graduate Study for College Teaching	329,000	SI
2. Medicine	287,000	I
3. Nursing (R.N. Training)	229,000	SI

The 5 Investigative Majors with the Best Job-Opening Potential

Major	Total Annual Openings of Related Jobs	Personality Types
4. Computer Science	142,000	IRC
5. Computer Engineering	126,000	IRC

The 5 Artistic Majors with the Best Job-Opening Potential

Major	Total Annual Openings of Related Jobs	Personality Types
1. Early Childhood Education	105,000	SA
2. Communications Studies/Speech	62,000	AE
3. Public Relations	52,000	EAS
4. Industrial Design	42,000	A
5. Journalism and Mass Communications	38,000	A

The 5 Social Majors with the Best Job-Opening Potential

Major	Total Annual Openings of Related Jobs	Personality Types
1. Graduate Study for College Teaching	329,000	SI
2. Nursing (R.N. Training)	229,000	SI
3. Early Childhood Education	105,000	SA
4. Human Resources Management	84,000	ESC
5. Industrial and Labor Relations	49,000	ESC

The 5 Enterprising Majors with the Best Job-Opening Potential

Major	Total Annual Openings of Related Jobs	Personality Types
1. Business Management	481,000	EC
2. Public Administration	310,000	EC
3. International Business	246,000	EC
4. Accounting	173,000	CE
5. Transportation and Logistics Management	85,000	EC

The 5 Conventional Majors with the Best Job-Opening Potential

Major	Total Annual Openings of Related Jobs	Personality Types
1. Business Management	481,000	EC
2. Public Administration	310,000	EC
3. International Business	246,000	EC
4. Accounting	173,000	CE
5. Finance	155,000	EC

Best Majors Lists by Demographic

We decided it would be interesting to include lists in this section that feature majors linked to jobs in which different types of people dominate. For example, what majors are associated with jobs that have the highest percentage of male workers? We're not saying that men should consider these majors over others, but it is interesting information to know.

In some cases, the lists can give you ideas for majors to consider that you might otherwise overlook. For example, perhaps women should consider some majors that prepare for jobs that traditionally have high percentages of men in them. Although these are not obvious ways of using these lists, the lists may give you some good ideas about majors to consider. The lists may also help you identify majors that work well for others in your situation—for example, majors that lead to plentiful opportunities for part-time work, if that is something you want to do at this stage of your career.

All of the lists in this section were created using a similar process. For each personality type, we sorted the 10 best majors according to a demographic criterion and discarded those whose related jobs did not have a high percentage of that criterion. For example, we sorted the majors based on the percentage of female workers in related jobs from highest to lowest percentage and discarded those with a figure less than 60 percent. We then ranked this subset of majors according to the usual economic criteria applied to related jobs—income, job growth, and job openings.

We used the same basic process for all six personality types and for four demographic characteristics (part-time, self-employed, women, and men. This would have created 24 lists in this section, but some lists do not appear because no majors met the criteria we set for them. For example, we found no Realistic majors related to jobs with a high percentage of part-time workers. The lists based on demographic characteristics are very interesting, and we hope you find them helpful.

Best Majors Related to Jobs with a High Percentage of Part-Time Workers

Look over the lists of the majors leading to jobs with high percentages (more than 15 percent) of part-time workers and you will find some interesting things. For example, a lot of the majors are in the health-care field. But several other industries—including business, education, and the arts—are also represented by the majors in these lists. On the other hand, the scientific and high-tech fields offer few opportunities for part-time work, so we were unable to include a list of Realistic majors in the set below.

In some cases, people work part time because they want the freedom of time this arrangement can provide, but others may do so because they can't find full-time employment in these jobs. These folks may work in other full- or part-time jobs to make ends meet. If you want to work part time now or in the future, these lists will help you identify majors that are more likely to lead to that opportunity. The earnings estimates in the following lists are based on a survey of both part-time *and* full-time workers. On average, part-time workers earn about 10 percent less per hour than full-time workers.

Best Investigative Majors Related to Jobs with a High Percentage of Part-Time Workers

Major	Percentage of Part-Time Workers in Related Jobs	Annual Earnings of Related Jobs	Percent Growth of Related Jobs	Annual Openings of Related Jobs	Personality Types
1. Graduate Study for College Teaching	24.8%	$57,770	32.2%	329,000	SI
2. Medicine	25.6%	$144,916	24.0%	287,000	I
3. Physician Assisting	23.1%	$74,980	50.0%	10,000	IS
4. Pharmacy	29.9%	$94,520	24.8%	16,000	ICR
5. Nursing (R.N. Training)	30.1%	$57,280	29.4%	229,000	SI

Best Artistic Majors Related to Jobs with a High Percentage of Part-Time Workers

Major	Percentage of Part-Time Workers in Related Jobs	Annual Earnings of Related Jobs	Percent Growth of Related Jobs	Annual Openings of Related Jobs	Personality Types
1. Public Relations	18.7%	$55,966	21.9%	52,000	EAS
2. Communications Studies/Speech	30.1%	$48,357	20.2%	62,000	AE
3. Early Childhood Education	27.0%	$29,250	30.1%	105,000	SA
4. Advertising	24.4%	$48,594	17.4%	33,000	EA
5. Drama/Theater Arts	28.8%	$56,310	16.9%	11,000	AES
6. Film/Cinema Studies	26.0%	$51,199	16.8%	18,000	AES
7. Art	32.0%	$55,182	12.5%	29,000	A
8. English	30.7%	$43,702	14.5%	34,000	A
9. Industrial Design	32.0%	$42,091	14.4%	42,000	A
10. Journalism and Mass Communications	30.4%	$43,942	14.2%	38,000	A

Best Social Majors Related to Jobs with a High Percentage of Part-Time Workers

Major	Percentage of Part-Time Workers in Related Jobs	Annual Earnings of Related Jobs	Percent Growth of Related Jobs	Annual Openings of Related Jobs	Personality Types
1. Graduate Study for College Teaching	24.8%	$57,770	32.2%	329,000	SI
2. Physician Assisting	23.1%	$74,980	50.0%	10,000	IS
3. Physical Therapy	21.4%	$66,200	36.8%	13,000	SRI
4. Nursing (R.N. Training)	30.1%	$57,280	29.4%	229,000	SI
5. Occupational Therapy	39.4%	$60,470	33.7%	7,000	SR
6. Early Childhood Education	27.0%	$29,250	30.1%	105,000	SA
7. Human Resources Management	22.6%	$50,296	24.0%	84,000	ESC
8. Industrial and Labor Relations	22.4%	$49,299	25.7%	49,000	ESC

Best Enterprising Majors Related to Jobs with a High Percentage of Part-Time Workers

Major	Percentage of Part-Time Workers in Related Jobs	Annual Earnings of Related Jobs	Percent Growth of Related Jobs	Annual Openings of Related Jobs	Personality Types
1. Accounting	22.0%	$54,500	20.0%	173,000	CE
2. Human Resources Management	22.6%	$50,296	24.0%	84,000	ESC

Best Conventional Majors Related to Jobs with a High Percentage of Part-Time Workers

Major	Percentage of Part-Time Workers in Related Jobs	Annual Earnings of Related Jobs	Percent Growth of Related Jobs	Annual Openings of Related Jobs	Personality Types
1. Pharmacy	29.9%	$94,520	24.8%	16,000	ICR
2. Accounting	22.0%	$54,500	20.0%	173,000	CE
3. Finance	17.5%	$70,359	14.4%	155,000	EC

Best Majors Related to Jobs with a High Percentage of Self-Employed Workers

About 8 percent of all working people are self-employed. Although you may think of the self-employed as having similar jobs, they actually work in an enormous range of situations, fields, and work environments that you may not have considered.

However, only a small number of college majors—only one Realistic major, one Investigative major, and no Social majors at all—are linked to jobs with an above-average percentage of self-employed workers.

Where the following lists give earnings estimates, keep in mind that figures are based on a survey that *does not include self-employed workers.* The median earnings for self-employed workers in these occupations may be significantly higher or lower.

The following lists contain majors linked to jobs in which more than 8 percent of the workers are self-employed.

Best Realistic Majors Related to Jobs with a High Percentage of Self-Employed Workers

Major	Percentage of Self-Employed Workers in Related Jobs	Annual Earnings of Related Jobs	Percent Growth of Related Jobs	Annual Openings of Related Jobs	Personaliy Types
1. Architecture	8.4%	$90,798	14.7%	22,000	ERI

Best Investigative Majors Related to Jobs with a High Percentage of Self-Employed Workers

Major	Percentage of Self-Employed Workers in Related Jobs	Annual Earnings of Related Jobs	Percent Growth of Related Jobs	Annual Openings of Related Jobs	Personaliy Types
1. Medicine	11.5%	$144,916	24.0%	287,000	I

Best Artistic Majors Related to Jobs with a High Percentage of Self-Employed Workers

Major	Percentage of Self-Employed Workers in Related Jobs	Annual Earnings of Related Jobs	Percent Growth of Related Jobs	Annual Openings of Related Jobs	Personaliy Types
1. Communications Studies/Speech	26.8%	$48,357	20.2%	62,000	AE
2. Drama/Theater Arts	24.1%	$56,310	16.9%	11,000	AES
3. Film/Cinema Studies	26.6%	$51,199	16.8%	18,000	AES
4. Art	58.4%	$55,182	12.5%	29,000	A
5. English	36.6%	$43,702	14.5%	34,000	A

Best Enterprising Majors Related to Jobs with a High Percentage of Self-Employed Workers

Major	Percentage of Self-Employed Workers in Related Jobs	Annual Earnings of Related Jobs	Percent Growth of Related Jobs	Annual Openings of Related Jobs	Personaliy Types
1. Accounting	9.3%	$54,500	20.0%	173,000	CE
2. Business Management	11.0%	$83,211	16.4%	481,000	EC
3. International Relations	16.1%	$144,875	14.7%	38,000	EC
4. Transportation and Logistics Management	8.8%	$101,203	15.2%	85,000	EC

Best Conventional Majors Related to Jobs with a High Percentage of Self-Employed Workers

Major	Percentage of Self-Employed Workers in Related Jobs	Annual Earnings of Related Jobs	Percent Growth of Related Jobs	Annual Openings of Related Jobs	Personaliy Types
1. Business Management	11.0%	$83,211	16.4%	481,000	EC
2. Accounting	9.3%	$54,500	20.0%	173,000	CE
3. Transportation and Logistics Management	8.8%	$101,203	15.2%	85,000	EC
4. International Relations	16.1%	$144,875	14.7%	38,000	EC

Best Majors Related to Jobs Employing a High Percentage of Women

To create the six lists that follow, we sorted the 10 best majors for each personality type according to the percentages of women and men in the workforces of the related jobs. These are our most controversial lists, and we knew we would create some controversy when we first included similar lists in our *Best Jobs* books. But these lists are not meant to restrict women or men from considering options for majors or jobs—our reason for including these lists is exactly the opposite. We hope the lists help people see possibilities that they might not otherwise have considered.

The fact is that jobs with high percentages (60 percent or higher) of women or high percentages of men offer good opportunities for both men and women if they want to do one of these jobs. So we suggest that women browse the lists of majors leading to jobs that employ high percentages of men and that men browse the lists of majors leading to jobs with high percentages of women. There are majors among both lists that have high income potential, and women or men who are interested in them should consider them.

It is interesting to compare the two sets of jobs related to the best majors—jobs with the highest percentage of men and jobs with the highest percentage of women—in terms of the economic measures that we use to rank these lists. The male-dominated jobs have much higher average earnings ($95,742) than the female-dominated jobs ($54,204). This is unfortunate but consistent with most other books in the *Best Jobs* series where we look at jobs by the sex of the workers. On the other hand, the female-dominated occupations have potential for greater job growth: 28.0 percent versus 20.2 percent. But job growth alone does not predict how likely it is that you'll be hired. The male-dominated occupations tend to be larger, with a larger turnover of workers, so almost twice as many annual job openings are expected in the male-dominated occupations related to the best majors compared to the female-dominated occupations: 139,125 openings compared to 69,938 openings.

Another reality of the workplace is that Realistic jobs tend to be dominated by men, and the Conventional jobs that are dominated by women tend to be clerical and secretarial jobs, for which a college degree is unnecessary. As a result, the following set of lists covers only four of the six RIASEC types: Investigative, Artistic, Social, and Enterprising.

Best Investigative Majors Related to Jobs with a High Percentage of Women

Major	Percentage of Women in Related Jobs	Annual Earnings of Related Jobs	Percent Growth of Related Jobs	Annual Openings of Related Jobs	Personality Types
1. Physician Assisting	71.7%	$74,980	50.0%	10,000	IS
2. Nursing (R.N. Training)	91.3%	$57,280	29.4%	229,000	SI

Best Artistic Majors Related to Jobs with a High Percentage of Women

Major	Percentage of Women in Related Jobs	Annual Earnings of Related Jobs	Percent Growth of Related Jobs	Annual Openings of Related Jobs	Personality Types
1. Early Childhood Education	97.7%	$29,250	30.1%	105,000	SA
2. Communications Studies/Speech	60.2%	$48,357	20.2%	62,000	AE

Best Social Majors Related to Jobs with a High Percentage of Women

Major	Percentage of Women in Related Jobs	Annual Earnings of Related Jobs	Percent Growth of Related Jobs	Annual Openings of Related Jobs	Personality Types
1. Physician Assisting	71.7%	$74,980	50.0%	10,000	IS
2. Nursing (R.N. Training)	91.3%	$57,280	29.4%	229,000	SI
3. Physical Therapy	62.7%	$66,200	36.8%	13,000	SRI
4. Early Childhood Education	97.7%	$29,250	30.1%	105,000	SA
5. Health Information Systems Administration	68.3%	$73,340	23.0%	33,000	ES
6. Hospital/Health Facilities Administration	68.3%	$73,340	23.0%	33,000	ES
7. Human Resources Management	70.6%	$50,296	24.0%	84,000	ESC
8. Occupational Therapy	90.3%	$60,470	33.7%	7,000	SR
9. Industrial and Labor Relations	70.5%	$49,299	25.7%	49,000	ESC

Best Enterprising Majors Related to Jobs with a High Percentage of Women

Major	Percentage of Women in Related Jobs	Annual Earnings of Related Jobs	Percent Growth of Related Jobs	Annual Openings of Related Jobs	Personality Types
1. Health Information Systems Administration	68.3%	$73,340	23.0%	33,000	ES
2. Hospital/Health Facilities Administration	68.3%	$73,340	23.0%	33,000	ES
3. Human Resources Management	70.6%	$50,296	24.0%	84,000	ESC

Best Majors Related to Jobs Employing a High Percentage of Men

If you have not already read the introduction to the previous group of lists, best majors leading to jobs with high percentages of women, consider doing so. Much of the content there applies to these lists as well. The previous set of lists includes none for the Realistic and Conventional personality types, and the following set of lists includes none for the Social type. This simply reflects the realities of the jobs that attract male college graduates.

We did not include these groups of lists with the assumption that men should consider only majors leading to jobs with high percentages of men or that women should consider only majors leading to jobs with high percentages of women. Instead, these lists are here because we think they are interesting and perhaps helpful in considering nontraditional career options. For example, some men would do very well in and enjoy some jobs that have high percentages of women but may not have considered the associated majors seriously. In a similar way, some women would very much enjoy and do well in some jobs that traditionally have been held by high percentages of men. We hope that these lists help you consider college majors that you previously did not consider seriously because of gender stereotypes.

Best Realistic Majors Related to Jobs with a High Percentage of Men

Major	Percentage of Men in Related Jobs	Annual Earnings of Related Jobs	Percent Growth of Related Jobs	Annual Openings of Related Jobs	Personality Types
1. Computer Science	75.3%	$82,718	38.0%	142,000	IRC
2. Computer Engineering	80.3%	$83,960	35.3%	126,000	IRC
3. Architecture	86.7%	$90,798	14.7%	22,000	ERI
4. Civil Engineering	90.1%	$84,707	15.0%	34,000	RIE
5. Landscape Architecture	91.0%	$100,030	14.0%	16,000	ERI
6. Petroleum Engineering	92.7%	$104,897	12.1%	16,000	ERI
7. Electrical Engineering	92.5%	$89,095	11.7%	38,000	IRE
8. Aeronautical/Aerospace Engineering	91.0%	$99,721	11.7%	21,000	IRE

Best Investigative Majors Related to Jobs with a High Percentage of Men

Major	Percentage of Men in Related Jobs	Annual Earnings of Related Jobs	Percent Growth of Related Jobs	Annual Openings of Related Jobs	Personality Types
1. Medicine	67.8%	$144,916	24.0%	287,000	I
2. Computer Science	75.3%	$82,718	38.0%	142,000	IRC
3. Computer Engineering	80.3%	$83,960	35.3%	126,000	IRC
4. Industrial Engineering	85.3%	$86,333	14.4%	28,000	EIR

Best Artistic Majors Related to Jobs with a High Percentage of Men

Major	Percentage of Men in Related Jobs	Annual Earnings of Related Jobs	Percent Growth of Related Jobs	Annual Openings of Related Jobs	Personality Types
1. Film/Cinema Studies	61.7%	$51,199	16.8%	18,000	AES

Best Enterprising Majors Related to Jobs with a High Percentage of Men

Major	Percentage of Men in Related Jobs	Annual Earnings of Related Jobs	Percent Growth of Related Jobs	Annual Openings of Related Jobs	Personality Types
1. International Business	72.0%	$94,442	16.6%	246,000	EC
2. Business Management	71.6%	$83,211	16.4%	481,000	EC
3. Public Administration	70.8%	$86,701	16.4%	310,000	EC
4. Transportation and Logistics Management	76.7%	$101,203	15.2%	85,000	EC
5. International Relations	76.3%	$144,875	14.7%	38,000	EC

Best Conventional Majors Related to Jobs with a High Percentage of Men

Major	Percentage of Men in Related Jobs	Annual Earnings of Related Jobs	Percent Growth of Related Jobs	Annual Openings of Related Jobs	Personality Types
1. International Business	72.0%	$94,442	16.6%	246,000	EC
2. Business Management	71.6%	$83,211	16.4%	481,000	EC
3. Public Administration	70.8%	$86,701	16.4%	310,000	EC
4. Transportation and Logistics Management	76.7%	$101,203	15.2%	85,000	EC
5. International Relations	76.3%	$144,875	14.7%	38,000	EC
6. Actuarial Science	71.6%	$82,800	22.2%	3,000	CI

Best Majors Related to Jobs at Different Levels of Education

The lists in this section organize the best majors associated with all six personality types into five groups based on the education or experience typically required for entry to related jobs. For each level of education or training, we provide one list that includes *all* related majors— not just the best 5 or 10, and not just those related to one personality type. Nevertheless, the list identifies the personality type or types for each major, and the majors are ranked by their total combined score for the earnings, growth, and number of openings for related jobs.

These lists can help you when you plan your education. For example, you might be thinking about a particular college major because the expected pay is very good, but the lists may help you identify a major that interests you more and offers even better potential for the same general educational requirements.

You may notice that many majors appear in more than one list. These double listings occur when a major is related to two or more jobs that require different levels of education. For example, Business Management appears in the list for the bachelor's degree because it is linked to Construction Managers and several other jobs at that level, and it also appears in the list for work experience plus degree because it is linked to Sales Managers and several other jobs at that level.

Best Majors Related to Jobs that Require a Bachelor's Degree

Of the 41 majors that meet the criteria for this book, 25 are linked to jobs that most commonly require a bachelor's degree. A bachelor's degree usually requires 120 to 130 semester hours to complete. A full-time student usually takes four to five years to complete a bachelor's degree, depending on the complexity of courses. Traditionally, people have thought of the bachelor's degree as a four-year degree. Some bachelor's degrees—like the Bachelor of Architecture—are considered a first professional degree and take five or more years to complete.

The following list shows the majors linked to jobs requiring the bachelor's degree. Although the personality types for these jobs include the Conventional and Enterprising types most frequently here, all of the RIASEC types are represented at least once among these majors. As in all the lists, the RIASEC types of the majors are represented by their initials because the full names would take up too much space.

Best Majors Related to Jobs that Require a Bachelor's Degree

Major	Annual Earnings of Related Jobs	Percent Growth of Related Jobs	Annual Openings of Related Jobs	Personality Types
1. Computer Engineering	$83,960	35.3%	126,000	IRC
2. Computer Science	$82,718	38.0%	142,000	IRC
3. Public Administration	$86,701	16.4%	310,000	EC
4. Business Management	$83,211	16.4%	481,000	EC
5. Transportation and Logistics Management	$101,203	15.2%	85,000	EC
6. Accounting	$54,500	20.0%	173,000	CE
7. Public Relations	$55,966	21.9%	52,000	EAS
8. Human Resources Management	$50,296	24.0%	84,000	ESC
9. Finance	$70,359	14.4%	155,000	EC
10. Early Childhood Education	$29,250	30.1%	105,000	SA
11. Industrial and Labor Relations	$49,299	25.7%	49,000	ESC
12. Civil Engineering	$84,707	15.0%	34,000	RIE

Best Majors Related to Jobs that Require a Bachelor's Degree

Major	Annual Earnings of Related Jobs	Percent Growth of Related Jobs	Annual Openings of Related Jobs	Personality Types
13. Communications Studies/Speech	$48,357	20.2%	62,000	AE
14. Physician Assisting	$74,980	50.0%	10,000	IS
15. Architecture	$90,798	14.7%	22,000	ERI
16. Electrical Engineering	$89,095	11.7%	38,000	IRE
17. Industrial Engineering	$86,333	14.4%	28,000	EIR
18. Landscape Architecture	$100,030	14.0%	16,000	ERI
19. Petroleum Engineering	$104,897	12.1%	16,000	ERI
20. Aeronautical/Aerospace Engineering	$99,721	11.7%	21,000	IRE
21. Film/Cinema Studies	$51,199	16.8%	18,000	AES
22. Industrial Design	$42,091	14.4%	42,000	A
23. English	$43,702	14.5%	34,000	A
24. Art	$55,182	12.5%	29,000	A
25. Journalism and Mass Communications	$43,942	14.2%	38,000	A

Best Majors Related to Jobs that Require Work Experience Plus Degree

Of the 41 best majors, 30 lead to jobs that require some work experience in addition to the degree. Most commonly these are managerial jobs. For example, Engineering Managers is a job linked to several engineering majors, plus the two architectural majors, but it is seldom an option for new graduates. Instead, the usual entry route is to get a job in engineering or architecture following a bachelor's degree in one of these majors, acquire work experience over some years, and then advance to management after demonstrating relevant knowledge and skills in managerial work assignments.

The presence of several managerial jobs causes the Enterprising personality type to dominate this list.

Best Majors Related to Jobs that Require Work Experience Plus Degree

Major	Annual Earnings of Related Jobs	Percent Growth of Related Jobs	Annual Openings of Related Jobs	Personality Types
1. Computer Engineering	$83,960	35.3%	126,000	IRC
2. Computer Science	$82,718	38.0%	142,000	IRC

(continued)

(continued)

Best Majors Related to Jobs that Require Work Experience Plus Degree

Major	Annual Earnings of Related Jobs	Percent Growth of Related Jobs	Annual Openings of Related Jobs	Personality Types
3. International Business	$94,442	16.6%	246,000	EC
4. Marketing	$92,429	20.0%	72,000	EC
5. Public Administration	$86,701	16.4%	310,000	EC
6. Transportation and Logistics Management	$101,203	15.2%	85,000	EC
7. Business Management	$83,211	16.4%	481,000	EC
8. International Relations	$144,875	14.7%	38,000	EC
9. Human Resources Management	$50,296	24.0%	84,000	ESC
10. Health Information Systems Administration	$73,340	23.0%	33,000	ES
11. Hospital/Health Facilities Administration	$73,340	23.0%	33,000	ES
12. Industrial and Labor Relations	$49,299	25.7%	49,000	ESC
13. Public Relations	$55,966	21.9%	52,000	EAS
14. Biochemistry	$74,650	26.2%	21,000	IR
15. Civil Engineering	$84,707	15.0%	34,000	RIE
16. Microbiology	$72,437	26.4%	21,000	IR
17. Finance	$70,359	14.4%	155,000	EC
18. Architecture	$90,798	14.7%	22,000	ERI
19. Electrical Engineering	$89,095	11.7%	38,000	IRE
20. Actuarial Science	$82,800	22.2%	3,000	CI
21. Industrial Engineering	$86,333	14.4%	28,000	EIR
22. Advertising	$48,594	17.4%	33,000	EA
23. Aeronautical/Aerospace Engineering	$99,721	11.7%	21,000	IRE
24. Landscape Architecture	$100,030	14.0%	16,000	ERI
25. Petroleum Engineering	$104,897	12.1%	16,000	ERI
26. Drama/Theater Arts	$56,310	16.9%	11,000	AES
27. Film/Cinema Studies	$51,199	16.8%	18,000	AES
28. Journalism and Mass Communications	$43,942	14.2%	38,000	A
29. English	$43,702	14.5%	34,000	A
30. Art	$55,182	12.5%	29,000	A

Best Majors Related to Jobs that Require a Master's Degree

Only four majors that meet the criteria for this book are linked to jobs that most commonly require a master's degree. This degree usually requires 33 to 60 semester hours beyond the bachelor's degree. An academic master's degree, such as a Master of Arts in International

Relations, usually requires 33 to 36 hours. A first professional degree in Occupational Therapy usually requires two and one-half years of full-time work, including supervised clinical training. Note that although Physical Therapy currently appears on this list, by 2020 the first professional degree required for this occupation will rise to the doctoral level.

The following list, in which the Social type dominates, ranks these four majors by the usual three economic criteria.

Best Majors Related to Jobs that Require a Master's Degree				
Major	Annual Earnings of Related Jobs	Percent Growth of Related Jobs	Annual Openings of Related Jobs	Personality Types
1. International Relations	$144,875	14.7%	38,000	EC
2. Physical Therapy	$66,200	36.8%	13,000	SRI
3. Graduate Study for College Teaching	$57,770	32.2%	329,000	SI
4. Occupational Therapy	$60,470	33.7%	7,000	SR

Best Majors Related to Jobs that Require a Doctoral Degree

The doctoral degree normally requires two or more years of full-time academic work beyond the bachelor's degree, including writing a dissertation that demonstrates mastery of research methods. Because of this emphasis on research, doctoral-level jobs tend to suit the Investigative personality type, but programs in the sciences often appeal additionally to the Realistic type.

Only four majors that meet the criteria for this book are linked to jobs requiring a doctoral degree, and they are ranked here by the earnings, job growth, and job openings of related jobs.

Best Majors Related to Jobs that Require a Doctoral Degree				
Major	Annual Earnings of Related Jobs	Percent Growth of Related Jobs	Annual Openings of Related Jobs	Personality Types
1. Computer Science	$82,718	38.0%	142,000	IRC
2. Graduate Study for College Teaching	$57,770	32.2%	329,000	SI
3. Biochemistry	$74,650	26.2%	21,000	IR
4. Microbiology	$72,437	26.4%	21,000	IR

Best Majors Related to Jobs that Require a First Professional Degree

The first professional degree normally requires a minimum of two years of education beyond the bachelor's degree and frequently requires three or more years. Programs that lead to health-care careers teach problem solving at both the theoretical and hands-on levels. As a result, these programs are attractive to people with the Investigative personality type.

Two majors that meet the criteria for this book are linked to jobs requiring a first professional degree and are ranked here.

	Annual Earnings of Related Jobs	Percent Growth of Related Jobs	Annual Openings of Related Jobs	Personality Types
Best Majors Related to Jobs that Require a First Professional Degree				
Major				
1. Medicine	$144,916	24.0%	287,000	I
2. Pharmacy	$94,520	24.8%	16,000	ICR

Best Majors Lists by Verbal and Math Skills

If you have ever applied for admission to a college, you are probably very aware of the verbal and math abilities you demonstrated on a standardized test. But have you thought about the relationship between verbal and math abilities and the different majors that are available in college?

One way to look at that relationship is to compare people's *intended* majors with their verbal and math scores on standardized tests. According to the College Board, in 2004–2005, the people with the highest verbal SAT scores intended to enroll in language and literature majors, library and archival sciences majors, and foreign/classical language majors. Those with the highest math SAT scores intended to enroll in mathematics majors, physical sciences majors, and engineering majors. These findings are not at all surprising, because people tend to plan enrollment in majors that seem consistent with their standardized test scores.

Another way to look at these abilities is to consider the verbal and math skills that are required for academic *success* when you're in the major. We don't have access to good data on this for a variety of majors, but you can make some inferences by looking at the Typical Sequence of College Courses listed for each major in Part IV. Note whether there are several courses related to writing, literature, or public speaking (verbal subjects) or whether the curriculum is rich in mathematical courses.

A third way to consider the relationship of these skills to college majors is to look at the *jobs* that people are preparing for by enrolling in the majors. We have good information about the skill requirements of jobs, and therefore for each major described in Part IV we list the verbal and math skills required by related jobs.

We used this job-related skill information to compile the sets of lists that follow. For each of the six personality types, we identified the majors linked to jobs that require a high level of verbal skill. First we list these highly verbal majors ordered by the level of verbal skill. Then we list them ordered by the standard "best jobs" criteria: earnings, job growth, and job openings. Finally, we list the majors linked to jobs that require a *low* level of verbal skills, also ranked by the three economic criteria. Those lists based on verbal skills are followed by another set of lists, similarly ordered, showing the majors linked to jobs that require a high and low level of mathematical skill.

The relationship between skills required in the major and skills required on the job is not exact. Students sometimes complain that they are required to study math at a level that they're never going to use on the job. Conversely, employers sometimes complain that graduates with excellent academic records are deficient in verbal skills they need at work. Nevertheless, the job-related skills are useful to know because one of the chief reasons you enroll in a major is to prepare for a job.

Best Majors Related to Jobs that Require a High Level of Verbal Skills

To rank the majors by their verbal skills, we looked at the ratings that O*NET gives to related jobs on two specific skills: Reading Comprehension and Writing. We took the average of these two ratings, represented it as a figure on a scale ranging from 0 to 100, and eliminated all majors linked to jobs scoring lower than 70.

Realistic Majors Related to Jobs that Require the Highest Level of Verbal Skills

Major	Level of Verbal Skills (Out of 100)	Personality Types
1. Biochemistry	82.0	IR
2. Microbiology	81.1	IR
3. Aeronautical/Aerospace Engineering	75.8	IRE
4. Civil Engineering	74.9	RIE
5. Petroleum Engineering	74.7	ERI
6. Electrical Engineering	74.2	IRE
7. Computer Engineering	74.1	IRC
8. Architecture	71.2	ERI

Investigative Majors Related to Jobs that Require the Highest Level of Verbal Skills

Major	Level of Verbal Skills (Out of 100)	Personality Types
1. Graduate Study for College Teaching	83.9	SI
2. Biochemistry	82.0	IR
3. Medicine	81.3	I
4. Microbiology	81.1	IR
5. Physician Assisting	76.1	IS
6. Computer Engineering	74.1	IRC
7. Nursing (R.N. Training)	72.1	SI
8. Pharmacy	72.1	ICR

Artistic Majors Related to Jobs that Require the Highest Level of Verbal Skills

Major	Level of Verbal Skills (Out of 100)	Personality Types
1. English	77.6	A
2. Journalism and Mass Communications	75.9	A

Social Majors Related to Jobs that Require the Highest Level of Verbal Skills

Major	Level of Verbal Skills (Out of 100)	Personality Types
1. Graduate Study for College Teaching	83.9	SI
2. Physical Therapy	78.4	SRI
3. Health Information Systems Administration	76.3	ES
4. Hospital/Health Facilities Administration	76.3	ES
5. Physician Assisting	76.1	IS
6. Occupational Therapy	75.6	SR
7. Nursing (R.N. Training)	72.1	SI

Enterprising Majors Related to Jobs that Require the Highest Level of Verbal Skills

Major	Level of Verbal Skills (Out of 100)	Personality Types
1. International Relations	81.1	EC
2. Health Information Systems Administration	76.3	ES
3. Hospital/Health Facilities Administration	76.3	ES

Conventional Majors Related to Jobs that Require the Highest Level of Verbal Skills

Major	Level of Verbal Skills (Out of 100)	Personality Types
1. International Relations	81.1	EC
2. Pharmacy	72.1	ICR
3. Actuarial Science	71.5	CI

The following lists rank the highly verbal majors by the earnings, job growth, and job openings of related jobs.

Best Realistic Majors Related to Jobs that Require a High Level of Verbal Skills

Major	Level of Verbal Skills	Annual Earnings of Related Jobs	Percent Growth of Related Jobs	Annual Openings of Related Jobs	Personality Types
1. Computer Engineering	74.1	$83,960	35.3%	126,000	IRC
2. Architecture	71.2	$90,798	14.7%	22,000	ERI
3. Civil Engineering	74.9	$84,707	15.0%	34,000	RIE
4. Electrical Engineering	74.2	$89,095	11.7%	38,000	IRE
5. Aeronautical/Aerospace Engineering	75.8	$99,721	11.7%	21,000	IRE
6. Biochemistry	82.0	$74,650	26.2%	21,000	IR
7. Microbiology	81.1	$72,437	26.4%	21,000	IR
8. Petroleum Engineering	74.7	$104,897	12.1%	16,000	ERI

Best Investigative Majors Related to Jobs that Require a High Level of Verbal Skills

Major	Level of Verbal Skills	Annual Earnings of Related Jobs	Percent Growth of Related Jobs	Annual Openings of Related Jobs	Personality Types
1. Computer Engineering	74.1	$83,960	35.3%	126,000	IRC
2. Graduate Study for College Teaching	83.9	$57,770	32.2%	329,000	SI
3. Medicine	81.3	$144,916	24.0%	287,000	I
4. Physician Assisting	76.1	$74,980	50.0%	10,000	IS
5. Nursing (R.N. Training)	72.1	$57,280	29.4%	229,000	SI
6. Biochemistry	82.0	$74,650	26.2%	21,000	IR
7. Microbiology	81.1	$72,437	26.4%	21,000	IR
8. Pharmacy	72.1	$94,520	24.8%	16,000	ICR

Best Artistic Majors Related to Jobs that Require a High Level of Verbal Skills

Major	Level of Verbal Skills	Annual Earnings of Related Jobs	Percent Growth of Related Jobs	Annual Openings of Related Jobs	Personality Types
1. Journalism and Mass Communications	75.9	$43,942	14.2%	38,000	A
2. English	77.6	$43,702	14.5%	34,000	A

Best Social Majors Related to Jobs that Require a High Level of Verbal Skills

Major	Level of Verbal Skills	Annual Earnings of Related Jobs	Percent Growth of Related Jobs	Annual Openings of Related Jobs	Personality Types
1. Physician Assisting	76.1	$74,980	50.0%	10,000	IS
2. Graduate Study for College Teaching	83.9	$57,770	32.2%	329,000	SI
3. Health Information Systems Administration	76.3	$73,340	23.0%	33,000	ES
4. Hospital/Health Facilities Administration	76.3	$73,340	23.0%	33,000	ES
5. Physical Therapy	78.4	$66,200	36.8%	13,000	SRI
6. Nursing (R.N. Training)	72.1	$57,280	29.4%	229,000	SI
7. Occupational Therapy	75.6	$60,470	33.7%	7,000	SR

Best Enterprising Majors Related to Jobs that Require a High Level of Verbal Skills

Major	Level of Verbal Skills	Annual Earnings of Related Jobs	Percent Growth of Related Jobs	Annual Openings of Related Jobs	Personality Types
1. International Relations	81.1	$144,875	14.7%	38,000	EC
2. Health Information Systems Administration	76.3	$73,340	23.0%	33,000	ES
3. Hospital/Health Facilities Administration	76.3	$73,340	23.0%	33,000	ES

Best Conventional Majors Related to Jobs that Require a High Level of Verbal Skills

Major	Level of Verbal Skills	Annual Earnings of Related Jobs	Percent Growth of Related Jobs	Annual Openings of Related Jobs	Personality Types
1. International Relations	81.1	$144,875	14.7%	38,000	EC
2. Pharmacy	72.1	$94,520	24.8%	16,000	ICR
3. Actuarial Science	71.5	$82,800	22.2%	3,000	CI

Best Majors Related to Jobs that Require a Low Level of Verbal Skills

Maybe verbal ability is not one of your strengths, and you're looking for a major that is compatible with your personality type but requires a relatively low level of verbal skills. To create the following list, we took the majors that did not exceed the cutoff score for the lists of highly verbal majors (a score of 70) and ranked them by their economic potential. The Enterprising and Conventional types appear here most frequently, suggesting that the business world may be a good setting for people who want to use verbal abilities at a comparatively low level.

Best Majors Related to Jobs that Require a Low Level of Verbal Skills

Major	Level of Verbal Skills	Annual Earnings of Related Jobs	Percent Growth of Related Jobs	Annual Openings of Related Jobs	Personality Types
1. Computer Science	69.9	$82,718	38.0%	142,000	IRC
2. International Business	68.0	$94,442	16.6%	246,000	EC
3. Public Administration	65.5	$86,701	16.4%	310,000	EC
4. Business Management	64.9	$83,211	16.4%	481,000	EC
5. Marketing	67.9	$92,429	20.0%	72,000	EC
6. Accounting	64.1	$54,500	20.0%	173,000	CE
7. Transportation and Logistics Management	64.2	$101,203	15.2%	85,000	EC
8. Human Resources Management	67.6	$50,296	24.0%	84,000	ESC
9. Public Relations	69.4	$55,966	21.9%	52,000	EAS
10. Early Childhood Education	63.6	$29,250	30.1%	105,000	SA
11. Finance	63.6	$70,359	14.4%	155,000	EC
12. Industrial and Labor Relations	66.0	$49,299	25.7%	49,000	ESC
13. Communications Studies/Speech	69.9	$48,357	20.2%	62,000	AE
14. Industrial Engineering	68.9	$86,333	14.4%	28,000	EIR
15. Drama/Theater Arts	66.0	$56,310	16.9%	11,000	AES
16. Landscape Architecture	69.5	$100,030	14.0%	16,000	ERI
17. Advertising	62.4	$48,594	17.4%	33,000	EA
18. Film/Cinema Studies	64.6	$51,199	16.8%	18,000	AES
19. Art	63.1	$55,182	12.5%	29,000	A
20. Industrial Design	64.5	$42,091	14.4%	42,000	A

Best Majors Related to Jobs that Require a High Level of Math Skills

All jobs in the O*NET database are rated on math skills, so we were able to use these ratings to assign math skill levels to each of the best majors. We eliminated majors that scored less than 60 on a scale from 0 to 100. This was a lower cutoff level than we used for verbal skills, but we needed to go lower to enable a reasonable number of majors to represent each personality type. Even at that level, no Artistic majors made the cut.

Realistic Majors Related to Jobs that Require the Highest Level of Math Skills

Major	Level of Math Skills (Out of 100)	Personality Types
1. Civil Engineering	79.9	RIE
2. Petroleum Engineering	79.2	ERI
3. Electrical Engineering	75.9	IRE
4. Aeronautical/Aerospace Engineering	74.4	IRE
5. Computer Engineering	73.8	IRC
6. Biochemistry	72.3	IR
7. Landscape Architecture	72.3	ERI
8. Microbiology	72.1	IR
9. Architecture	70.3	ERI
10. Computer Science	66.1	IRC

Investigative Majors Related to Jobs that Require the Highest Level of Math Skills

Major	Level of Math Skills (Out of 100)	Personality Types
1. Computer Engineering	73.8	IRC
2. Biochemistry	72.3	IR
3. Microbiology	72.1	IR
4. Industrial Engineering	71.2	EIR
5. Computer Science	66.1	IRC
6. Pharmacy	62.1	ICR
7. Graduate Study for College Teaching	61.9	SI

Social Majors Related to Jobs that Require the Highest Level of Math Skills

Major	Level of Math Skills (Out of 100)	Personality Types
1. Graduate Study for College Teaching	61.9	SI
2. Health Information Systems Administration	60.7	ES
3. Hospital/Health Facilities Administration	60.7	ES

Enterprising Majors Related to Jobs that Require the Highest Level of Math Skills

Major	Level of Math Skills (Out of 100)	Personality Types
1. Accounting	62.3	CE
2. Health Information Systems Administration	60.7	ES
3. Hospital/Health Facilities Administration	60.7	ES
4. International Business	60.1	EC

Conventional Majors Related to Jobs that Require the Highest Level of Math Skills

Major	Level of Math Skills (Out of 100)	Personality Types
1. Actuarial Science	89.0	CI
2. Accounting	62.3	CE
3. Pharmacy	62.1	ICR
4. International Business	60.1	EC
5. Finance	60.0	EC

The following lists rank the highly mathematical majors by the earnings, job growth, and job openings of related jobs.

Best Realistic Majors Related to Jobs that Require a High Level of Math Skills

Major	Level of Math Skills	Annual Earnings of Related Jobs	Percent Growth of Related Jobs	Annual Openings of Related Jobs	Personality Types
1. Computer Science	66.1	$82,718	38.0%	142,000	IRC
2. Computer Engineering	73.8	$83,960	35.3%	126,000	IRC
3. Architecture	70.3	$90,798	14.7%	22,000	ERI
4. Civil Engineering	79.9	$84,707	15.0%	34,000	RIE
5. Electrical Engineering	75.9	$89,095	11.7%	38,000	IRE
6. Aeronautical/Aerospace Engineering	74.4	$99,721	11.7%	21,000	IRE
7. Landscape Architecture	72.3	$100,030	14.0%	16,000	ERI
8. Petroleum Engineering	79.2	$104,897	12.1%	16,000	ERI
9. Biochemistry	72.3	$74,650	26.2%	21,000	IR
10. Microbiology	72.1	$72,437	26.4%	21,000	IR

Best Investigative Majors Related to Jobs that Require a High Level of Math Skills

Major	Level of Math Skills	Annual Earnings of Related Jobs	Percent Growth of Related Jobs	Annual Openings of Related Jobs	Personality Types
1. Computer Science	66.1	$82,718	38.0%	142,000	IRC
2. Computer Engineering	73.8	$83,960	35.3%	126,000	IRC
3. Graduate Study for College Teaching	61.9	$57,770	32.2%	329,000	SI
4. Industrial Engineering	71.2	$86,333	14.4%	28,000	EIR
5. Pharmacy	62.1	$94,520	24.8%	16,000	ICR
6. Biochemistry	72.3	$74,650	26.2%	21,000	IR
7. Microbiology	72.1	$72,437	26.4%	21,000	IR

Best Social Majors Related to Jobs that Require a High Level of Math Skills

Major	Level of Math Skills	Annual Earnings of Related Jobs	Percent Growth of Related Jobs	Annual Openings of Related Jobs	Personality Types
1. Graduate Study for College Teaching	61.9	$57,770	32.2%	329,000	SI
2. Health Information Systems Administration	60.7	$73,340	23.0%	33,000	ES
3. Hospital/Health Facilities Administration	60.7	$73,340	23.0%	33,000	ES

Best Enterprising Majors Related to Jobs that Require a High Level of Math Skills

Major	Level of Math Skills	Annual Earnings of Related Jobs	Percent Growth of Related Jobs	Annual Openings of Related Jobs	Personality Types
1. International Business	60.1	$94,442	16.6%	246,000	EC
2. Health Information Systems Administration	60.7	$73,340	23.0%	33,000	ES
3. Hospital/Health Facilities Administration	60.7	$73,340	23.0%	33,000	ES
4. Accounting	62.3	$54,500	20.0%	173,000	CE

Best Conventional Majors Related to Jobs that Require a High Level of Math Skills

Major	Level of Math Skills	Annual Earnings of Related Jobs	Percent Growth of Related Jobs	Annual Openings of Related Jobs	Personality Types
1. Pharmacy	62.1	$94,520	24.8%	16,000	ICR
2. International Business	60.1	$94,442	16.6%	246,000	EC
3. Accounting	62.3	$54,500	20.0%	173,000	CE
4. Actuarial Science	89.0	$82,800	22.2%	3,000	CI
5. Finance	60.0	$70,359	14.4%	155,000	EC

Best Majors Related to Jobs with a Low Level of Math Skills

If you find math uninteresting or too challenging, the following list may suggest majors that can suit this preference and also fit your personality type. These majors all failed to make the cutoff score (60) used to create the lists of highly mathematical majors, and they are ranked according to the usual economic criteria. The six personality types are represented almost equally here, but the most business-friendly types (Enterprising and Conventional) tend to rank highest.

Don't assume from this list that you can enter these majors without a good background in math or complete them by taking only low-level math courses. Some of these majors typically include courses in statistics or even calculus! However, the *jobs* that these majors usually lead to generally do not require workers to use a high level of math skill.

Why is there sometimes such a disconnect between course requirements and work tasks? The curriculum developers who design the majors want you to be able to understand the people you'll work with. In many jobs, you do not use a lot of math but work with people who do, so with a background in mathematical concepts you can understand how these other workers produce their results and can tell the difference between meaningful and misleading results. You can challenge the output of those workers and ask them intelligent questions. For example, physicians need to understand the procedures of medical researchers, and marketers need to understand how market research works, even if they are not engaged in it. A background in math also makes it possible for you to specialize in research—although, if you are looking at this list, you probably are not interested in such math-intense pursuits.

Best Majors Related to Jobs that Require a Low Level of Math Skills

Major	Level of Math Skills	Annual Earnings of Related Jobs	Percent Growth of Related Jobs	Annual Openings of Related Jobs	Personality Types
1. Medicine	57.9	$144,916	24.0%	287,000	I
2. Nursing (R.N. Training)	57.4	$57,280	29.4%	229,000	SI
3. Business Management	57.9	$83,211	16.4%	481,000	EC
4. Public Administration	55.0	$86,701	16.4%	310,000	EC
5. Marketing	56.7	$92,429	20.0%	72,000	EC
6. Transportation and Logistics Management	56.5	$101,203	15.2%	85,000	EC
7. Human Resources Management	49.0	$50,296	24.0%	84,000	ESC
8. Physical Therapy	35.6	$66,200	36.8%	13,000	SRI
9. Physician Assisting	59.6	$74,980	50.0%	10,000	IS
10. Early Childhood Education	39.6	$29,250	30.1%	105,000	SA
11. Public Relations	42.8	$55,966	21.9%	52,000	EAS

(continued)

(continued)

Best Majors Related to Jobs that Require a Low Level of Math Skills

Major	Level of Math Skills	Annual Earnings of Related Jobs	Percent Growth of Related Jobs	Annual Openings of Related Jobs	Personality Types
12. Industrial and Labor Relations	46.6	$49,299	25.7%	49,000	ESC
13. International Relations	59.5	$144,875	14.7%	38,000	EC
14. Occupational Therapy	45.4	$60,470	33.7%	7,000	SR
15. Communications Studies/Speech	32.4	$48,357	20.2%	62,000	AE
16. Drama/Theater Arts	35.9	$56,310	16.9%	11,000	AES
17. Advertising	50.9	$48,594	17.4%	33,000	EA
18. Film/Cinema Studies	39.0	$51,199	16.8%	18,000	AES
19. Art	57.0	$55,182	12.5%	29,000	A
20. Industrial Design	53.1	$42,091	14.4%	42,000	A

Bonus Lists: Best Majors that May Appeal to Other Aspects of Your Personality

The six Holland types provide a convenient way of describing personalities, but most of us are familiar with other aspects of personality, many of which are arguably relevant to career choice. The O*NET database provides ratings that allowed us to compile several lists based on these other dimensions of personality. All of the following lists are based on the 41 majors that met the criteria for this book. For each major in these lists, we also list the one, two, or three Holland types that characterize the major.

Best Majors for Introverts and Extroverts

The psychologist Carl Jung described two kinds of people: **extroverts**, whose psychic energy flows inward, gained from other people; and **introverts**, whose psychic energy flows outward, gained from solitude. Nowadays the concept of psychic energy is not taken literally, but psychologists continue to recognize that some people are stimulated by social settings and feel most comfortable there, whereas others are more energetic and productive when they can escape distractions caused by other people. So psychologists still speak of introverts and extroverts, and in the field of career development it can be useful to consider whether you lean toward one of these personality types.

For example, if you are an introvert, you are likely to fit better in a job where you can focus on the task without being distracted by ringing telephones, office chit-chat, and frequent meetings. On the other hand, if you are an extrovert, you probably don't mind multitasking and enjoy chatting up your co-workers and clients. (For a detailed look at introversion and its relationship to career choice, see *200 Best Jobs for Introverts* from JIST Publishing.)

These two personality types align with the six Holland types to some extent: Extroverts have much in common with Social personalities and introverts have much in common with Realistic personalities.

The O*NET database does not rate jobs for introversion and extroversion as it does for the six Holland types. Nevertheless, we were able to compute introversion and extroversion ratings for jobs related to majors by looking at the O*NET ratings for two aspects of the jobs: the value Independence, which is defined as doing work alone, and the work-context feature called Contact with Others, which represents how much the job requires workers to be in contact with others—face-to-face, by telephone, or otherwise. O*NET provides ratings for both features on a scale of 1 to 5, so to compute an introversion score we subtracted the rating for Contact with Others from 5 (thus getting a measure of how much the job *does not* involve contact with others), took the average of this figure and the Independence rating, and then represented that average on a scale from 0 to 100. For an extroversion score we subtracted the introversion score from 100.

These scores for major-related jobs enabled us to identify the 20 most introverted majors and the 20 most extroverted majors, and then we used the three standard economic measures to rank each set and produce the following two lists. If you tend toward introversion or extroversion, the majors on one of these lists may appeal to you.

Best Majors for Introverts

Major	Rating for Introversion	Annual Earnings of Related Jobs	Percent Growth of Related Jobs	Annual Openings of Related Jobs	Personality Types
1. Computer Engineering	36.2	$83,960	35.3%	126,000	IRC
2. Computer Science	37.9	$82,718	38.0%	142,000	IRC
3. International Relations	33.7	$144,875	14.7%	38,000	EC
4. Accounting	38.4	$54,500	20.0%	173,000	CE
5. Civil Engineering	35.4	$84,707	15.0%	34,000	RIE
6. Architecture	33.7	$90,798	14.7%	22,000	ERI
7. Communications Studies/Speech	37.3	$48,357	20.2%	62,000	AE
8. Finance	33.7	$70,359	14.4%	155,000	EC
9. Biochemistry	52.4	$74,650	26.2%	21,000	IR
10. Microbiology	41.6	$72,437	26.4%	21,000	IR
11. Electrical Engineering	38.3	$89,095	11.7%	38,000	IRE
12. Industrial Engineering	30.6	$86,333	14.4%	28,000	EIR
13. Actuarial Science	52.0	$82,800	22.2%	3,000	CI

(continued)

(continued)

Best Majors for Introverts

Major	Rating for Introversion	Annual Earnings of Related Jobs	Percent Growth of Related Jobs	Annual Openings of Related Jobs	Personality Types
14. Landscape Architecture	31.4	$100,030	14.0%	16,000	ERI
15. Aeronautical/Aerospace Engineering	36.9	$99,721	11.7%	21,000	IRE
16. Industrial Design	42.4	$42,091	14.4%	42,000	A
17. Petroleum Engineering	31.1	$104,897	12.1%	16,000	ERI
18. English	41.5	$43,702	14.5%	34,000	A
19. Journalism and Mass Communications	38.0	$43,942	14.2%	38,000	A
20. Art	46.6	$55,182	12.5%	29,000	A

Best Majors for Extroverts

Major	Rating for Extroversion	Annual Earnings of Related Jobs	Percent Growth of Related Jobs	Annual Openings of Related Jobs	Personality Types
1. Medicine	79.6	$144,916	24.0%	287,000	I
2. Graduate Study for College Teaching	88.7	$57,770	32.2%	329,000	SI
3. Business Management	75.5	$83,211	16.4%	481,000	EC
4. International Business	73.0	$94,442	16.6%	246,000	EC
5. Nursing (R.N. Training)	92.0	$57,280	29.4%	229,000	SI
6. Pharmacy	76.1	$94,520	24.8%	16,000	ICR
7. Public Administration	78.3	$86,701	16.4%	310,000	EC
8. Physician Assisting	82.5	$74,980	50.0%	10,000	IS
9. Marketing	81.4	$92,429	20.0%	72,000	EC
10. Physical Therapy	83.5	$66,200	36.8%	13,000	SRI
11. Transportation and Logistics Management	77.4	$101,203	15.2%	85,000	EC
12. Early Childhood Education	81.7	$29,250	30.1%	105,000	SA
13. Health Information Systems Administration	77.1	$73,340	23.0%	33,000	ES
14. Hospital/Health Facilities Administration	77.1	$73,340	23.0%	33,000	ES
15. Human Resources Management	76.8	$50,296	24.0%	84,000	ESC
16. Occupational Therapy	86.0	$60,470	33.7%	7,000	SR
17. Industrial and Labor Relations	77.8	$49,299	25.7%	49,000	ESC
18. Public Relations	77.8	$55,966	21.9%	52,000	EAS
19. Advertising	80.1	$48,594	17.4%	33,000	EA
20. Drama/Theater Arts	76.2	$56,310	16.9%	11,000	AES

Best Majors for Persistent People

Some people tend to stick to a task even in the face of obstacles. Whether you call them dedicated or pig-headed, they seem to represent a distinct personality type. Because the O*NET database rates jobs on Persistence (as a work style), we were able to compute scores for majors based on their related jobs and to identify the 20 majors most hospitable to persistent people. We then ranked these majors by the usual three economic criteria to produce the following list.

Major	Rating for Persistence	Annual Earnings of Related Jobs	Percent Growth of Related Jobs	Annual Openings of Related Jobs	Personality Types
1. Medicine	86.5	$144,916	24.0%	287,000	I
2. Computer Science	77.8	$82,718	38.0%	142,000	IRC
3. Graduate Study for College Teaching	79.2	$57,770	32.2%	329,000	SI
4. Public Administration	76.4	$86,701	16.4%	310,000	EC
5. Nursing (R.N. Training)	77.8	$57,280	29.4%	229,000	SI
6. Physician Assisting	83.0	$74,980	50.0%	10,000	IS
7. Transportation and Logistics Management	82.5	$101,203	15.2%	85,000	EC
8. International Relations	90.2	$144,875	14.7%	38,000	EC
9. Biochemistry	87.4	$74,650	26.2%	21,000	IR
10. Health Information Systems Administration	82.7	$73,340	23.0%	33,000	ES
11. Hospital/Health Facilities Administration	82.7	$73,340	23.0%	33,000	ES
12. Microbiology	86.6	$72,437	26.4%	21,000	IR
13. Finance	77.4	$70,359	14.4%	155,000	EC
14. Occupational Therapy	80.0	$60,470	33.7%	7,000	SR
15. Communications Studies/Speech	83.3	$48,357	20.2%	62,000	AE
16. Advertising	91.9	$48,594	17.4%	33,000	EA
17. Drama/Theater Arts	82.4	$56,310	16.9%	11,000	AES
18. Film/Cinema Studies	80.3	$51,199	16.8%	18,000	AES
19. Journalism and Mass Communications	87.8	$43,942	14.2%	38,000	A
20. English	87.7	$43,702	14.5%	34,000	A

Best Majors for Sensitive People

Another work style used to rate jobs in O*NET is Concern for Others, which is defined as being sensitive to others' needs and feelings and being understanding and helpful on the job. We used these ratings to identify the 20 majors most suited to sensitive people, and then we ranked this set of majors by the earnings, job growth, and job openings of the related occupations.

You may think the sensitive personality type has a lot in common with the Social personality type, but the majors listed here are also associated with other Holland types. For example, the majors Public Relations and Advertising are considered Enterprising and Artistic; they are included in the following list, probably because the jobs associated with them need workers who are sensitive to consumers' attitudes and reactions.

Best Majors for Sensitive People

Major	Rating for Concern for Others	Annual Earnings	Percent Growth	Annual Openings	Personality Types
1. Medicine	94.2	$144,916	24.0%	287,000	I
2. Graduate Study for College Teaching	78.5	$57,770	32.2%	329,000	SI
3. Business Management	82.0	$83,211	16.4%	481,000	EC
4. International Business	84.0	$94,442	16.6%	246,000	EC
5. Nursing (R.N. Training)	94.2	$57,280	29.4%	229,000	SI
6. Public Administration	84.3	$86,701	16.4%	310,000	EC
7. Pharmacy	79.0	$94,520	24.8%	16,000	ICR
8. Physician Assisting	98.2	$74,980	50.0%	10,000	IS
9. Marketing	74.4	$92,429	20.0%	72,000	EC
10. Transportation and Logistics Management	79.0	$101,203	15.2%	85,000	EC
11. Early Childhood Education	88.2	$29,250	30.1%	105,000	SA
12. Physical Therapy	97.7	$66,200	36.8%	13,000	SRI
13. Health Information Systems Administration	89.0	$73,340	23.0%	33,000	ES
14. Hospital/Health Facilities Administration	89.0	$73,340	23.0%	33,000	ES
15. Human Resources Management	84.6	$50,296	24.0%	84,000	ESC
16. International Relations	73.5	$144,875	14.7%	38,000	EC
17. Occupational Therapy	98.2	$60,470	33.7%	7,000	SR
18. Industrial and Labor Relations	80.6	$49,299	25.7%	49,000	ESC
19. Public Relations	78.3	$55,966	21.9%	52,000	EAS
20. Advertising	78.4	$48,594	17.4%	33,000	EA

Best Majors for People with Self-Control

The O*NET database rates jobs on a work style called Self-Control, which is defined as maintaining composure, keeping emotions in check, controlling anger, and avoiding aggressive behavior, even in very difficult situations. This tendency to stay as cool as the other side of the pillow may be regarded as a personality type, so we thought it would be interesting to see which majors are a good fit.

We identified the 20 majors with related jobs rated highest on Self-Control, and it's interesting to note that the four highest-rated were all in the health-care field. Then we sorted the 20 majors by the three usual economic measures to produce the following list.

Best Majors for People with Self-Control

Major	Rating for Self-Control	Annual Earnings	Percent Growth	Annual Openings	Personality Types
1. Medicine	92.2	$144,916	24.0%	287,000	I
2. Graduate Study for College Teaching	81.3	$57,770	32.2%	329,000	SI
3. Business Management	83.7	$83,211	16.4%	481,000	EC
4. International Business	87.2	$94,442	16.6%	246,000	EC
5. Nursing (R.N. Training)	95.2	$57,280	29.4%	229,000	SI
6. Public Administration	87.2	$86,701	16.4%	310,000	EC
7. Marketing	80.8	$92,429	20.0%	72,000	EC
8. Physician Assisting	90.5	$74,980	50.0%	10,000	IS
9. Physical Therapy	91.3	$66,200	36.8%	13,000	SRI
10. Transportation and Logistics Management	84.6	$101,203	15.2%	85,000	EC
11. Early Childhood Education	90.4	$29,250	30.1%	105,000	SA
12. Health Information Systems Administration	89.0	$73,340	23.0%	33,000	ES
13. Hospital/Health Facilities Administration	89.0	$73,340	23.0%	33,000	ES
14. Human Resources Management	83.9	$50,296	24.0%	84,000	ESC
15. International Relations	81.8	$144,875	14.7%	38,000	EC
16. Occupational Therapy	88.0	$60,470	33.7%	7,000	SR
17. Industrial and Labor Relations	83.9	$49,299	25.7%	49,000	ESC
18. Public Relations	81.7	$55,966	21.9%	52,000	EAS
19. Advertising	82.7	$48,594	17.4%	33,000	EA
20. Drama/Theater Arts	80.6	$56,310	16.9%	11,000	AES

Best Majors for Stress-Tolerant People

Workplace stress can be emotionally draining and can even have serious consequences for your health. But some people have a personality that allows them to tolerate stressful work situations, and we thought that they deserve a list of majors especially suitable for them. (We also thought that the rest of us deserve a whole book about careers that lack these pressures, *150 Best Low-Stress Jobs* from JIST Publishing.)

To create the list, we identified the 20 majors with related jobs that are rated highest on the O*NET work style Stress Tolerance, which is defined as accepting criticism and dealing calmly and effectively with high-stress situations. The major rated highest for requiring stress tolerance (with a score of 93.3) is Physician Assisting; evidently it is more stressful to assist a physician than to be one. As in the other lists in this section, we ordered the 20 majors by three economic criteria so you can see which are best overall.

Best Majors for Stress-Tolerant People

Major	Rating for Stress Tolerance	Annual Earnings	Percent Growth	Annual Openings	Personality Types
1. Medicine	90.6	$144,916	24.0%	287,000	I
2. Nursing (R.N. Training)	90.0	$57,280	29.4%	229,000	SI
3. Business Management	82.2	$83,211	16.4%	481,000	EC
4. International Business	87.1	$94,442	16.6%	246,000	EC
5. Public Administration	86.6	$86,701	16.4%	310,000	EC
6. Pharmacy	83.0	$94,520	24.8%	16,000	ICR
7. Physician Assisting	93.3	$74,980	50.0%	10,000	IS
8. Transportation and Logistics Management	88.4	$101,203	15.2%	85,000	EC
9. Biochemistry	81.0	$74,650	26.2%	21,000	IR
10. Early Childhood Education	81.8	$29,250	30.1%	105,000	SA
11. Health Information Systems Administration	83.0	$73,340	23.0%	33,000	ES
12. Hospital/Health Facilities Administration	83.0	$73,340	23.0%	33,000	ES
13. International Relations	93.4	$144,875	14.7%	38,000	EC
14. Human Resources Management	84.5	$50,296	24.0%	84,000	ESC
15. Industrial and Labor Relations	82.8	$49,299	25.7%	49,000	ESC
16. Occupational Therapy	87.8	$60,470	33.7%	7,000	SR
17. Advertising	90.1	$48,594	17.4%	33,000	EA
18. Drama/Theater Arts	86.7	$56,310	16.9%	11,000	AES
19. Film/Cinema Studies	85.8	$51,199	16.8%	18,000	AES
20. Art	79.9	$55,182	12.5%	29,000	A

Best Majors for Flexible People

Our rapidly changing economy has made flexibility a very useful personality trait in the workplace. Some jobs are particularly demanding of flexibility, and the O*NET database provides guidance on this matter by rating all occupations on a work style called Adaptability/Flexibility. This trait is defined as being open to change (positive or negative) and to considerable variety in the workplace. Using these ratings, we were able to identify the 20 majors leading to jobs with the highest need for flexible people. We ordered these 20 majors by the economic rewards of the related jobs and produced the following list.

Best Majors for Flexible People

Major	Rating for Adaptability/ Flexibility	Annual Earnings	Percent Growth	Annual Openings	Personality Types
1. Medicine	81.1	$144,916	24.0%	287,000	I
2. Computer Science	79.7	$82,718	38.0%	142,000	IRC
3. Business Management	78.6	$83,211	16.4%	481,000	EC
4. International Business	77.8	$94,442	16.6%	246,000	EC
5. Public Administration	79.5	$86,701	16.4%	310,000	EC
6. Nursing (R.N. Training)	92.3	$57,280	29.4%	229,000	SI
7. Physician Assisting	86.2	$74,980	50.0%	10,000	IS
8. Transportation and Logistics Management	85.2	$101,203	15.2%	85,000	EC
9. Health Information Systems Administration	89.8	$73,340	23.0%	33,000	ES
10. Hospital/Health Facilities Administration	89.8	$73,340	23.0%	33,000	ES
11. International Relations	86.7	$144,875	14.7%	38,000	EC
12. Biochemistry	78.7	$74,650	26.2%	21,000	IR
13. Early Childhood Education	82.3	$29,250	30.1%	105,000	SA
14. Physical Therapy	86.7	$66,200	36.8%	13,000	SRI
15. Occupational Therapy	95.0	$60,470	33.7%	7,000	SR
16. Advertising	90.8	$48,594	17.4%	33,000	EA
17. Drama/Theater Arts	89.2	$56,310	16.9%	11,000	AES
18. Film/Cinema Studies	87.2	$51,199	16.8%	18,000	AES
19. Industrial Design	82.9	$42,091	14.4%	42,000	A
20. Art	82.3	$55,182	12.5%	29,000	A

Best Majors for Detail-Oriented People

Some workers tend to be careful about detail and thorough in completing work tasks. These workers are attracted to jobs where it is important to get the details right. Such jobs can be identified in the O*NET database by their high ratings on a work style called Attention to Detail, so we used these ratings to extract the 20 majors whose related jobs are most detail-oriented. As you might expect, many of these majors are linked to the Conventional personality type, but all the other personality types are also represented here at least once. Like the other lists in this section, this one is ordered to show which majors are best in terms of economic criteria.

Best Majors for Detail-Oriented People

Major	Rating for Attention to Detail	Annual Earnings	Percent Growth	Annual Openings	Personality Types
1. Medicine	96.2	$144,916	24.0%	287,000	I
2. Nursing (R.N. Training)	92.0	$57,280	29.4%	229,000	SI
3. International Business	88.7	$94,442	16.6%	246,000	EC
4. Public Administration	88.1	$86,701	16.4%	310,000	EC
5. Pharmacy	92.0	$94,520	24.8%	16,000	ICR
6. Health Information Systems Administration	98.7	$73,340	23.0%	33,000	ES
7. Hospital/Health Facilities Administration	98.7	$73,340	23.0%	33,000	ES
8. Human Resources Management	87.4	$50,296	24.0%	84,000	ESC
9. Physician Assisting	95.2	$74,980	50.0%	10,000	IS
10. Industrial and Labor Relations	90.3	$49,299	25.7%	49,000	ESC
11. Public Relations	91.8	$55,966	21.9%	52,000	EAS
12. Accounting	90.2	$54,500	20.0%	173,000	CE
13. Actuarial Science	97.5	$82,800	22.2%	3,000	CI
14. Advertising	95.4	$48,594	17.4%	33,000	EA
15. Drama/Theater Arts	91.5	$56,310	16.9%	11,000	AES
16. Film/Cinema Studies	90.8	$51,199	16.8%	18,000	AES
17. Art	90.1	$55,182	12.5%	29,000	A
18. English	88.3	$43,702	14.5%	34,000	A
19. Industrial Design	97.2	$42,091	14.4%	42,000	A
20. Journalism and Mass Communications	88.8	$43,942	14.2%	38,000	A

Best Majors for Innovators

Some workers like to develop new ideas and solve work-related problems by thinking in creative and unorthodox ways. This tendency is considered to be an aspect of the Artistic personality type, but it also can be useful in the scientific and business fields. We used the O*NET database to discover the 20 majors linked to jobs with the highest ratings for the work style Innovation. Then we ordered the majors by earnings, job growth, and job openings to produce the following list. It comes as no surprise that Artistic majors are more prominent in this list than in any other list in this section.

Best Majors for Innovators

Major	Rating for Innovation	Annual Earnings	Percent Growth	Annual Openings	Personality Types
1. Computer Engineering	75.7	$83,960	35.3%	126,000	IRC
2. Computer Science	76.3	$82,718	38.0%	142,000	IRC
3. Graduate Study for College Teaching	75.2	$57,770	32.2%	329,000	SI
4. International Business	76.5	$94,442	16.6%	246,000	EC
5. Public Administration	75.7	$86,701	16.4%	310,000	EC
6. Transportation and Logistics Management	76.9	$101,203	15.2%	85,000	EC
7. Health Information Systems Administration	81.5	$73,340	23.0%	33,000	ES
8. Hospital/Health Facilities Administration	81.5	$73,340	23.0%	33,000	ES
9. International Relations	80.4	$144,875	14.7%	38,000	EC
10. Early Childhood Education	76.0	$29,250	30.1%	105,000	SA
11. Occupational Therapy	82.7	$60,470	33.7%	7,000	SR
12. Communications Studies/Speech	76.0	$48,357	20.2%	62,000	AE
13. Actuarial Science	79.5	$82,800	22.2%	3,000	CI
14. Advertising	83.9	$48,594	17.4%	33,000	EA
15. Drama/Theater Arts	78.7	$56,310	16.9%	11,000	AES
16. Film/Cinema Studies	77.5	$51,199	16.8%	18,000	AES
17. Industrial Design	83.9	$42,091	14.4%	42,000	A
18. Journalism and Mass Communications	78.4	$43,942	14.2%	38,000	A
19. English	79.4	$43,702	14.5%	34,000	A
20. Art	78.1	$55,182	12.5%	29,000	A

Best Majors for Analytical Thinkers

Maybe you know someone who likes to analyze information and use logic to address work-related issues and problems. This trait is one aspect of the Investigative personality type but, according to O*NET, it also characterizes many jobs that attract Realistic, Enterprising, and Conventional workers. We isolated the 20 majors with related jobs rated highest on the measure Analytical Thinking and sorted them by the usual economic criteria. It's interesting to note that the Social personality type appears only once and the Artistic personality type does not appear at all in the following list.

Best Majors for Analytical Thinkers

Major	Rating for Analytical Thinking	Annual Earnings	Percent Growth	Annual Openings	Personality Types
1. Medicine	87.9	$144,916	24.0%	287,000	I
2. International Business	85.2	$94,442	16.6%	246,000	EC
3. Public Administration	83.2	$86,701	16.4%	310,000	EC
4. Computer Engineering	88.7	$83,960	35.3%	126,000	IRC
5. Business Management	80.8	$83,211	16.4%	481,000	EC
6. Computer Science	88.8	$82,718	38.0%	142,000	IRC
7. Graduate Study for College Teaching	83.1	$57,770	32.2%	329,000	SI
8. International Relations	81.1	$144,875	14.7%	38,000	EC
9. Accounting	89.2	$54,500	20.0%	173,000	CE
10. Architecture	82.1	$90,798	14.7%	22,000	ERI
11. Civil Engineering	82.1	$84,707	15.0%	34,000	RIE
12. Biochemistry	89.4	$74,650	26.2%	21,000	IR
13. Microbiology	87.7	$72,437	26.4%	21,000	IR
14. Electrical Engineering	82.3	$89,095	11.7%	38,000	IRE
15. Industrial Engineering	87.0	$86,333	14.4%	28,000	EIR
16. Aeronautical/Aerospace Engineering	87.5	$99,721	11.7%	21,000	IRE
17. Landscape Architecture	81.8	$100,030	14.0%	16,000	ERI
18. Petroleum Engineering	84.2	$104,897	12.1%	16,000	ERI
19. Finance	80.8	$70,359	14.4%	155,000	EC
20. Actuarial Science	97.2	$82,800	22.2%	3,000	CI

Best Majors Related to Jobs Not Behind a Desk

Some people have what might be called an antsy personality. They don't like being stuck behind a desk and they enjoy work that involves physical activity. We created an entire book for these people, *175 Best Jobs Not Behind a Desk,* based on the O*NET ratings for Physical Activity and (lack of) Sitting. The following list identifies the 20 majors that are linked to jobs with the highest level of activity and ranks them by the usual economic criteria.

It's worth noting that the major on this list rated highest on physical activity, Physical Therapy, has an activity score of only 56.4 on a scale of 0 to 100. Many of the majors are rated down in the 30s. The fact is that we live in an information-based economy, and even health-care jobs involve a large amount of paperwork. Much of the growth in our economy is in Dilbert-type settings, so any list of the best jobs or best majors includes many options that are not highly active. Nevertheless, a list such as the following can help you avoid the most sedentary choices.

Best Majors Related to Jobs Not Behind a Desk

Major	Rating for Activity	Annual Earnings	Percent Growth	Annual Openings	Personality Types
1. Medicine	42.8	$144,916	24.0%	287,000	I
2. Graduate Study for College Teaching	33.1	$57,770	32.2%	329,000	SI
3. Business Management	37.0	$83,211	16.4%	481,000	EC
4. International Business	35.6	$94,442	16.6%	246,000	EC
5. Public Administration	35.5	$86,701	16.4%	310,000	EC
6. Pharmacy	49.6	$94,520	24.8%	16,000	ICR
7. Nursing (R.N. Training)	56.4	$57,280	29.4%	229,000	SI
8. Physician Assisting	53.2	$74,980	50.0%	10,000	IS
9. Biochemistry	32.1	$74,650	26.2%	21,000	IR
10. Health Information Systems Administration	42.9	$73,340	23.0%	33,000	ES
11. Hospital/Health Facilities Administration	42.9	$73,340	23.0%	33,000	ES
12. Early Childhood Education	56.9	$29,250	30.1%	105,000	SA
13. Microbiology	32.7	$72,437	26.4%	21,000	IR
14. Physical Therapy	68.3	$66,200	36.8%	13,000	SRI
15. Industrial Engineering	34.5	$86,333	14.4%	28,000	EIR
16. Landscape Architecture	34.3	$100,030	14.0%	16,000	ERI
17. Petroleum Engineering	32.9	$104,897	12.1%	16,000	ERI
18. Occupational Therapy	61.6	$60,470	33.7%	7,000	SR
19. Advertising	31.9	$48,594	17.4%	33,000	EA
20. Drama/Theater Arts	34.5	$56,310	16.9%	11,000	AES

Best Majors Related to World-Improving Jobs

Some people want to do work that makes the world a better place by easing suffering, increasing knowledge, promoting safety and security, improving the natural environment, or creating things of beauty. The O*NET database does not provide ratings that are useful in identifying world-improving jobs, but the editors at JIST used the criteria in the previous sentence to create a list that became the centerpiece of the book *150 Best Jobs for a Better World*. We used this same list to identify majors related to world-improving jobs; 21 majors met these criteria. We then sorted these majors by their economic potential to produce the following list of the highest-ranking 20 majors.

Best Majors Related to World-Improving Jobs

Major	Annual Earnings	Percent Growth	Annual Openings	Personality Types
1. Medicine	$144,916	24.0%	287,000	I
2. Graduate Study for College Teaching	$57,770	32.2%	329,000	SI
3. Business Management	$83,211	16.4%	481,000	EC
4. Public Administration	$86,701	16.4%	310,000	EC
5. Nursing (R.N. Training)	$57,280	29.4%	229,000	SI
6. Pharmacy	$94,520	24.8%	16,000	ICR
7. Physician Assisting	$74,980	50.0%	10,000	IS
8. Biochemistry	$74,650	26.2%	21,000	IR
9. Microbiology	$72,437	26.4%	21,000	IR
10. Physical Therapy	$66,200	36.8%	13,000	SRI
11. Architecture	$90,798	14.7%	22,000	ERI
12. Early Childhood Education	$29,250	30.1%	105,000	SA
13. Finance	$70,359	14.4%	155,000	EC
14. Occupational Therapy	$60,470	33.7%	7,000	SR
15. Communications Studies/Speech	$48,357	20.2%	62,000	AE
16. Landscape Architecture	$100,030	14.0%	16,000	ERI
17. Film/Cinema Studies	$51,199	16.8%	18,000	AES
18. Drama/Theater Arts	$56,310	16.9%	11,000	AES
19. English	$43,702	14.5%	34,000	A
20. Journalism and Mass Communications	$43,942	14.2%	38,000	A

PART IV

Descriptions of the Best College Majors for Your Personality

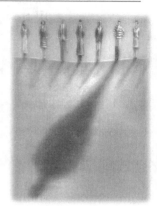

This part provides descriptions for all the majors included in one or more of the lists in Part III, plus the jobs related to these majors. The introduction gives more details on how to use and interpret the descriptions of majors, but here is some additional information:

◎ The descriptions are divided into six sections, based on the primary RIASEC code of the majors. Within each section, majors are arranged in alphabetical order by name. This approach allows you to find a description quickly if you know the major's correct title from one of the lists in Part III. It also allows you to browse easily among majors with a similar primary personality type.

◎ Five additional majors are described here: African-American Studies, American Studies, Area Studies, Humanities, and Women's Studies. These majors are related to Graduate Study for College Teaching but, unlike that pseudo-major, are specific majors linked to specific college teaching jobs. Some graduates of these programs go into fields other than college teaching, sometimes by earning a degree in a different field.

◎ The pseudo-major Graduate Study for College Teaching is linked to 38 postsecondary teaching jobs. Because their major work tasks are so similar, we have included only their individual definitions.

◎ Consider the descriptions of majors in this section as a first step in exploring educational options. When you find a major that interests you, turn to Appendix A for suggestions about resources for further exploration.

◎ Appendix C can give you more context to understand the GOE work groups referred to in the descriptions; you'll find the complete outline of the GOE taxonomy there. The skills referenced in the job descriptions are defined in Appendix D, and the work-related values are defined in Appendix E.

◎ If you are using this section to browse for interesting options, we suggest you begin with the table of contents. Part III features many interesting lists that will help you identify titles of majors to explore in more detail. If you have not browsed the lists in Part III, consider spending some time there. The lists are interesting and will help you identify majors you can find described in the material that follows. The titles of majors in Part III are also listed in the table of contents.

Realistic Major

Civil Engineering

Personality Type:
Realistic–Investigative–Enterprising

Useful Facts About the Major

Prepares individuals to apply mathematical and scientific principles to the design, development, and operational evaluation of structural, load-bearing, material moving, transportation, water resource, and material control systems and environmental safety measures.

Related CIP Program: 14.0801 Civil Engineering, General

Specializations in the Major: Environmental engineering; geotechnical engineering; structural engineering; transportation engineering; water resources.

Typical Sequence of College Courses: English composition, technical writing, calculus, differential equations, general chemistry, introduction to computer science, general physics, introduction to electric circuits, engineering graphics, statics, dynamics, materials engineering, introduction to civil engineering, numerical analysis, fluid mechanics, engineering surveying and measurement, environmental engineering and design, soil mechanics, engineering economics, analysis of structures, highway and transportation engineering, reinforced concrete design, steel design, water resources and hydraulic engineering, senior design project.

Typical Sequence of High School Courses: English, algebra, geometry, trigonometry, pre-calculus, calculus, chemistry, physics, computer science.

Career Snapshot

Civil engineers design and supervise construction of roads, buildings, bridges, dams, airports, water-supply systems, and many other projects that affect the quality of our environment. They apply principles of physics and other sciences to devise engineering solutions that are technically effective, as well as being economically and environmentally sound. A bachelor's degree is the usual way to enter the field. Engineering is also a good way to prepare for a later position in management. Employment opportunities tend to rise and fall with the economy.

Useful Averages for the Related Jobs

- **Annual Earnings:** $84,707
- **Growth:** 15.0%
- **Self-Employed:** 3.0%
- **Part-Time:** 8.7%
- **Verbal Skill Rating:** 74.9
- **Math Skill Rating:** 79.9

Other Details About the Related Jobs

Total Annual Job Openings: 34,000

Interest Area: 15 Scientific Research, Engineering, and Mathematics

Skills—Science; operations analysis; technology design; mathematics; installation; management of financial resources. **Values**—Authority; creativity; autonomy; ability utilization; social status; responsibility. **Work Conditions**—Outdoors; sitting; exposed to weather.

Related Jobs

1. Civil Engineers

Personality Type:
Realistic–Investigative–Conventional

Earnings: $68,600
Growth: 16.5%
Annual Openings: 19,000

Most Common Education/Training Level:
Bachelor's degree

Perform engineering duties in planning, designing, and overseeing construction and maintenance of building structures and facilities, such as roads, railroads, airports, bridges, harbors, channels, dams, irrigation projects, pipelines, power plants, water and sewage systems, and waste disposal units. Includes architectural, structural, traffic, ocean, and geo-technical engineers. Analyze survey reports, maps, drawings, blueprints, aerial photography, and other topographical or geologic data to plan projects. Plan and design transportation or hydraulic systems and structures, following construction and government standards and using design software and drawing tools. Compute load and grade requirements, water flow rates, and material stress factors to determine design specifications. Inspect project sites to monitor progress and ensure conformance to design specifications and safety or sanitation standards. Direct construction, operations, and maintenance activities at project site. Direct or participate in surveying to lay out installations and establish reference points, grades, and elevations to guide construction. Estimate quantities and cost of materials, equipment, or labor to determine project feasibility. Prepare or present public reports on topics such as bid proposals, deeds, environmental impact statements, or property and right-of-way descriptions. Test soils and materials to determine the adequacy and strength of foundations, concrete, asphalt, or steel. Provide technical advice regarding design, construction, or program modifications and structural repairs to industrial and managerial personnel. Conduct studies of traffic patterns or environmental conditions to identify engineering problems and assess the potential impact of projects.

2. Engineering Managers

Personality Type:
Enterprising–Investigative–Realistic

Earnings: $105,430
Growth: 13.0%
Annual Openings: 15,000

Most Common Education/Training Level:
Work experience plus degree

Plan, direct, or coordinate activities in such fields as architecture and engineering or research and development in these fields. Confer with management, production, and marketing staff to discuss project specifications and procedures. Coordinate and direct projects, making detailed plans to accomplish goals and directing the integration of technical activities. Analyze technology, resource needs, and market demand to plan and assess the feasibility of projects. Plan and direct the installation, testing, operation, maintenance, and repair of facilities and equipment. Direct, review, and approve product design and changes. Recruit employees; assign, direct, and evaluate their work; and oversee the development and maintenance of staff competence. Prepare budgets, bids, and contracts and direct the negotiation of research contracts. Develop and implement policies, standards, and procedures for the engineering and technical work performed in the department, service, laboratory, or firm. Review and recommend or approve contracts and cost estimates. Perform administrative functions such as reviewing and writing reports, approving expenditures, enforcing rules, and making decisions about the purchase of materials or services. Present and explain proposals, reports, and findings to clients. Consult or negotiate with clients to prepare project specifications. Set scientific and technical goals within broad outlines provided by top management. Administer highway planning, construction, and maintenance. Direct the engineering of water control, treatment, and distribution projects. Plan, direct, and coordinate survey work with other staff activities, certifying survey work and writing land legal descriptions. Confer with and report to officials and the public to provide information and solicit support for projects.

Investigative Majors

Aeronautical/Aerospace Engineering

Personality Type:
Investigative–Realistic–Enterprising

Useful Facts About the Major

Prepares individuals to apply mathematical and scientific principles to the design, development, and operational evaluation of aircraft, space vehicles, and their systems; applied research on flight characteristics; and the development of systems and procedures for the launching, guidance, and control of air and space vehicles.

Related CIP Program: 14.0201 Aerospace, Aeronautical, and Astronautical Engineering

Specializations in the Major: Airframes and aerodynamics; propulsion; spacecraft; testing.

Typical Sequence of College Courses: English composition, technical writing, calculus, differential equations, introduction to computer science, general chemistry, general physics, thermodynamics, introduction to electric circuits, introduction to aerospace engineering, statics, dynamics, materials engineering, fluid mechanics, aircraft systems and propulsion, flight control systems, aerodynamics, aircraft structural design, aircraft stability and control, experimental aerodynamics, senior design project.

Typical Sequence of High School Courses: English, algebra, geometry, trigonometry, precalculus, calculus, chemistry, physics, computer science.

Career Snapshot

Engineers apply scientific principles to real-world problems, finding the optimal solution that balances elegant technology with realistic cost. Aeronautical/aerospace engineers need to learn the specific principles of air flow and resistance and the workings of various kinds of propulsion systems. Most enter the job market with a bachelor's degree. Some later move into managerial positions. Job outlook is good because for many years other engineering fields were perceived as having a better outlook. Best opportunities are expected in jobs related to defense as opposed to commercial aviation.

Useful Averages for the Related Jobs

- **Annual Earnings:** $99,721
- **Growth:** 11.5%
- **Self-Employed:** 0.4%
- **Part-Time:** 8.0%
- **Verbal Skill Rating:** 75.8
- **Math Skill Rating:** 74.4

Other Details About the Related Jobs

Total Annual Job Openings: 21,000

Interest Area: 15 Scientific Research, Engineering, and Mathematics

Skills—Science; technology design; operations analysis; management of financial resources; mathematics; judgment and decision making. **Values**—Authority; creativity; autonomy; ability utilization; social status; compensation. **Work Conditions**—Indoors, environmentally controlled; sitting.

Related Jobs

1. Aerospace Engineers

Personality Type:
Investigative–Realistic–Conventional

Earnings: $87,610
Growth: 8.3%
Annual Openings: 6,000

Most Common Education/Training Level:
Bachelor's degree

Perform a variety of engineering work in designing, constructing, and testing aircraft, missiles, and spacecraft. May conduct basic and applied research to evaluate adaptability of materials and equipment to aircraft design and manufacture. May recommend improvements in testing equipment and techniques. Formulate conceptual design of aeronautical or aerospace products or systems to meet customer requirements. Direct and coordinate activities of engineering or technical personnel designing, fabricating, modifying, or testing aircraft or aerospace products. Develop design criteria for aeronautical or aerospace products or systems, including testing methods, production costs, quality standards, and completion dates. Plan and conduct experimental, environmental, operational, and stress tests on models and prototypes of aircraft and aerospace systems and equipment. Evaluate product data and design from inspections and reports for conformance to engineering principles, customer requirements, and quality standards. Formulate mathematical models or other methods of computer analysis to develop, evaluate, or modify design according to customer engineering requirements. Write technical reports and other documentation, such as handbooks and bulletins, for use by engineering staff, management, and customers. Analyze project requests and proposals and engineering data to determine feasibility, productibility, cost, and production time of aerospace or aeronautical product. Review performance reports and documentation from customers and field engineers and inspect malfunctioning or damaged products to determine problem. Direct research and development programs. Evaluate and approve selection of vendors by study of past performance and new advertisements. Plan and coordinate activities concerned with investigating and resolving customers' reports of technical problems with aircraft or aerospace vehicles. Maintain records of performance reports for future reference.

2. Engineering Managers

Personality Type:
Enterprising–Investigative–Realistic

Earnings: $105,430
Growth: 13.0%
Annual Openings: 15,000

Most Common Education/Training Level:
Work experience plus degree

Plan, direct, or coordinate activities in such fields as architecture and engineering or research and development in these fields. Confer with management, production, and marketing staff to discuss project specifications and procedures. Coordinate and direct projects, making detailed plans to accomplish goals and directing the integration of technical activities. Analyze technology, resource needs, and market demand to plan and assess the feasibility of projects. Plan and direct the installation, testing, operation, maintenance, and repair of facilities and equipment. Direct, review, and approve product design and changes. Recruit employees; assign, direct, and evaluate their work; and

Investigative

oversee the development and maintenance of staff competence. Prepare budgets, bids, and contracts and direct the negotiation of research contracts. Develop and implement policies, standards, and procedures for the engineering and technical work performed in the department, service, laboratory, or firm. Review and recommend or approve contracts and cost estimates. Perform administrative functions such as reviewing and writing reports, approving expenditures, enforcing rules, and making decisions about the purchase of materials or services. Present and explain proposals, reports, and findings to clients. Consult or negotiate with clients to prepare project specifications. Set scientific and technical goals within broad outlines provided by top management. Administer highway planning, construction, and maintenance. Direct the engineering of water control, treatment, and distribution projects. Plan, direct, and coordinate survey work with other staff activities, certifying survey work and writing land legal descriptions. Confer with and report to officials and the public to provide information and solicit support for projects.

Biochemistry

Personality Type: Investigative–Realistic

Useful Facts About the Major

Focuses on the scientific study of the chemistry of living systems, their fundamental chemical substances and reactions, and their chemical pathways and information transfer systems, with particular reference to carbohydrates, proteins, lipids, and nucleic acids.

Related CIP Program: 26.0202 Biochemistry

Specializations in the Major: Forensic chemistry; pharmacological chemistry; recombinant DNA; research.

Typical Sequence of College Courses: English composition, calculus, introduction to computer science, general chemistry, general biology, organic chemistry, general physics, analytical chemistry, general microbiology, introduction to biochemistry, cell biology, molecular biology, physical chemistry, genetics.

Typical Sequence of High School Courses: English, algebra, trigonometry, biology, geometry, chemistry, physics, computer science, precalculus, calculus.

Career Snapshot

Biochemistry studies the fundamental chemical processes that support life. The recent growth of the pharmaceutical industry and of genetic engineering technology has fueled the demand for biochemistry majors, especially at the graduate level, but there will be a lot of competition for jobs that are supported by grants, either at universities or in other settings. Better opportunities are expected for those with bachelor's degrees who seek work in nonresearch jobs such as sales, marketing, and clinical laboratory testing.

Useful Averages for the Related Jobs

- **Annual Earnings:** $74,650
- **Growth:** 26.4%
- **Self-Employed:** 0.6%
- **Part-Time:** 13.8%
- **Verbal Skill Rating:** 82.0
- **Math Skill Rating:** 72.3

Other Details About the Related Jobs

Total Annual Job Openings: 21,000

Interest Area: 15 Scientific Research, Engineering, and Mathematics

Skills—Science; reading comprehension; writing; complex problem solving; active learning; mathematics. **Values**—Creativity; social status; responsibility; ability utilization; autonomy; achievement. **Work Conditions**—Indoors, environmentally controlled; exposed to disease or infections.

Related Jobs

1. Biochemists and Biophysicists

Personality Type:
Investigative–Realistic–Conventional

Earnings: $76,320
Growth: 21.0%
Annual Openings: 1,000

Most Common Education/Training Level:
Doctoral degree

Investigative

Study the chemical composition and physical principles of living cells and organisms, their electrical and mechanical energy, and related phenomena. May conduct research to further understanding of the complex chemical combinations and reactions involved in metabolism, reproduction, growth, and heredity. May determine the effects of foods, drugs, serums, hormones, and other substances on tissues and vital processes of living organisms. Design and perform experiments with equipment such as lasers, accelerators, and mass spectrometers. Analyze brain functions such as learning, thinking, memory, and the dynamics of seeing and hearing. Share research findings by writing scientific articles and by making presentations at scientific conferences. Develop and test new drugs and medications intended for commercial distribution. Develop methods to process, store, and use foods, drugs, and chemical compounds. Develop new methods to study the mechanisms of biological processes. Examine the molecular and chemical aspects of immune system functioning. Investigate the nature, composition, and expression of genes and research how genetic engineering can impact these processes. Determine the three-dimensional structure of biological macromolecules. Prepare reports and recommendations based upon research outcomes. Design and build laboratory equipment needed for special research projects. Isolate, analyze, and synthesize vitamins, hormones, allergens, minerals, and enzymes and determine their effects on body functions. Research cancer treatment, using radiation and nuclear particles. Research transformations of substances in cells, using atomic isotopes. Study how light is absorbed in processes such as photosynthesis or vision. Analyze foods to determine their nutritional values and the effects of cooking, canning, and processing on these values. Study spatial configurations of submicroscopic molecules such as proteins, using X rays and electron microscopes. Teach and advise undergraduate and graduate students and supervise their research. Investigate the transmission of electrical impulses along nerves and muscles. Research how characteristics of plants and animals are carried through successive generations. Investigate damage to cells and tissues caused by X rays and nuclear particles. Research the chemical effects of substances such as drugs, serums, hormones, and food on tissues and vital processes. Develop and execute tests to detect diseases, genetic disorders, or other abnormalities. Produce pharmaceutically and industrially useful proteins, using recombinant DNA technology.

2. Medical Scientists, Except Epidemiologists

Personality Type: Investigative–Realistic–Social

Earnings: $61,680
Growth: 34.1%
Annual Openings: 15,000

Most Common Education/Training Level: Doctoral degree

Conduct research dealing with the understanding of human diseases and the improvement of human health. Engage in clinical investigation or other research, production, technical writing, or related activities. Conduct research to develop methodologies, instrumentation, and procedures for medical application, analyzing data and presenting findings. Plan and direct studies to investigate human or animal disease, preventive methods, and treatments for disease. Follow strict safety procedures when handling toxic materials to avoid contamination. Evaluate effects of drugs, gases, pesticides, parasites, and microorganisms at various levels. Teach principles of medicine and medical and laboratory procedures to physicians, residents, students, and technicians. Prepare and analyze organ, tissue, and cell samples to identify toxicity, bacteria, or microorganisms or to study cell structure. Standardize drug dosages, methods of immunization, and procedures for manufacture of drugs and medicinal compounds. Investigate cause, progress, life cycle, or mode of transmission of diseases or parasites. Confer with health department, industry personnel, physicians, and others to develop health safety standards and public health improvement programs. Study animal and human health and physiological processes. Consult with and advise physicians, educators, researchers, and others regarding medical applications of physics, biology, and chemistry. Use equipment such as atomic absorption spectrometers, electron microscopes, flow cytometers, and chromatography systems.

3. Natural Sciences Managers

Personality Type:
Investigative–Enterprising–Realistic

Earnings: $100,080
Growth: 13.6%
Annual Openings: 5,000

Most Common Education/Training Level:
Work experience plus degree

Plan, direct, or coordinate activities in such fields as life sciences, physical sciences, mathematics, and statistics and research and development in these fields. Confer with scientists, engineers, regulators, and others to plan and review projects and to provide technical assistance. Develop client relationships and communicate with clients to explain proposals, present research findings, establish specifications, or discuss project status. Plan and direct research, development, and production activities. Prepare project proposals. Design and coordinate successive phases of problem analysis, solution proposals, and testing. Review project activities and prepare and review research, testing, and operational reports. Hire, supervise, and evaluate engineers, technicians, researchers, and other staff. Determine scientific and technical goals within broad outlines provided by top management and make detailed plans to accomplish these goals. Develop and implement policies, standards, and procedures for the architectural, scientific, and technical work performed to ensure regulatory compliance and operations enhancement. Develop innovative technology and train staff for its implementation. Provide for stewardship of plant and animal resources and habitats, studying land use; monitoring animal populations; and providing shelter, resources, and medical treatment for animals. Conduct own research in field of expertise. Recruit personnel and oversee the development and maintenance of staff competence. Advise and assist in obtaining patents or meeting other legal requirements. Prepare and administer budget, approve and review expenditures, and prepare financial reports. Make presentations at professional meetings to further knowledge in the field.

Investigative

Computer Engineering

Personality Type:
Investigative–Realistic–Conventional

Useful Facts About the Major

Prepares individuals to apply mathematical and scientific principles to the design, development, and operational evaluation of computer hardware and software systems and related equipment and facilities; and the analysis of specific problems of computer applications to various tasks.

Related CIP Program: 14.0901 Computer Engineering, General

Specializations in the Major: Hardware design; software/systems design; systems analysis.

Typical Sequence of College Courses: English composition, technical writing, calculus, differential equations, general chemistry, introduction to computer science, general physics, introduction to engineering, introduction to electric circuits, engineering circuit analysis, numerical analysis, electrical networks, electronics, computer architecture, algorithms and data structures, digital system design, software engineering, operating systems, microcomputer systems, senior design project.

Typical Sequence of High School Courses: English, algebra, geometry, trigonometry, pre-calculus, calculus, chemistry, physics, computer science.

Career Snapshot

Computer engineers use their knowledge of scientific principles to design computers, networks of computers, and systems (such as telecommunications) that include computers. They need to understand both hardware and software, and they may build prototypes of new systems. The usual entry route is via a bachelor's degree. Opportunities for employment are good despite foreign competition, especially in nonmanufacturing jobs related to systems design. Some engineers go into management, and the computer industry provides many opportunities for creative and motivated engineers to become entrepreneurs.

Useful Averages for the Related Jobs

- **Annual Earnings:** $83,960
- **Growth:** 35.1%
- **Self-Employed:** 2.5%
- **Part-Time:** 12.3%
- **Verbal Skill Rating:** 74.1
- **Math Skill Rating:** 73.8

Other Details About the Related Jobs

Total Annual Job Openings: 126,000

Interest Area: 11 Information Technology; 15 Scientific Research, Engineering, and Mathematics

Skills—Programming; technology design; troubleshooting; systems analysis; operations analysis; quality control analysis. **Values**—Creativity; ability utilization; authority; working conditions; responsibility; social status. **Work Conditions**—Indoors, environmentally controlled; sitting.

Related Jobs

1. Computer Hardware Engineers

Personality Type:
Investigative–Realistic–Conventional

Earnings: $88,470
Growth: 10.1%
Annual Openings: 5,000

Most Common Education/Training Level:
Bachelor's degree

Research, design, develop, and test computer or computer-related equipment for commercial, industrial, military, or scientific use. May supervise the manufacturing and installation of computer or computer-related equipment and components. Update knowledge and skills to keep up with rapid advancements in computer technology. Provide technical support to designers, marketing and sales departments, suppliers, engineers, and other team members throughout the product development and implementation process. Test and verify hardware and support peripherals to ensure that they meet specifications and requirements, analyzing and recording test data. Monitor functioning of equipment and make necessary modifications to ensure system operates in conformance with specifications. Analyze information to determine, recommend, and plan layout, including type of computers and peripheral equipment modifications. Build, test, and modify product prototypes, using working models or theoretical models constructed using computer simulation. Analyze user needs and recommend appropriate hardware. Direct technicians, engineering designers, or other technical support personnel as needed. Confer with engineering staff and consult specifications to evaluate interface between hardware and software and operational and performance requirements of overall system.

Select hardware and material, assuring compliance with specifications and product requirements. Store, retrieve, and manipulate data for analysis of system capabilities and requirements. Write detailed functional specifications that document the hardware development process and support hardware introduction. Specify power supply requirements and configuration, drawing on system performance expectations and design specifications. Provide training and support to system designers and users. Assemble and modify existing pieces of equipment to meet special needs. Evaluate factors such as reporting formats required, cost constraints, and need for security restrictions to determine hardware configuration. Design and develop computer hardware and support peripherals, including central processing units (CPUs), support logic, microprocessors, custom integrated circuits, and printers and disk drives. Recommend purchase of equipment to control dust, temperature, and humidity in area of system installation.

2. Computer Software Engineers, Applications

Personality Type:
Realistic–Investigative–Conventional

Earnings: $79,780
Growth: 48.4%
Annual Openings: 54,000

Most Common Education/Training Level:
Bachelor's degree

Develop, create, and modify general computer applications software or specialized utility programs. Analyze user needs and develop software solutions. Design software or customize software for client use with the aim of optimizing operational efficiency. May analyze and design databases within an application area, working individually or coordinating database

Investigative

development as part of a team. Confer with systems analysts, engineers, programmers, and others to design system and to obtain information on project limitations and capabilities, performance requirements, and interfaces. Modify existing software to correct errors, allow it to adapt to new hardware, or improve its performance. Analyze user needs and software requirements to determine feasibility of design within time and cost constraints. Consult with customers about software system design and maintenance. Coordinate software system installation and monitor equipment functioning to ensure specifications are met. Design, develop, and modify software systems, using scientific analysis and mathematical models to predict and measure outcome and consequences of design. Develop and direct software system testing and validation procedures, programming, and documentation. Analyze information to determine, recommend, and plan computer specifications and layouts and peripheral equipment modifications. Supervise the work of programmers, technologists, and technicians and other engineering and scientific personnel. Obtain and evaluate information on factors such as reporting formats required, costs, and security needs to determine hardware configuration. Determine system performance standards. Train users to use new or modified equipment. Store, retrieve, and manipulate data for analysis of system capabilities and requirements. Specify power supply requirements and configuration. Recommend purchase of equipment to control dust, temperature, and humidity in area of system installation.

3. Computer Software Engineers, Systems Software

Personality Type:
Investigative–Realistic–Conventional

Earnings: $85,370
Growth: 43.0%
Annual Openings: 37,000

Most Common Education/Training Level: Bachelor's degree

Research, design, develop, and test operating systems–level software, compilers, and network distribution software for medical, industrial, military, communications, aerospace, business, scientific, and general computing applications. Set operational specifications and formulate and analyze software requirements. Apply principles and techniques of computer science, engineering, and mathematical analysis. Modify existing software to correct errors, to adapt it to new hardware, or to upgrade interfaces and improve performance. Design and develop software systems, using scientific analysis and mathematical models to predict and measure outcome and consequences of design. Consult with engineering staff to evaluate interface between hardware and software, develop specifications and performance requirements, and resolve customer problems. Analyze information to determine, recommend, and plan installation of a new system or modification of an existing system. Develop and direct software system testing and validation procedures. Direct software programming and development of documentation. Consult with customers or other departments on project status, proposals, and technical issues such as software system design and maintenance. Advise customer about, or perform, maintenance of software system. Coordinate installation of software system. Monitor functioning of equipment to ensure system operates in conformance with specifications. Store, retrieve, and manipulate data for analysis of system capabilities and requirements. Confer with data-processing and project managers to obtain information on limitations and capabilities for data-processing projects. Prepare reports and correspondence concerning project specifications, activities, and status. Evaluate factors such as reporting formats required, cost constraints, and need for security restrictions to determine hardware configuration. Supervise and assign work to programmers, designers, technologists and technicians, and other engineering and scientific personnel. Train users to use new or modified equipment. Utilize microcontrollers to develop control signals; implement control algorithms; and measure process variables such as temperatures, pressures, and positions. Recommend purchase of equipment to control dust, temperature, and humidity in area of system installation. Specify power supply requirements and configuration.

4. Computer Specialists, All Other

Personality Type: No data available

Earnings: $68,570
Growth: 19.0%
Annual Openings: 15,000

Most Common Education/Training Level: Associate degree

Job Specializations

Computer Systems Engineers/Architects. Design and develop solutions to complex applications problems, system administration issues, or network concerns. Perform systems management and integration functions. Perform security analyses of developed or packaged software components. Perform ongoing hardware and software maintenance operations, including installing or upgrading hardware or software. Complete models and simulations, using manual or automated tools, to analyze or predict system performance under different operating conditions. Define and analyze objectives, scope, issues, or organizational impact of information systems. Develop efficient and effective system controllers. Develop application-specific software. Configure servers to meet functional specifications. Verify stability, interoperability, portability, security, or scalability of system architecture. Train system users in system operation or maintenance. Provide guidelines for implementing secure systems to customers or installation teams. Provide technical guidance or support for the development or troubleshooting of systems. Monitor system operation to detect potential problems. Communicate project information through presentations, technical reports, or white papers. Communicate with staff or clients to understand specific system requirements. Investigate system component suitability for specified purposes and make recommendations regarding component use. Identify system data, hardware, or software components required to meet user needs. Evaluate existing systems to determine effectiveness and suggest changes to meet organizational requirements. Evaluate current or emerging technologies to consider factors such as cost, portability, compatibility, or usability. Establish functional or system standards to ensure operational requirements, quality requirements, and design constraints are addressed. Document design specifications, installation instructions, and other system-related information. Direct the analysis, development, and operation of complete computer systems. Direct the installation of operating systems, network or application software, or computer or network hardware. Develop system engineering, software engineering, system integration, or distributed system architectures. Design and conduct hardware or software tests.

Investigative

Network Designers. Determine user requirements and design specifications for computer networks. Plan and implement network upgrades. Develop network-related documentation. Design, build, or operate equipment configuration prototypes, including network hardware, software, servers, or server operation systems. Coordinate network operations, maintenance, repairs, or upgrades. Adjust network sizes to meet volume or capacity demands. Communicate with vendors to gather information about products, to alert them to future needs, to resolve problems, or to address system maintenance issues. Coordinate installation of new equipment. Coordinate network or design activities with designers of associated networks. Design, organize, and deliver product awareness, skills transfer, and product education sessions for staff and suppliers. Determine specific network hardware or software requirements, such as platforms, interfaces, bandwidths, or routine schemas. Develop disaster recovery plans. Communicate with customers, sales staff, or marketing staff to determine customer needs. Explain design specifications to integration or test engineers. Develop plans or budgets for network equipment replacement. Prepare design presentations and proposals for staff or customers. Supervise engineers and other staff in the design or implementation of network solutions. Use network computer-aided design (CAD) software packages to optimize network designs. Develop or maintain project reporting systems. Participate in network technology upgrade or expansion projects, including installation of hardware and software and integration testing. Research and test new or modified hardware or software products to determine performance and interoperability. Develop and implement solutions for network problems. Prepare or monitor project schedules, budgets, or cost control systems. Monitor and analyze network performance and data input/output reports to detect problems, identify inefficient use of computer resources, or perform capacity planning. Evaluate network designs to determine whether customer requirements are met efficiently and effectively. Estimate time and materials needed to complete projects. Develop or recommend network security measures, such as firewalls, network security audits, or automated security probes.

Software Quality Assurance Engineers and Testers. Develop and execute software test plans in order to identify software problems and their causes. Develop or specify standards, methods, or procedures to determine product quality or release readiness. Update automated test scripts to ensure currency. Conduct software compatibility tests with programs, hardware, operating systems, or network environments. Create or maintain databases of known test defects. Design test plans, scenarios, scripts, or procedures. Design or develop automated testing tools. Perform initial debugging procedures by reviewing configuration files, logs, or code pieces to determine breakdown source. Visit beta testing sites to evaluate software performance. Monitor bug resolution efforts and track successes. Document test procedures to ensure replicability and compliance with standards. Evaluate or recommend software for testing or bug tracking. Identify program deviance from standards and suggest modifications to ensure compliance. Identify, analyze, and document problems with program function, output, online screen, or content. Install and configure recreations of software production environments to allow testing of software performance. Install, maintain, or use software testing programs. Investigate customer problems referred by technical support. Review software documentation to ensure technical accuracy, compliance, or completeness or to mitigate risks. Participate in product design reviews to provide input on functional requirements, product designs, schedules, or potential problems. Develop testing programs that address areas such as database impacts, software scenarios, regression testing, negative testing, error or bug retests, or usability. Plan test schedules or strategies in accordance with project scope or delivery dates. Provide feedback and recommendations to developers on software usability and functionality. Test system modifications to prepare for implementation. Collaborate with field staff or customers to evaluate or diagnose problems and recommend possible solutions. Provide technical support during software installation or configuration. Conduct historical analyses of test results. Coordinate user or third-party testing. Document software defects, using a bug tracking system, and report defects to software developers.

Web Administrators. Manage Web environment design, deployment, development, and maintenance activities. Perform testing and quality assurance of Web sites and Web applications. Gather, analyze, or document user feedback to locate or resolve sources of problems. Perform user testing or usage analyses to determine Web sites' effectiveness or usability. Set up or maintain monitoring tools on Web servers or Web sites. Check and analyze operating system or application logfiles regularly to verify proper system performance. Develop testing routines and procedures. Evaluate testing routines or procedures for adequacy, sufficiency, and effectiveness. Test issues such as system integration, performance, and system security on a regular schedule or after any major program modifications. Determine sources of Web page or server problems and take action to correct such problems. Track, compile, and analyze Web site usage data. Recommend Web site improvements and develop budgets to support recommendations. Identify or address interoperability requirements. Evaluate or recommend server hardware or software. Develop or implement procedures for ongoing Web site revision. Implement updates, upgrades, and patches in a timely manner to limit loss of service. Identify, standardize, and communicate levels of access and security. Implement Web site security measures, such as firewalls or message encryption. Collaborate with Web developers to create and operate internal and external Web sites or to manage projects such as e-marketing campaigns. Develop Web site performance metrics. Correct testing-identified problems or recommend actions for their resolution. Provide training or technical assistance in Web site implementation or use. Back up or modify applications and related data to provide for disaster recovery. Test backup or recovery plans regularly and resolve any problems. Document application and Web site changes or change procedures. Document installation or configuration procedures to allow maintenance and repetition. Test new software packages for use in Web operations or other applications. Inform Web site users of problems, problem resolutions, or application changes and updates. Monitor Web developments through continuing education; reading; or participation in professional conferences, workshops, or groups.

Web Developers. Develop and design Web applications and Web sites. Create and specify architectural and technical parameters. Direct Web site content creation, enhancement, and maintenance. Recommend and implement performance improvements. Perform or direct Web site updates. Develop and document style guidelines for Web site content. Renew domain name registrations. Design and implement Web site security measures such as firewalls or message encryption. Establish appropriate server directory trees. Identify or maintain links to and from other Web sites and check links to ensure proper functioning. Create searchable indices for Web page content. Back up files from Web sites to local directories for instant recovery in case of problems. Write supporting code for Web applications or Web sites. Register Web sites with search engines to increase Web site traffic. Respond to user e-mail inquiries or set up automated systems to send responses. Collaborate with management or users to develop e-commerce strategies and to integrate these strategies with Web sites. Communicate with network personnel or Web site hosting agencies to address hardware or software issues affecting Web sites. Evaluate or recommend server hardware or software. Develop or implement procedures for ongoing Web site revision. Perform Web site tests according to planned schedules or after any Web site or product revisions. Create Web models or prototypes that include physical, interface, logical, or data models. Maintain understanding of current Web technologies or programming practices through continuing education; reading; or participation in professional conferences, workshops, or groups. Identify problems uncovered by testing or customer feedback and correct problems or refer problems to appropriate personnel for correction. Research, document, rate, or select alternatives for Web architecture or technologies. Write, design, or edit Web page content or direct others producing content. Document technical factors such as server load, bandwidth, database performance, and browser and device types. Design, build, or maintain Web sites, using authoring or scripting languages, content creation tools, management

tools, and digital media. Confer with management or development teams to prioritize needs, resolve conflicts, develop content criteria, or choose solutions.

5. Engineering Managers

Personality Type:
Enterprising–Investigative–Realistic

Earnings: $105,430
Growth: 13.0%
Annual Openings: 15,000

Most Common Education/Training Level: Work experience plus degree

Plan, direct, or coordinate activities in such fields as architecture and engineering or research and development in these fields. Confer with management, production, and marketing staff to discuss project specifications and procedures. Coordinate and direct projects, making detailed plans to accomplish goals and directing the integration of technical activities. Analyze technology, resource needs, and market demand to plan and assess the feasibility of projects. Plan and direct the installation, testing, operation, maintenance, and repair of facilities and equipment. Direct, review, and approve product design and changes. Recruit employees; assign, direct, and evaluate their work; and oversee the development and maintenance of staff competence. Prepare budgets, bids, and contracts and direct the negotiation of research contracts. Develop and implement policies, standards, and procedures for the engineering and technical work performed in the department, service, laboratory, or firm. Review and recommend or approve contracts and cost estimates. Perform administrative functions such as reviewing and writing reports, approving expenditures, enforcing rules, and making decisions about the purchase of materials or services. Present and explain proposals, reports, and findings to clients. Consult or negotiate with clients to prepare project specifications. Set scientific and technical goals within broad outlines provided by top management. Administer highway planning, construction, and maintenance. Direct the engineering of water control, treatment, and distribution projects. Plan, direct, and coordinate survey work with other staff activities, certifying survey work and writing land legal descriptions. Confer with and report to officials and the public to provide information and solicit support for projects.

Investigative

Computer Science

Personality Type:
Investigative–Realistic–Conventional

Useful Facts About the Major

Focuses on computers, computing problems and solutions, and the design of computer systems and user interfaces from a scientific perspective.

Related CIP Programs: 11.0701 Computer Science; 11.0802 Data Modeling/Warehousing and Database Administration

Specializations in the Major: Business programming; database programming; programming for the Internet; scientific programming; security and disaster recovery; systems programming.

Typical Sequence of College Courses: English composition, calculus, introduction to economics, statistics for business and social sciences, introduction to computer science, programming in a language (e.g., C, PASCAL, COBOL), algorithms and data structures, software engineering, operating systems, database systems, theory of computer languages, computer architecture, artificial intelligence.

Typical Sequence of High School Courses: English, algebra, geometry, trigonometry, precalculus, calculus, chemistry, physics, computer science.

Career Snapshot

Computer science teaches you not only specific languages, but the principles by which languages are created, the structures used to store data, and the logical structures by which programs solve problems. Job outlook is best for roles that are not easily outsourced to overseas workers, such as systems administration and information security.

Useful Averages for the Related Jobs

- **Annual Earnings:** $82,718
- **Growth:** 37.8%
- **Self-Employed:** 2.5%
- **Part-Time:** 10.9%
- **Verbal Skill Rating:** 69.9
- **Math Skill Rating:** 66.1

Other Details About the Related Jobs

Total Annual Job Openings: 142,000

Interest Area: 11 Information Technology

Skills—Programming; systems analysis; technology design; troubleshooting; operations analysis; quality control analysis. **Values**—Creativity; ability utilization; authority; working conditions; responsibility; social status. **Work Conditions**—Indoors, environmentally controlled; sitting.

Related Jobs

1. Computer and Information Scientists, Research

Personality Type: No data available

Earnings: $93,950
Growth: 25.6%
Annual Openings: 2,000

Most Common Education/Training Level:
Doctoral degree

Conduct research into fundamental computer and information science as theorists, designers, or inventors. Solve or develop solutions to problems in the field of computer hardware and software. Evaluate project plans and proposals to assess feasibility issues. Direct daily operations of departments, coordinating project activities with other departments. Consult with users, management, vendors, and technicians to determine computing needs and system requirements. Participate in staffing decisions and direct training of subordinates. Participate in multidisciplinary projects in areas such as virtual reality, human-computer interaction, or robotics. Meet with managers, vendors, and others to solicit cooperation and resolve problems. Maintain network hardware and software, direct network security measures, and monitor networks to ensure availability to system users. Develop performance standards and evaluate work in light of established standards. Develop and interpret organizational goals, policies, and procedures. Approve, prepare, monitor, and adjust operational budgets. Design computers and the software that runs them. Analyze problems to develop solutions involving computer hardware and software. Apply theoretical expertise and innovation to create or apply new technology, such as adapting principles for applying computers to new uses. Conduct logical analyses of business, scientific, engineering, and other technical problems, formulating mathematical models of problems for solution by computers. Assign or schedule tasks in order to meet work priorities and goals.

2. Computer and Information Systems Managers

Personality Type:
Enterprising–Conventional–Investigative

Earnings: $101,580
Growth: 25.9%
Annual Openings: 25,000

Most Common Education/Training Level:
Work experience plus degree

Plan, direct, or coordinate activities in such fields as electronic data processing, information systems, systems analysis, and computer programming. Manage backup, security, and user help systems. Consult with users, management, vendors, and technicians to assess computing needs and system requirements. Direct daily operations of department, analyzing workflow, establishing priorities, developing standards, and setting deadlines. Assign and review the work of systems analysts, programmers, and other computer-related workers. Stay abreast of advances in technology. Develop computer information resources, providing for data security and control, strategic computing, and disaster recovery. Review and approve all systems charts and programs prior to their implementation. Evaluate the organization's technology use and needs and recommend improvements, such as hardware and software upgrades. Control operational budget and expenditures. Meet with department heads, managers, supervisors, vendors, and others to solicit cooperation and resolve problems. Develop and interpret organizational goals, policies, and procedures. Recruit, hire, train, and supervise staff or participate in staffing decisions. Review project plans to plan and coordinate project activity. Evaluate

Investigative

data-processing proposals to assess project feasibility and requirements. Prepare and review operational reports or project progress reports. Purchase necessary equipment.

3. Computer Software Engineers, Applications

Personality Type:
Realistic–Investigative–Conventional

Earnings: $79,780
Growth: 48.4%
Annual Openings: 54,000

Most Common Education/Training Level:
Bachelor's degree

Develop, create, and modify general computer applications software or specialized utility programs. Analyze user needs and develop software solutions. Design software or customize software for client use with the aim of optimizing operational efficiency. May analyze and design databases within an application area, working individually or coordinating database development as part of a team. Confer with systems analysts, engineers, programmers, and others to design system and to obtain information on project limitations and capabilities, performance requirements, and interfaces. Modify existing software to correct errors, allow it to adapt to new hardware, or improve its performance. Analyze user needs and software requirements to determine feasibility of design within time and cost constraints. Consult with customers about software system design and maintenance. Coordinate software system installation and monitor equipment functioning to ensure specifications are met. Design, develop, and modify software systems, using scientific analysis and mathematical models to predict and measure outcome and consequences of design. Develop and direct software system testing and validation

procedures, programming, and documentation. Analyze information to determine, recommend, and plan computer specifications and layouts and peripheral equipment modifications. Supervise the work of programmers, technologists, and technicians and other engineering and scientific personnel. Obtain and evaluate information on factors such as reporting formats required, costs, and security needs to determine hardware configuration. Determine system performance standards. Train users to use new or modified equipment. Store, retrieve, and manipulate data for analysis of system capabilities and requirements. Specify power supply requirements and configuration. Recommend purchase of equipment to control dust, temperature, and humidity in area of system installation.

4. Computer Software Engineers, Systems Software

Personality Type:
Investigative–Realistic–Conventional

Earnings: $85,370
Growth: 43.0%
Annual Openings: 37,000

Most Common Education/Training Level:
Bachelor's degree

Research, design, develop, and test operating systems–level software, compilers, and network distribution software for medical, industrial, military, communications, aerospace, business, scientific, and general computing applications. Set operational specifications and formulate and analyze software requirements. Apply principles and techniques of computer science, engineering, and mathematical analysis. Modify existing software to correct errors, to adapt it to new hardware, or to upgrade interfaces and improve performance. Design and develop software systems, using scientific analysis and mathematical models to predict and measure outcome and consequences of design. Consult with engineering staff to evaluate interface between hardware and software, develop specifications and performance requirements, and resolve customer problems. Analyze information to determine, recommend, and plan installation of a new system or modification of an existing system. Develop and direct software system testing and validation procedures. Direct software programming and development of documentation. Consult with customers or other departments on project status, proposals, and technical issues such as software system design and maintenance. Advise customer about, or perform, maintenance of software system. Coordinate installation of software system. Monitor functioning of equipment to ensure system operates in conformance with specifications. Store, retrieve, and manipulate data for analysis of system capabilities and requirements. Confer with data-processing and project managers to obtain information on limitations and capabilities for data-processing projects. Prepare reports and correspondence concerning project specifications, activities, and status. Evaluate factors such as reporting formats required, cost constraints, and need for security restrictions to determine hardware configuration. Supervise and assign work to programmers, designers, technologists and technicians, and other engineering and scientific personnel. Train users to use new or modified equipment. Utilize microcontrollers to develop control signals; implement control algorithms; and measure process variables such as temperatures, pressures, and positions. Recommend purchase of equipment to control dust, temperature, and humidity in area of system installation. Specify power supply requirements and configuration.

5. Computer Specialists, All Other

Personality Type: No data available

Earnings: $68,570
Growth: 19.0%
Annual Openings: 15,000

Most Common Education/Training Level:
Associate degree

Job Specializations

Computer Systems Engineers/Architects. Design and develop solutions to complex applications problems, system administration issues, or network concerns. Perform systems management and integration functions. Perform security analyses of developed or packaged software components. Perform ongoing hardware and software maintenance operations, including installing or upgrading hardware or software. Complete models and simulations, using manual or automated tools, to analyze or predict system performance under different operating conditions. Define and analyze objectives, scope, issues, or organizational impact of information systems. Develop efficient and effective system controllers. Develop application-specific software. Configure servers to meet functional specifications. Verify stability, interoperability, portability, security, or scalability of system architecture. Train system users in system operation or maintenance. Provide guidelines for implementing secure systems to customers or installation teams. Provide technical guidance or support for the development or troubleshooting of systems. Monitor system operation to detect potential problems. Communicate project information through presentations, technical reports, or white papers. Communicate with staff or clients to understand specific system requirements. Investigate system component suitability for specified purposes and make

Investigative

recommendations regarding component use. Identify system data, hardware, or software components required to meet user needs. Evaluate existing systems to determine effectiveness and suggest changes to meet organizational requirements. Evaluate current or emerging technologies to consider factors such as cost, portability, compatibility, or usability. Establish functional or system standards to ensure operational requirements, quality requirements, and design constraints are addressed. Document design specifications, installation instructions, and other system-related information. Direct the analysis, development, and operation of complete computer systems. Direct the installation of operating systems, network or application software, or computer or network hardware. Develop system engineering, software engineering, system integration, or distributed system architectures. Design and conduct hardware or software tests.

Network Designers. Determine user requirements and design specifications for computer networks. Plan and implement network upgrades. Develop network-related documentation. Design, build, or operate equipment configuration prototypes, including network hardware, software, servers, or server operation systems. Coordinate network operations, maintenance, repairs, or upgrades. Adjust network sizes to meet volume or capacity demands. Communicate with vendors to gather information about products, to alert them to future needs, to resolve problems, or to address system maintenance issues. Coordinate installation of new equipment. Coordinate network or design activities with designers of associated networks. Design, organize, and deliver product awareness, skills transfer, and product education sessions for staff and suppliers. Determine specific network hardware or software requirements, such as platforms, interfaces, bandwidths, or routine

schemas. Develop disaster recovery plans. Communicate with customers, sales staff, or marketing staff to determine customer needs. Explain design specifications to integration or test engineers. Develop plans or budgets for network equipment replacement. Prepare design presentations and proposals for staff or customers. Supervise engineers and other staff in the design or implementation of network solutions. Use network computer-aided design (CAD) software packages to optimize network designs. Develop or maintain project reporting systems. Participate in network technology upgrade or expansion projects, including installation of hardware and software and integration testing. Research and test new or modified hardware or software products to determine performance and interoperability. Develop and implement solutions for network problems. Prepare or monitor project schedules, budgets, or cost control systems. Monitor and analyze network performance and data input/output reports to detect problems, identify inefficient use of computer resources, or perform capacity planning. Evaluate network designs to determine whether customer requirements are met efficiently and effectively. Estimate time and materials needed to complete projects. Develop or recommend network security measures, such as firewalls, network security audits, or automated security probes.

Software Quality Assurance Engineers and Testers. Develop and execute software test plans in order to identify software problems and their causes. Develop or specify standards, methods, or procedures to determine product quality or release readiness. Update automated test scripts to ensure currency. Conduct software compatibility tests with programs, hardware, operating systems, or network environments. Create or maintain databases of known test defects. Design test plans, scenarios, scripts, or procedures. Design or develop automated testing tools. Perform initial debugging procedures by reviewing configuration files, logs, or code pieces to determine breakdown source. Visit beta testing sites to evaluate software performance. Monitor bug resolution efforts and track successes. Document test procedures to ensure replicability and compliance with standards. Evaluate or recommend software for testing or bug tracking. Identify program deviance from standards and suggest modifications to ensure compliance. Identify, analyze, and document problems with program function, output, online screen, or content. Install and configure recreations of software production environments to allow testing of software performance. Install, maintain, or use software testing programs. Investigate customer problems referred by technical support. Review software documentation to ensure technical accuracy, compliance, or completeness or to mitigate risks. Participate in product design reviews to provide input on functional requirements, product designs, schedules, or potential problems. Develop testing programs that address areas such as database impacts, software scenarios, regression testing, negative testing, error or bug retests, or usability. Plan test schedules or strategies in accordance with project scope or delivery dates. Provide feedback and recommendations to developers on software usability and functionality. Test system modifications to prepare for implementation. Collaborate with field staff or customers to evaluate or diagnose problems and recommend possible solutions. Provide technical support during software installation or configuration. Conduct historical analyses of test results. Coordinate user or third-party testing. Document software defects, using a bug tracking system, and report defects to software developers.

Web Administrators. Manage Web environment design, deployment, development, and maintenance activities. Perform testing and quality assurance of Web sites and Web applications. Gather, analyze, or document user feedback to locate or resolve sources of problems. Perform user testing or usage analyses to determine Web sites' effectiveness or usability. Set up or maintain monitoring tools on Web servers or Web sites. Check and analyze operating system or application logfiles regularly to verify proper system performance. Develop testing routines and procedures. Evaluate testing routines or procedures for adequacy, sufficiency, and effectiveness. Test issues such as system integration, performance, and system security on a regular schedule or after any major program modifications. Determine sources of Web page or server problems and take action to correct such problems. Track, compile, and analyze Web site usage data. Recommend Web site improvements and develop budgets to support recommendations. Identify or address interoperability requirements. Evaluate or recommend server hardware or software. Develop or implement procedures for ongoing Web site revision. Implement updates, upgrades, and patches in a timely manner to limit loss of service. Identify, standardize, and communicate levels of access and security. Implement Web site security measures, such as firewalls or message encryption. Collaborate with Web developers to create and operate internal and external Web sites or to manage projects such as e-marketing campaigns. Develop Web site performance metrics. Correct testing-identified problems or recommend actions for their resolution. Provide training or technical assistance in Web site implementation or use. Back up or modify applications and related data to provide for disaster recovery. Test backup or recovery plans regularly and resolve any problems. Document application and Web site changes or change procedures. Document installation or configuration procedures to allow maintenance and repetition. Test new software packages for use in Web operations or other applications. Inform Web site users of problems, problem resolutions, or application changes and updates. Monitor Web developments through continuing education; reading; or participation in professional conferences, workshops, or groups.

Web Developers. Develop and design Web applications and Web sites. Create and specify architectural and technical parameters. Direct Web site content creation, enhancement, and maintenance. Recommend and implement performance improvements. Perform or direct Web site updates. Develop and document style guidelines for Web site content. Renew domain name registrations. Design and implement Web site security measures such as firewalls or message encryption. Establish appropriate server directory trees. Identify or maintain links to and from other Web sites and check links to ensure proper functioning. Create searchable indices for Web page content. Back up files from Web sites to local directories for instant recovery in case of problems. Write supporting code for Web applications or Web sites. Register Web sites with search engines to increase Web site traffic. Respond to user e-mail inquiries or set up automated systems to send responses. Collaborate with management or users to develop e-commerce strategies and to integrate these strategies with Web sites. Communicate with network personnel or Web site hosting agencies to address hardware or software issues affecting Web sites. Evaluate or recommend server hardware or software. Develop or implement procedures for ongoing Web site revision. Perform Web site tests according to planned schedules or after any Web site or product revisions. Create

Web models or prototypes that include physical, interface, logical, or data models. Maintain understanding of current Web technologies or programming practices through continuing education; reading; or participation in professional conferences, workshops, or groups. Identify problems uncovered by testing or customer feedback and correct problems or refer problems to appropriate personnel for correction. Research, document, rate, or select alternatives for Web architecture or technologies. Write, design, or edit Web page content or direct others producing content. Document technical factors such as server load, bandwidth, database performance, and browser and device types. Design, build, or maintain Web sites, using authoring or scripting languages, content creation tools, management tools, and digital media. Confer with management or development teams to prioritize needs, resolve conflicts, develop content criteria, or choose solutions.

6. Database Administrators

Personality Type:
Investigative–Conventional–Realistic

Earnings: $64,670
Growth: 38.2%
Annual Openings: 9,000

Most Common Education/Training Level:
Bachelor's degree

Coordinate changes to computer databases; test and implement the database, applying knowledge of database management systems. May plan, coordinate, and implement security measures to safeguard computer databases. Develop standards and guidelines to guide the use and acquisition of software and to protect vulnerable information. Modify existing databases and database management systems or direct programmers and analysts to make changes. Test programs or databases, correct errors, and make necessary modifications. Plan, coordinate, and implement security measures to safeguard information in computer files against accidental or unauthorized damage, modification, or disclosure. Approve, schedule, plan, and supervise the installation and testing of new products and improvements to computer systems, such as the installation of new databases. Train users and answer questions. Establish and calculate optimum values for database parameters, using manuals and calculator. Specify users and user access levels for each segment of database. Develop data model describing data elements and how they are used, following procedures and using pen, template, or computer software. Develop methods for integrating different products so they work properly together, such as customizing commercial databases to fit specific needs. Review project requests

describing database user needs to estimate time and cost required to accomplish project. Review procedures in database management system manuals for making changes to database. Work as part of a project team to coordinate database development and determine project scope and limitations. Select and enter codes to monitor database performance and to create production database. Identify and evaluate industry trends in database systems to serve as a source of information and advice for upper management. Write and code logical and physical database descriptions and specify identifiers of database to management system or direct others in coding descriptions. Review workflow charts developed by programmer analyst to understand tasks computer will perform, such as updating records. Revise company definition of data as defined in data dictionary.

Investigative

Electrical Engineering

Personality Type:
Investigative–Realistic–Enterprising

Useful Facts About the Major

Prepares individuals to apply mathematical and scientific principles to the design, development, and operational evaluation of electrical, electronic, and related communications systems and their components, including electrical power generation systems, and the analysis of problems such as superconduction, wave propagation, energy storage and retrieval, and reception and amplification.

Related CIP Program: 14.1001 Electrical, Electronics, and Communications Engineering

Specializations in the Major: Aerospace applications; broadcasting; communications; computers; controls; power generation/transmission.

Typical Sequence of College Courses: English composition, technical writing, calculus, differential equations, introduction to computer science, general chemistry, general physics, introduction to engineering, introduction to electric circuits, engineering circuit analysis, signals and systems, semiconductor devices, digital systems, logic design, electromagnetic fields, communication systems, control systems, senior design project.

Typical Sequence of High School Courses: English, algebra, geometry, trigonometry, precalculus, calculus, chemistry, physics, computer science.

Career Snapshot

Electrical engineers apply principles of physics, chemistry, and materials science to the generation, transmission, and use of electric power. They may develop huge dynamos or tiny chips. Usually they enter the field with a bachelor's degree. Management may be an option later in their careers. Electricity is not likely to be replaced as a power source anytime soon, and new electronic devices are being developed constantly, so the job outlook for electrical engineers is expected to be good despite foreign competition.

Useful Averages for the Related Jobs

- **Annual Earnings:** $89,095
- **Growth:** 11.7%
- **Self-Employed:** 2.2%
- **Part-Time:** 9.9%
- **Verbal Skill Rating:** 74.2
- **Math Skill Rating:** 75.9

Other Details About the Related Jobs

Total Annual Job Openings: 38,000

Interest Area: 15 Scientific Research, Engineering, and Mathematics

Skills—Technology design; science; operations analysis; installation; troubleshooting; mathematics. **Values**—Creativity; ability utilization; authority; autonomy; responsibility; social status. **Work Conditions**—Indoors, environmentally controlled; sitting.

Related Jobs

1. Electrical Engineers

Personality Type:
Investigative–Realistic–Conventional

Earnings: $75,930
Growth: 11.8%
Annual Openings: 12,000

Most Common Education/Training Level: Bachelor's degree

Design, develop, test, or supervise the manufacturing and installation of electrical equipment, components, or systems for commercial, industrial, military, or scientific use. Confer with engineers, customers, and others to discuss existing or potential engineering projects and products. Design, implement, maintain, and improve electrical instruments, equipment, facilities, components, products, and systems for commercial, industrial, and domestic purposes. Operate computer-assisted engineering and design software and equipment to perform engineering tasks. Direct and coordinate manufacturing, construction, installation, maintenance, support, documentation, and testing activities to ensure compliance with specifications, codes, and customer requirements. Perform detailed calculations to compute and establish manufacturing, construction, and installation standards and specifications. Inspect completed installations and observe operations to ensure conformance to design and equipment specifications and compliance with operational and safety standards. Plan and implement research methodology and procedures to apply principles of electrical theory to engineering projects. Prepare specifications for purchase of materials and equipment. Supervise and train project team members as necessary. Investigate and test vendors' and competitors' products. Oversee project production efforts to assure projects are completed satisfactorily, on time, and within budget. Prepare and study technical drawings, specifications of electrical systems, and topographical maps to ensure that installation and operations conform to standards and customer requirements. Investigate customer or public complaints, determine nature and extent of problem, and recommend remedial measures. Plan layout of electric-power-generating plants and distribution lines and stations. Assist in developing capital project programs for new equipment and major repairs. Develop budgets, estimating labor, material, and construction costs. Compile data and write reports regarding existing and potential engineering studies and projects. Collect data relating to commercial and residential development, population, and power system interconnection to determine operating efficiency of electrical systems. Conduct field surveys and study maps, graphs, diagrams, and other data to identify and correct power system problems.

2. Electronics Engineers, Except Computer

Personality Type:
Investigative–Realistic–Conventional

Earnings: $81,050
Growth: 9.7%
Annual Openings: 11,000

Most Common Education/Training Level: Bachelor's degree

Research, design, develop, and test electronic components and systems for commercial, industrial, military, or scientific use, utilizing knowledge of electronic theory and materials properties. Design electronic circuits and components for use in fields such as telecommunications, aerospace guidance and propulsion control, acoustics, or instruments and controls. Design electronic components, software, products, or systems for commercial, industrial, medical, military, or scientific applications. Provide technical support and instruction to staff or customers regarding equipment standards, assisting

Investigative

with specific, difficult in-service engineering. Operate computer-assisted engineering and design software and equipment to perform engineering tasks. Analyze system requirements, capacity, cost, and customer needs to determine feasibility of project and develop system plan. Confer with engineers, customers, vendors, or others to discuss existing and potential engineering projects or products. Review and evaluate work of others inside and outside the organization to ensure effectiveness, technical adequacy, and compatibility in the resolution of complex engineering problems. Determine material and equipment needs and order supplies. Inspect electronic equipment, instruments, products, and systems to ensure conformance to specifications, safety standards, and applicable codes and regulations. Evaluate operational systems, prototypes, and proposals and recommend repair or design modifications based on factors such as environment, service, cost, and system capabilities. Prepare documentation containing information such as confidential descriptions and specifications of proprietary hardware and software, product development and introduction schedules, product costs, and information about product performance weaknesses. Direct and coordinate activities concerned with manufacture, construction, installation, maintenance, operation, and modification of electronic equipment, products, and systems. Develop and perform operational, maintenance, and testing procedures for electronic products, components, equipment, and systems. Plan and develop applications and modifications for electronic properties used in components, products, and systems to improve technical performance. Plan and implement research, methodology, and procedures to apply principles of electronic theory to engineering projects. Prepare engineering sketches and specifications for construction, relocation, and installation of equipment, facilities, products, and systems.

3. Engineering Managers

Personality Type:
Enterprising–Investigative–Realistic

Earnings: $105,430
Growth: 13.0%
Annual Openings: 15,000

Most Common Education/Training Level:
Work experience plus degree

Plan, direct, or coordinate activities in such fields as architecture and engineering or research and development in these fields. Confer with management, production, and marketing staff to discuss project specifications and procedures. Coordinate and direct projects, making detailed plans to accomplish goals and directing the integration of technical activities. Analyze technology, resource needs, and market demand to plan and assess the feasibility of projects. Plan and direct the installation, testing, operation, maintenance, and repair of facilities and equipment. Direct, review, and approve product design and changes. Recruit employees; assign, direct, and evaluate their work; and oversee the development and maintenance of staff competence. Prepare budgets, bids, and contracts and direct the negotiation of research contracts. Develop and implement policies, standards, and procedures for the engineering and technical work performed in the department, service, laboratory, or firm. Review and recommend or approve contracts and cost estimates. Perform administrative functions such as reviewing and writing reports, approving expenditures, enforcing rules, and making decisions about the purchase of materials or services. Present and explain proposals, reports, and findings to clients. Consult or negotiate with clients to prepare project specifications. Set scientific and technical goals within broad outlines provided by top management. Administer highway planning, construction, and maintenance. Direct the engineering of water control, treatment, and distribution projects. Plan, direct, and coordinate survey work with other staff activities, certifying survey work and writing land legal descriptions. Confer with and report to officials and the public to provide information and solicit support for projects.

Investigative

Medicine

Personality Type: Investigative

Useful Facts About the Major

Prepares individuals for the independent professional practice of medicine, involving the prevention, diagnosis, and treatment of illnesses, injuries, and other disorders of the human body.

Related CIP Programs: 51.1201 Medicine (MD); 51.1901 Osteopathic Medicine/Osteopathy (DO)

Specializations in the Major: Emergency medicine; family medicine; internal medicine; obstetrics/gynecology; pediatrics; psychiatry; radiology; surgery.

Typical Sequence of College Courses: English composition, introduction to psychology, college algebra, calculus, introduction to sociology, oral communication, general chemistry, general biology, introduction to computer science, organic chemistry, human anatomy and physiology, general microbiology, genetics, introduction to biochemistry, pathology, pharmacology, abnormal psychology, medical interviewing techniques, patient examination and evaluation, clinical laboratory procedures, ethics in health care, clinical experience in internal medicine, clinical experience in emergency medicine, clinical experience in obstetrics/gynecology, clinical experience in family medicine, clinical experience in psychiatry, clinical experience in surgery, clinical experience in pediatrics, clinical experience in geriatrics.

Typical Sequence of High School Courses: English, algebra, geometry, trigonometry, precalculus, biology, computer science, public speaking, chemistry, foreign language, physics.

Career Snapshot

Medicine requires long years of education—four years of college, four years of medical school, and three to eight years of internship and residency, depending on the specialty. Once you enter medical school, hands-on learning style becomes as important as theoretical learning. Entrance to medical school is highly competitive. Although "pre-med" is often referred to as a major, many students meet the entry requirements for medical school while majoring in a nonscientific subject. This may be helpful to demonstrate that you are a well-rounded person and to prepare you for another career in case you are not admitted to medical school. Today, physicians are more likely than in the past to work as salaried employees of group practices or HMOs. Best opportunities are expected in rural and low-income areas.

Useful Averages for the Related Jobs

- ◎ **Annual Earnings:** $144,916
- ◎ **Growth:** 24.0%
- ◎ **Self-Employed:** 11.5%
- ◎ **Part-Time:** 25.6%
- ◎ **Verbal Skill Rating:** 81.3
- ◎ **Math Skill Rating:** 57.9

Other Details About the Related Jobs

Total Annual Job Openings: 287,000

Interest Area: 08 Health Science

Skills—Science; social perceptiveness; reading comprehension; complex problem solving; judgment and decision making; persuasion. **Values**—Social service; social status; recognition; ability utilization; responsibility; achievement. **Work Conditions**—Exposed to disease or infections; exposed to radiation.

Related Jobs

1. Anesthesiologists

Personality Type: Investigative–Realistic–Social

Earnings: More than $145,600
Growth: 24.0%
Annual Openings: 41,000

Most Common Education/Training Level: First professional degree

Administer anesthetics during surgery or other medical procedures. Administer anesthetic or sedation during medical procedures, using local, intravenous, spinal, or caudal methods. Monitor patient before, during, and after anesthesia and counteract adverse reactions or complications. Provide and maintain life support and airway management and help prepare patients for emergency surgery. Record type and amount of anesthesia and patient condition throughout procedure. Examine patient; obtain medical history; and use diagnostic tests to determine risk during surgical, obstetrical, and other medical procedures. Position patient on operating table to maximize patient comfort and surgical accessibility. Decide when patients have recovered or stabilized enough to be sent to another room or ward or to be sent home following outpatient surgery. Coordinate administration of anesthetics with surgeons during operation. Confer with other medical professionals to determine type and method of anesthetic or sedation to render patient insensible to pain. Coordinate and direct work of nurses, medical technicians, and other health-care providers. Order laboratory tests, X rays, and other diagnostic procedures. Diagnose illnesses, using examinations, tests, and reports. Manage anesthesiological services, coordinating

them with other medical activities and formulating plans and procedures. Provide medical care and consultation in many settings, prescribing medication and treatment and referring patients for surgery. Inform students and staff of types and methods of anesthesia administration, signs of complications, and emergency methods to counteract reactions. Schedule and maintain use of surgical suite, including operating, wash-up, and waiting rooms and anesthetic and sterilizing equipment. Instruct individuals and groups on ways to preserve health and prevent disease. Conduct medical research to aid in controlling and curing disease, to investigate new medications, and to develop and test new medical techniques.

2. Family and General Practitioners

Personality Type: Investigative–Social–Enterprising

Earnings: More than $145,600
Growth: 24.0%
Annual Openings: 41,000

Most Common Education/Training Level: First professional degree

Diagnose, treat, and help prevent diseases and injuries that commonly occur in the general population. Prescribe or administer treatment, therapy, medication, vaccination, and other specialized medical care to treat or prevent illness, disease, or injury. Order, perform, and interpret tests and analyze records, reports, and examination information to diagnose patients' condition. Monitor the patients' conditions and progress and re-evaluate treatments as necessary. Explain procedures and discuss test results or prescribed treatments with patients. Collect, record, and maintain patient information, such as medical history, reports, and examination results. Advise patients and community

Investigative

members concerning diet, activity, hygiene, and disease prevention. Refer patients to medical specialists or other practitioners when necessary. Direct and coordinate activities of nurses, students, assistants, specialists, therapists, and other medical staff. Coordinate work with nurses, social workers, rehabilitation therapists, pharmacists, psychologists, and other health-care providers. Deliver babies. Operate on patients to remove, repair, or improve functioning of diseased or injured body parts and systems. Plan, implement, or administer health programs or standards in hospital, business, or community for information, prevention, or treatment of injury or illness. Prepare reports for government or management of birth, death, and disease statistics; workforce evaluations; or medical status of individuals. Conduct research to study anatomy and develop or test medications, treatments, or procedures to prevent or control disease or injury.

3. Internists, General

Personality Type:
Investigative–Social–Enterprising

Earnings: More than $145,600
Growth: 24.0%
Annual Openings: 41,000

Most Common Education/Training Level:
First professional degree

Diagnose and provide non-surgical treatment of diseases and injuries of internal organ systems. Provide care mainly for adults who have a wide range of problems associated with the internal organs. Treat internal disorders, such as hypertension; heart disease; diabetes; and problems of the lung, brain, kidney, and gastrointestinal tract. Analyze records, reports, test results, or examination information to diagnose medical condition of patient. Prescribe or

administer medication, therapy, and other specialized medical care to treat or prevent illness, disease, or injury. Provide and manage long-term, comprehensive medical care, including diagnosis and non-surgical treatment of diseases, for adult patients in an office or hospital. Manage and treat common health problems, such as infections, influenza, and pneumonia, as well as serious, chronic, and complex illnesses, in adolescents, adults, and the elderly. Monitor patients' conditions and progress and re-evaluate treatments as necessary. Collect, record, and maintain patient information, such as medical history, reports, and examination results. Make diagnoses when different illnesses occur together or in situations where the diagnosis may be obscure. Explain procedures and discuss test results or prescribed treatments with patients. Advise patients and community members concerning diet, activity, hygiene, and disease prevention. Refer patient to medical specialist or other practitioner when necessary. Immunize patients to protect them from preventable diseases. Advise surgeon of a patient's risk status and recommend appropriate intervention to minimize risk. Direct and coordinate activities of nurses, students, assistants, specialists, therapists, and other medical staff. Provide consulting services to other doctors caring for patients with special or difficult problems. Operate on patients to remove, repair, or improve functioning of diseased or injured body parts and systems. Plan, implement, or administer health programs in hospitals, businesses, or communities for prevention and treatment of injuries or illnesses. Conduct research to develop or test medications, treatments, or procedures to prevent or control disease or injury. Prepare government or organizational reports on birth, death, and disease statistics; workforce evaluations; or the medical status of individuals.

4. Obstetricians and Gynecologists

Personality Type:
Investigative–Enterprising–Social

Earnings: More than $145,600
Growth: 24.0%
Annual Openings: 41,000

Most Common Education/Training Level:
First professional degree

Diagnose, treat, and help prevent diseases of women, especially those affecting the reproductive system and the process of childbirth. Care for and treat women during prenatal, natal, and post-natal periods. Explain procedures and discuss test results or prescribed treatments with patients. Treat diseases of female organs. Monitor patients' condition and progress and re-evaluate treatments as necessary. Perform cesarean sections or other surgical procedures as needed to preserve patients' health and deliver babies safely. Prescribe or administer therapy, medication, and other specialized medical care to treat or prevent illness, disease, or injury. Analyze records, reports, test results, or examination information to diagnose medical condition of patient. Collect, record, and maintain patient information, such as medical histories, reports, and examination results. Advise patients and community members concerning diet, activity, hygiene, and disease prevention. Refer patient to medical specialist or other practitioner when necessary. Consult with, or provide consulting services to, other physicians. Direct and coordinate activities of nurses, students, assistants, specialists, therapists, and other medical staff. Plan, implement, or administer health programs in hospitals, businesses, or communities for prevention and treatment of injuries or illnesses. Prepare government and organizational reports on birth, death, and disease statistics; workforce evaluations; or the medical status of individuals. Conduct research to develop or test medications, treatments, or procedures to prevent or control disease or injury.

5. Pediatricians, General

Personality Type:
Investigative–Enterprising–Social

Earnings: $138,130
Growth: 24.0%
Annual Openings: 41,000

Most Common Education/Training Level:
First professional degree

Diagnose, treat, and help prevent children's diseases and injuries. Examine patients or order, perform, and interpret diagnostic tests to obtain information on medical condition and determine diagnosis. Examine children regularly to assess their growth and development. Prescribe or administer treatment, therapy, medication, vaccination, and other specialized medical care to treat or prevent illness, disease, or injury in infants and children. Collect, record, and maintain patient information, such as medical history, reports, and examination results. Advise patients, parents or guardians, and community members concerning diet, activity, hygiene, and disease prevention. Treat children who have minor illnesses, acute and chronic health problems, and growth and development concerns. Explain procedures and discuss test results or prescribed treatments with patients and parents or guardians. Monitor patients' condition and progress and re-evaluate treatments as necessary. Plan and execute medical care programs to aid in the mental and physical growth and development of children and adolescents. Refer patient to medical specialist or other practitioner when necessary. Direct and coordinate activities of

Investigative

nurses, students, assistants, specialists, therapists, and other medical staff. Provide consulting services to other physicians. Plan, implement, or administer health programs or standards in hospital, business, or community for information, prevention, or treatment of injury or illness. Operate on patients to remove, repair, or improve functioning of diseased or injured body parts and systems. Conduct research to study anatomy and develop or test medications, treatments, or procedures to prevent or control disease or injury. Prepare reports for government or management of birth, death, and disease statistics; workforce evaluations; or medical status of individuals.

6. Psychiatrists

Personality Type: Investigative–Artistic–Social

Earnings: More than $145,600
Growth: 24.0%
Annual Openings: 41,000

Most Common Education/Training Level:
First professional degree

Diagnose, treat, and help prevent disorders of the mind. Analyze and evaluate patient data and test findings to diagnose nature and extent of mental disorder. Prescribe, direct, and administer psychotherapeutic treatments or medications to treat mental, emotional, or behavioral disorders. Collaborate with physicians, psychologists, social workers, psychiatric nurses, or other professionals to discuss treatment plans and progress. Gather and maintain patient information and records, including social and medical history obtained from patients, relatives, and other professionals. Counsel outpatients and other patients during office visits. Design individualized care plans, using a variety of treatments. Examine or conduct laboratory or diagnostic tests on patient to provide informa-

tion on general physical condition and mental disorder. Advise and inform guardians, relatives, and significant others of patients' conditions and treatment. Review and evaluate treatment procedures and outcomes of other psychiatrists and medical professionals. Teach, conduct research, and publish findings to increase understanding of mental, emotional, and behavioral states and disorders. Prepare and submit case reports and summaries to government and mental health agencies. Serve on committees to promote and maintain community mental health services and delivery systems.

7. Surgeons

Personality Type: Investigative–Realistic–Social

Earnings: More than $145,600
Growth: 24.0%
Annual Openings: 41,000

Most Common Education/Training Level:
First professional degree

Treat diseases, injuries, and deformities by invasive methods, such as manual manipulation, or by using instruments and appliances. Analyze patient's medical history, medication allergies, physical condition, and examination results to verify operation's necessity and to determine best procedure. Operate on patients to correct deformities, repair injuries, prevent and treat diseases, or improve or restore patients' functions. Follow established surgical techniques during the operation. Prescribe preoperative and postoperative treatments and procedures, such as sedatives, diets, antibiotics, and preparation and treatment of the patient's operative area. Examine patient to provide information on medical condition and surgical risk. Diagnose bodily disorders and orthopedic conditions and provide treatments, such as medicines and surgeries, in clinics, hospital wards, and operating rooms. Direct and coordinate activities of nurses, assistants, specialists, residents, and other medical staff. Provide consultation and surgical assistance to other physicians and surgeons. Refer patient to medical specialist or other practitioners when necessary. Examine instruments, equipment, and operating room to ensure sterility. Prepare case histories. Manage surgery services, including planning, scheduling and coordination, determination of procedures, and procurement of supplies and equipment. Conduct research to develop and test surgical techniques that can improve operating procedures and outcomes.

Investigative

Microbiology

Personality Type: Investigative–Realistic

Useful Facts About the Major

Focuses on the scientific study of one-celled organisms and colonies and subcellular genetic matter and their ecological interactions with human beings and other life.

Related CIP Programs: 26.0503 Medical Microbiology and Bacteriology; 26.0502 Microbiology, General; 26.0506 Mycology; 26.0505 Parasitology; 26.0504 Virology

Specializations in the Major: Algae; bacteria; fungi (mycology); immunology; virology.

Typical Sequence of College Courses: English composition, calculus, introduction to computer science, general chemistry, general biology, organic chemistry, general physics, general microbiology, genetics, introduction to biochemistry, immunology, bacterial physiology, bacterial genetics.

Typical Sequence of High School Courses: English, biology, algebra, geometry, trigonometry, pre-calculus, chemistry, physics, computer science, calculus.

Career Snapshot

A bachelor's degree in microbiology or bacteriology may be an entry route to clinical laboratory work or to nonresearch work in industry or government. It also is good preparation for medical school. For a position in research or college teaching, a graduate degree is expected.

Useful Averages for the Related Jobs

- **Annual Earnings:** $72,437
- **Growth:** 26.1%
- **Self-Employed:** 0.6%
- **Part-Time:** 13.8%
- **Verbal Skill Rating:** 81.1
- **Math Skill Rating:** 72.1

Other Details About the Related Jobs

Total Annual Job Openings: 21,000

Interest Area: 15 Scientific Research, Engineering, and Mathematics

Skills—Science; writing; reading comprehension; complex problem solving; management of financial resources; active learning. **Values**—Creativity; social status; ability utilization; responsibility; authority; autonomy. **Work Conditions**—Indoors, environmentally controlled; exposed to disease or infections.

Related Jobs

1. Medical Scientists, Except Epidemiologists

Personality Type: Investigative–Realistic–Social

Earnings: $61,680
Growth: 34.1%
Annual Openings: 15,000

Most Common Education/Training Level: Doctoral degree

Conduct research dealing with the understanding of human diseases and the improvement of human health. Engage in clinical investigation or other research, production, technical writing, or related activities. Conduct research to develop methodologies, instrumentation, and procedures for medical application, analyzing data and presenting findings. Plan and direct studies to investigate human or animal disease, preventive methods, and treatments for disease. Follow strict safety procedures when handling toxic materials to avoid contamination. Evaluate effects of drugs, gases, pesticides, parasites, and microorganisms at various levels. Teach principles of medicine and medical and laboratory procedures to physicians, residents, students, and technicians. Prepare and analyze organ, tissue, and cell samples to identify toxicity, bacteria, or microorganisms or to study cell structure. Standardize drug dosages, methods of immunization, and procedures for manufacture of drugs and medicinal compounds. Investigate cause, progress, life cycle, or mode of transmission of diseases or parasites. Confer with health department, industry personnel, physicians, and others to develop health safety standards and public health improvement programs. Study animal and human health and physiological processes. Consult with and advise physicians, educators, researchers, and others regarding medical applications of physics, biology, and chemistry. Use equipment such as atomic absorption spectrometers, electron microscopes, flow cytometers, and chromatography systems.

2. Microbiologists

Personality Type:
Investigative–Realistic–Conventional

Earnings: $57,980
Growth: 17.2%
Annual Openings: 1,000

Most Common Education/Training Level:
Doctoral degree

Investigate the growth, structure, development, and other characteristics of microscopic organisms, such as bacteria, algae, or fungi. Includes medical microbiologists who study the relationship between organisms and disease or the effects of antibiotics on microorganisms. Isolate and make cultures of bacteria or other microorganisms in prescribed media, controlling moisture, aeration, temperature, and nutrition. Perform tests on water, food, and the environment to detect harmful microorganisms and to obtain information about sources of pollution and contamination. Examine physiological, morphological, and cultural characteristics, using microscope, to identify and classify microorganisms in human, water, and food specimens. Provide laboratory services for health departments, for community environmental health programs, and for physicians needing information for diagnosis and treatment. Observe action of microorganisms upon living tissues of plants, higher animals, and other microorganisms and on dead organic matter. Investigate the relationship between organisms and disease, including the control of epidemics and the effects of antibiotics on microorganisms. Supervise biological technologists and technicians and other scientists. Study growth, structure, development, and general characteristics of bacteria and other microorganisms to understand their relationship to human, plant, and animal health. Prepare technical reports and recommendations based upon research outcomes. Study the structure and function of human, animal, and plant tissues, cells, pathogens, and toxins. Use a variety of specialized equipment such as electron microscopes, gas chromatographs and high-pressure liquid chromatographs, electrophoresis units, thermocyclers, fluorescence-activated cell sorters, and phosphoimagers. Conduct chemical analyses of substances such as acids, alcohols, and enzymes. Research use of bacteria and microorganisms to develop

Investigative

vitamins, antibiotics, amino acids, grain alcohol, sugars, and polymers.

3. Natural Sciences Managers

Personality Type:
Investigative–Enterprising–Realistic

Earnings: $100,080
Growth: 13.6%
Annual Openings: 5,000

Most Common Education/Training Level:
Work experience plus degree

Plan, direct, or coordinate activities in such fields as life sciences, physical sciences, mathematics, and statistics and research and development in these fields. Confer with scientists, engineers, regulators, and others to plan and review projects and to provide technical assistance. Develop client relationships and communicate with clients to explain proposals, present research findings, establish specifications, or discuss project status. Plan and direct research, development, and production activities. Prepare project proposals. Design and coordinate successive phases of problem analysis, solution proposals, and testing. Review project activities and prepare and review research, testing, and operational reports. Hire, supervise, and evaluate engineers, technicians, researchers, and other staff. Determine scientific and technical goals within broad outlines provided by top management and make detailed plans to accomplish these goals. Develop and implement policies, standards, and procedures for the architectural, scientific, and technical work performed to ensure regulatory compliance and operations enhancement. Develop innovative technology and train staff for its implementation. Provide for stewardship of plant and animal resources and habitats, studying land use; monitoring animal populations; and providing shelter, resources, and medical treatment for animals. Conduct own research in field of expertise. Recruit personnel and oversee the development and maintenance of staff competence. Advise and assist in obtaining patents or meeting other legal requirements. Prepare and administer budget, approve and review expenditures, and prepare financial reports. Make presentations at professional meetings to further knowledge in the field.

Pharmacy

Personality Type:
Investigative–Conventional–Realistic

Useful Facts About the Major

Prepares individuals for the independent or employed practice of preparing and dispensing drugs and medications in consultation with prescribing physicians and other health care professionals and for managing pharmacy practices and counseling patients.

Related CIP Program: 51.2001 Pharmacy (PharmD [USA], PharmD or BS/BPharm [Canada])

Specializations in the Major: Pharmaceutical chemistry; pharmacology; pharmacy administration.

Typical Sequence of College Courses: English composition, introduction to psychology, calculus, introduction to sociology, oral communication, general chemistry, general biology, organic chemistry, introduction to biochemistry, human anatomy and physiology, pharmaceutical calculations, pharmacology, pharmaceutics, microbiology and immunology, patient assessment and education, medicinal chemistry, therapeutics, pharmacy law and ethics, pharmacokinetics, electrical inspection.

Typical Sequence of High School Courses: English, algebra, geometry, trigonometry, biology, computer science, public speaking, chemistry, calculus, physics, foreign language.

Career Snapshot

Pharmacists dispense medications as prescribed by physicians and other health practitioners and give advice to patients about how to use medications. Pharmacists must be knowledgeable about the chemical and physical properties of drugs, how they behave in the body, and how they may interact with other drugs and substances. Schools of pharmacy take about four years to complete and usually require at least one or two years of prior college work. Some pharmacists go on to additional graduate training to prepare for research, administration, or college teaching. Some find work in sales for pharmaceutical companies or in marketing research for managed-care organizations. The job outlook for pharmacists is expected to be good, thanks to the aging of the population, combined with the shift of medical care from the scalpel to the pill.

Useful Averages for the Related Job

- ◎ **Annual Earnings:** $94,520
- ◎ **Growth:** 24.6%
- ◎ **Self-Employed:** 1.7%
- ◎ **Part-Time:** 29.9%
- ◎ **Verbal Skill Rating:** 72.1
- ◎ **Math Skill Rating:** 62.1

Other Details About the Related Job

Total Annual Job Openings: 16,000

Interest Area: 08 Health Science

Skills—Science; reading comprehension; instructing; critical thinking; speaking; writing. **Values**—Authority; social service; social status; ability utilization; achievement; working conditions. **Work Conditions**—Exposed to disease or infections; indoors, environmentally controlled.

Investigative

Related Job

Pharmacists

Personality Type:
Investigative–Conventional–Realistic

Earnings: $94,520
Growth: 24.6%
Annual Openings: 16,000

Most Common Education/Training Level:
First professional degree

Compound and dispense medications, following prescriptions issued by physicians, dentists, or other authorized medical practitioners. Review prescriptions to assure accuracy, to ascertain the needed ingredients, and to evaluate their suitability. Provide information and advice regarding drug interactions, side effects, dosage, and proper medication storage. Analyze prescribing trends to monitor patient compliance and to prevent excessive usage or harmful interactions. Order and purchase pharmaceutical supplies, medical supplies, and drugs, maintaining stock and storing and handling it properly. Maintain records, such as pharmacy files; patient profiles; charge system files; inventories; control records for radioactive nuclei; and registries of poisons, narcotics, and controlled drugs. Provide specialized services to help patients manage conditions such as diabetes, asthma, smoking cessation, or high blood pressure. Advise customers on the selection of medication brands, medical equipment, and health-care supplies. Collaborate with other health-care professionals to plan, monitor, review, and evaluate the quality and effectiveness of drugs and drug regimens, providing advice on drug applications and characteristics. Compound and dispense medications as prescribed by doctors and dentists by calculating, weighing, measuring, and mixing ingredients or oversee these activities. Offer health promotion and prevention activities, for example, training people to use devices such as blood pressure or diabetes monitors. Refer patients to other health professionals and agencies when appropriate. Prepare sterile solutions and infusions for use in surgical procedures, emergency rooms, or patients' homes. Plan, implement, and maintain procedures for mixing, packaging, and labeling pharmaceuticals according to policy and legal requirements to ensure quality, security, and proper disposal. Assay radiopharmaceuticals, verify rates of disintegration, and calculate the volume required to produce the desired results to ensure proper dosages. Manage pharmacy operations, hiring and supervising staff, performing administrative duties, and buying and selling non-pharmaceutical merchandise. Work in hospitals, in clinics, or for Health Management Organizations (HMOs), dispensing prescriptions, serving as a medical team consultant, or specializing in specific drug therapy areas such as oncology or nuclear pharmacotherapy.

Physician Assisting

Personality Type: Investigative–Social

Useful Facts About the Major

Prepares individuals to practice medicine, including diagnoses and treatment therapies, under the supervision of a physician.

Related CIP Program: 51.0912 Physician Assistant

Specializations in the Major: Emergency medicine; family medicine; internal medicine; pediatrics.

Typical Sequence of College Courses: English composition, college algebra, general chemistry, general biology, introduction to psychology, human growth and development, general microbiology, human physiology, human anatomy, pharmacology, medical interviewing techniques, patient examination and evaluation, clinical laboratory procedures, ethics in health care, clinical experience in internal medicine, clinical experience in emergency medicine, clinical experience in obstetrics/gynecology, clinical experience in family medicine, clinical experience in psychiatry, clinical experience in surgery, clinical experience in pediatrics, clinical experience in geriatrics.

Typical Sequence of High School Courses: English, algebra, geometry, trigonometry, precalculus, biology, computer science, public speaking, chemistry, foreign language.

Career Snapshot

Physician assistants work under the supervision of physicians, but in some cases they provide care in settings where a physician may be present only a couple of days per week. They perform many of the diagnostic, therapeutic, and preventative functions that we are used to associating with physicians. The typical educational program results in a bachelor's degree. It often takes only two years to complete, but entrants usually must have at least two years of prior college and often must have work experience in the field of health care. Employment opportunities are expected to be good.

Useful Averages for the Related Job

- **Annual Earnings:** $74,980
- **Growth:** 49.6%
- **Self-Employed:** 1.3%
- **Part-Time:** 23.1%
- **Verbal Skill Rating:** 76.1
- **Math Skill Rating:** 59.6

Other Details About the Related Job

Total Annual Job Openings: 10,000

Interest Area: 08 Health Science

Skills—Science; instructing; writing; reading comprehension; critical thinking; complex problem solving. **Values**—Social service; authority; achievement; ability utilization; social status; coworkers. **Work Conditions**—Indoors; exposed to disease or infections; environmentally controlled.

Related Job

Physician Assistants

Personality Type: Investigative–Social–Artistic

Earnings: $74,980
Growth: 49.6%
Annual Openings: 10,000

Investigative

Most Common Education/Training Level:
Bachelor's degree

Under the supervision of a physician, provide health-care services typically performed by a physician. Conduct complete physicals, provide treatment, and counsel patients. May, in some cases, prescribe medication. Must graduate from an accredited educational program for physician assistants. Examine patients to obtain information about their physical condition. Make tentative diagnoses and decisions about management and treatment of patients. Interpret diagnostic test results for deviations from normal. Obtain, compile, and record patient medical data, including health history, progress notes, and results of physical examination. Administer or order diagnostic tests, such as X-ray, electrocardiogram, and laboratory tests. Prescribe therapy or medication with physician approval. Perform therapeutic procedures, such as injections, immunizations, suturing and wound care, and infection management. Instruct and counsel patients about prescribed therapeutic regimens, normal growth and development, family planning, emotional problems of daily living, and health maintenance. Provide physicians with assistance during surgery or complicated medical procedures. Supervise and coordinate activities of technicians and technical assistants. Visit and observe patients on hospital rounds or house calls, updating charts, ordering therapy, and reporting back to physician. Order medical and laboratory supplies and equipment.

Artistic Majors

Art

Personality Type: Artistic

Useful Facts About the Major

Focuses on the introductory study and appreciation of the visual arts and may prepare individuals to generally function as creative artists in the visual and plastic media.

Related CIP Programs: 50.0701 Art/Art Studies, General; 50.0711 Ceramic Arts and Ceramics; 50.0705 Drawing; 50.0712 Fiber, Textile, and Weaving Arts; 50.0702 Fine/Studio Arts, General; 50.0706 Intermedia/Multimedia; 50.0713 Metal and Jewelry Arts; 50.0708 Painting; 50.0710 Printmaking; 50.0709 Sculpture

Specializations in the Major: Art education; ceramics; painting; screenprinting; sculpture; studio art.

Typical Sequence of College Courses: English composition, foreign language, art and culture, basic drawing, color and design, two-dimensional design, three-dimensional design, art history: prehistoric to Renaissance, art history: Renaissance to modern, figure drawing, a medium (e.g., painting, sculpture, ceramics), art practicum.

Typical Sequence of High School Courses: English, foreign language, literature, history, art.

Career Snapshot

Only a few highly talented and motivated artists are able to support themselves by producing and selling their artworks. But many other graduates of art programs find work in education—as private instructors, school teachers, and university instructors of art and art history. College teaching requires a master's degree. Some graduates apply their artistic skills to crafts or to commercial applications such as illustration or cartooning.

Useful Averages for the Related Jobs

- **Annual Earnings:** $55,182
- **Growth:** 12.2%
- **Self-Employed:** 58.4%
- **Part-Time:** 32.0%
- **Verbal Skill Rating:** 63.1
- **Math Skill Rating:** 57.0

Other Details About the Related Jobs

Total Annual Job Openings: 29,000

Interest Area: 03 Arts and Communication

Skills—Persuasion; speaking; active listening; instructing; reading comprehension; learning strategies. **Values**—Creativity; authority; ability utilization; achievement; autonomy; responsibility. **Work Conditions**—Indoors, environmentally controlled; sitting.

Related Jobs

1. Art Directors

Personality Type:
Artistic–Enterprising–Realistic

Earnings: $68,100
Growth: 11.5%
Annual Openings: 10,000

Artistic

Most Common Education/Training Level:
Work experience plus degree

Formulate design concepts and presentation approaches and direct workers engaged in art work, layout design, and copy writing for visual communications media, such as magazines, books, newspapers, and packaging. Formulate basic layout design or presentation approach and specify material details, such as style and size of type, photographs, graphics, animation, video, and sound. Review and approve proofs of printed copy and art and copy materials developed by staff members. Manage own accounts and projects, working within budget and scheduling requirements. Confer with creative, art, copywriting, or production department heads to discuss client requirements and presentation concepts and to coordinate creative activities. Present final layouts to clients for approval. Confer with clients to determine objectives; budget; background information; and presentation approaches, styles, and techniques. Hire, train, and direct staff members who develop design concepts into art layouts or who prepare layouts for printing. Work with creative directors to develop design solutions. Review illustrative material to determine whether it conforms to standards and specifications. Attend photo shoots and printing sessions to ensure that the products needed are obtained. Create custom illustrations or other graphic elements. Mark up, paste, and complete layouts and write typography instructions to prepare materials for typesetting or printing. Negotiate with printers and estimators to determine what services will be performed. Conceptualize and help design interfaces for multimedia games, products, and devices. Prepare detailed storyboards showing sequence and timing of story development for television production.

2. Craft Artists

Personality Type: No data available

Earnings: $24,090
Growth: 10.6%
Annual Openings: 1,000

Most Common Education/Training Level:
Long-term on-the-job training

Create or reproduce hand-made objects for sale and exhibition, using a variety of techniques such as welding, weaving, pottery, and needlecraft. Create functional or decorative objects by hand, using a variety of methods and materials. Cut, shape, fit, join, mold, or otherwise process materials, using hand tools, power tools, or machinery. Attend craft shows to market products. Select materials for use based on strength, color, texture, balance, weight, size, malleability, and other characteristics. Apply finishes to objects being crafted. Develop concepts or creative ideas for craft objects. Set specifications for materials, dimensions, and finishes. Confer with customers to assess customer needs or obtain feedback. Fabricate patterns or templates to guide craft production. Create prototypes or models of objects to be crafted. Sketch or draw objects to be crafted. Advertise products and work, using media such as Internet advertising and brochures. Develop product packaging, display, and pricing strategies. Research craft trends, venues, and customer buying patterns in order to inspire designs and marketing strategies. Develop designs, using specialized computer software.

3. Fine Artists, Including Painters, Sculptors, and Illustrators

Personality Type:
Artistic–Realistic–Enterprising

Earnings: $41,970
Growth: 10.2%
Annual Openings: 4,000

Most Common Education/Training Level:
Long-term on-the-job training

Create original artwork, using any of a wide variety of mediums and techniques such as painting and sculpture. Use materials such as pens and ink, watercolors, charcoal, oil, or computer software to create artwork. Integrate and develop visual elements, such as line, space, mass, color, and perspective, to produce desired effects such as the illustration of ideas, emotions, or moods. Confer with clients, editors, writers, art directors, and other interested parties regarding the nature and content of artwork to be produced. Submit preliminary or finished artwork or project plans to clients for approval, incorporating changes as necessary. Maintain portfolios of artistic work to demonstrate styles, interests, and abilities. Create finished artwork as decoration or to elucidate or substitute for spoken or written messages. Cut, bend, laminate, arrange, and fasten individual or mixed raw and manufactured materials and products to form works of art. Monitor events, trends, and other circumstances; research specific subject areas; attend art exhibitions; and read art publications to develop ideas and keep current on art world activities. Study different techniques to learn how to apply them to artistic endeavors. Render drawings, illustrations, and sketches of buildings, manufactured products, or models, working from sketches, blueprints, memory, models, or reference materials. Create sculptures, statues, and other three-dimensional artwork by using abrasives and tools to shape, carve, and fabricate materials such as clay, stone, wood, or metal. Create sketches, profiles, or likenesses of posed subjects or photographs, using any combination

of freehand drawing, mechanical assembly kits, and computer imaging. Study styles, techniques, colors, textures, and materials used in works undergoing restoration to ensure consistency during the restoration process. Develop project budgets for approval, estimating timelines and material costs. Shade and fill in sketch outlines and backgrounds, using a variety of media such as watercolors, markers, and transparent washes, labeling designated colors when necessary. Collaborate with engineers, mechanics, and other technical experts as necessary to build and install creations.

4. Multi-Media Artists and Animators

Personality Type: No data available

Earnings: $51,350
Growth: 14.1%
Annual Openings: 14,000

Most Common Education/Training Level:
Bachelor's degree

Create special effects, animation, or other visual images, using film, video, computers, or other electronic tools and media, for use in products or creations such as computer games, movies, music videos, and commercials. Design complex graphics and animation, using independent judgment, creativity, and computer equipment. Create two-dimensional and three-dimensional images depicting objects in motion or illustrating a process, using computer animation or modeling programs. Make objects or characters appear lifelike by manipulating light, color, texture, shadow, and transparency or manipulating static images to give the illusion of motion. Apply story development, directing, cinematography, and editing to animation to create storyboards that show the flow of the animation and map out key scenes and characters. Assemble, typeset, scan, and produce digital

Artistic

camera-ready art or film negatives and printer's proofs. Script, plan, and create animated narrative sequences under tight deadlines, using computer software and hand-drawing techniques. Create basic designs, drawings, and illustrations for product labels, cartons, direct mail, or television. Create pen-and-paper images to be scanned, edited, colored, textured, or animated by computer. Develop briefings, brochures, multimedia presentations, Web pages, promotional products, technical illustrations, and computer artwork for use in products, technical manuals, literature, newsletters, and slide shows.

Use models to simulate the behavior of animated objects in the finished sequence. Create and install special effects as required by the script, mixing chemicals and fabricating needed parts from wood, metal, plaster, and clay. Participate in design and production of multimedia campaigns, handling budgeting and scheduling and assisting with such responsibilities as production coordination, background design, and progress tracking. Convert real objects to animated objects through modeling, using techniques such as optical scanning. Implement and maintain configuration control systems.

Communications Studies/Speech

Personality Type: Artistic–Enterprising

Useful Facts About the Major

Focuses on the scientific, humanistic, and critical study of human communication in a variety of formats, media, and contexts.

Related CIP Program: 09.0101 Communication Studies/Speech Communication and Rhetoric

Specializations in the Major: Business communications; speech/rhetoric.

Typical Sequence of College Courses: Public speaking, introduction to psychology, English composition, communications theory, introduction to mass communication, argumentation and critical thinking, interpersonal communication, rhetorical tradition and techniques.

Typical Sequence of High School Courses: English, public speaking, foreign language, applied communications, social science.

Career Snapshot

This major is sometimes offered in the same department as mass communications or theater, but it is not designed to teach a technical skill such as television production or acting. Instead, it teaches how effective communication depends on a combination of verbal and nonverbal elements. Students work in various media and learn how to strike a balance between covering the subject matter, appealing to the listener or reader, and projecting the intended image of the speaker or writer. Graduates of communication and speech programs may go on to careers in sales, public relations, law, or teaching.

Useful Averages for the Related Jobs

- **Annual Earnings:** $48,357
- **Growth:** 21.3%
- **Self-Employed:** 26.8%
- **Part-Time:** 30.1%
- **Verbal Skill Rating:** 69.9
- **Math Skill Rating:** 32.4

Other Details About the Related Jobs

Total Annual Job Openings: 62,000

Interest Area: 03 Arts and Communication; 07 Government and Public Administration

Skills—Writing; persuasion; reading comprehension; active listening; critical thinking; social perceptiveness. **Values**—Creativity; recognition; ability utilization; achievement; autonomy; responsibility. **Work Conditions**—Sitting; spend time making repetitive motions.

Related Jobs

1. Court Reporters

Personality Type: Artistic–Conventional–Social

Earnings: $45,610
Growth: 14.8%
Annual Openings: 3,000

Most Common Education/Training Level: Postsecondary vocational training

Use verbatim methods and equipment to capture, store, retrieve, and transcribe pretrial and trial proceedings or other information. Includes stenocaptioners who operate computerized stenographic captioning equipment to provide captions of live or prerecorded broadcasts for hearing-impaired viewers. Take notes

Artistic

in shorthand or use a stenotype or shorthand machine that prints letters on a paper tape. Provide transcripts of proceedings upon request of judges, lawyers, or the public. Record verbatim proceedings of courts, legislative assemblies, committee meetings, and other proceedings, using computerized recording equipment, electronic stenograph machines, or stenomasks. Transcribe recorded proceedings in accordance with established formats. Ask speakers to clarify inaudible statements. File a legible transcript of records of a court case with the court clerk's office. File and store shorthand notes of court session. Respond to requests during court sessions to read portions of the proceedings already recorded. Record depositions and other proceedings for attorneys. Verify accuracy of transcripts by checking copies against original records of proceedings and accuracy of rulings by checking with judges. Record symbols on computer disks or CD-ROM; then translate and display them as text in computer-aided transcription process.

2. Public Address System and Other Announcers

Personality Type: Social–Artistic–Enterprising

Earnings: $24,990
Growth: 3.8%
Annual Openings: 2,000

Most Common Education/Training Level: Long-term on-the-job training

Make announcements over loudspeaker at sporting or other public events. May act as master of ceremonies or disc jockey at weddings, parties, clubs, or other gathering places. Greet attendees and serve as masters of ceremonies at banquets, store openings, and other events. Preview any music intended to be broadcast over the public address system. Inform patrons of coming events at a specific venue.

Meet with event directors to review schedules and exchange information about details such as national anthem performers and starting line-ups. Announce programs and player substitutions or other changes to patrons. Read prepared scripts describing acts or tricks presented during performances. Improvise commentary on items of interest, such as background and history of an event or past records of participants. Instruct and calm crowds during emergencies. Learn to pronounce the names of players, coaches, institutional personnel, officials, and other individuals involved in an event. Study the layout of an event venue in order to be able to give accurate directions in the event of an emergency. Review and announce crowd control procedures before the beginning of each event. Provide running commentaries of event activities, such as play-by-play descriptions or explanations of official decisions. Organize team information, such as statistics and tournament records, to ensure accessibility for use during events. Furnish information concerning plays to scoreboard operators.

3. Public Relations Specialists

Personality Type: Enterprising–Artistic–Social

Earnings: $47,350
Growth: 22.9%
Annual Openings: 38,000

Most Common Education/Training Level: Bachelor's degree

Engage in promoting or creating good will for individuals, groups, or organizations by writing or selecting favorable publicity material and releasing it through various communications media. May prepare and arrange displays and make speeches. Prepare or edit organizational publications for internal and external audiences, including employee newsletters and stockholders' reports. Respond to requests for information from the media or designate another appropriate spokesperson or information source. Establish and maintain cooperative relationships with representatives of community, consumer, employee, and public interest groups. Plan and direct development and communication of informational programs to maintain favorable public and stockholder perceptions of an organization's accomplishments and agenda. Confer with production and support personnel to produce or coordinate production of advertisements and promotions. Arrange public appearances, lectures, contests, or exhibits for clients to increase product and service awareness and to promote goodwill. Study the objectives, promotional policies, and needs of organizations to develop public relations strategies that will influence public opinion or promote ideas, products, and services. Consult with advertising agencies or staff to arrange promotional campaigns in all types of media for products, organizations, or individuals. Confer with other managers to identify trends and key group interests and concerns or to provide advice on business decisions. Coach client representatives in effective communication with the public and with employees. Prepare and deliver speeches to further public relations objectives. Purchase advertising space and time as required to promote client's product or agenda. Plan and conduct market and public opinion research to test products or determine potential for product success, communicating results to client or management.

4. Technical Writers

Personality Type:
Artistic–Investigative–Conventional

Earnings: $58,050
Growth: 23.2%
Annual Openings: 5,000

Most Common Education/Training Level: Bachelor's degree

Write technical materials, such as equipment manuals, appendices, or operating and maintenance instructions. May assist in layout work. Organize material and complete writing assignment according to set standards regarding order, clarity, conciseness, style, and terminology. Maintain records and files of work and revisions. Edit, standardize, or make changes to material prepared by other writers or establishment personnel. Confer with customer representatives, vendors, plant executives, or publisher to establish technical specifications and to determine subject material to be developed for publication. Review published materials and recommend revisions or changes in scope, format, content, and methods of reproduction and binding. Select photographs, drawings, sketches, diagrams, and charts to illustrate material. Study drawings, specifications, mockups, and product samples to integrate and delineate technology, operating procedure, and production sequence and detail. Interview production and engineering personnel and read journals and other material to become familiar with product technologies and production methods. Observe production, developmental, and experimental activities to determine operating procedure and detail. Arrange for typing, duplication, and distribution of material. Assist in laying out material for publication. Analyze developments in specific field to determine need for revisions in previously published materials and development of new material. Review manufacturer's and trade catalogs, drawings, and other data relative

Artistic

to operation, maintenance, and service of equipment. Draw sketches to illustrate specified materials or assembly sequence.

5. Writers and Authors

Personality Type: Artistic–Enterprising–Social

Earnings: $48,640
Growth: 17.7%
Annual Openings: 14,000

Most Common Education/Training Level:
Bachelor's degree

Job Specializations

Copy Writers. Write advertising copy for use by publication or broadcast media to promote sale of goods and services. Write advertising copy for use by publication, broadcast, or Internet media to promote the sale of goods and services. Present drafts and ideas to clients. Discuss with the client the product, advertising themes and methods, and any changes that should be made in advertising copy. Consult with sales, media, and marketing representatives to obtain information on product or service and discuss style and length of advertising copy. Vary language and tone of messages based on product and medium. Edit or rewrite existing copy as necessary and submit copy for approval by supervisor. Write to customers in their terms and on their level so that the advertiser's sales message is more readily received. Write articles; bulletins; sales letters; speeches; and other related informative, marketing, and promotional material. Invent names for products and write the slogans that appear on packaging, brochures, and other promotional material. Review advertising trends, consumer surveys, and other data regarding marketing of goods and services to determine the best way to promote products. Develop advertising campaigns for a wide range of clients, working with an advertising agency's cre-

ative director and art director to determine the best way to present advertising information. Conduct research and interviews to determine which of a product's selling features should be promoted.

Poets, Lyricists and Creative Writers. Create original written works, such as scripts, essays, prose, poetry, or song lyrics, for publication or performance. Revise written material to meet personal standards and to satisfy needs of clients, publishers, directors, or producers. Choose subject matter and suitable form to express personal feelings and experiences or ideas or to narrate stories or events. Plan project arrangements or outlines and organize material accordingly. Prepare works in appropriate format for publication and send them to publishers or producers. Follow appropriate procedures to get copyrights for completed work. Write fiction or nonfiction prose such as short stories, novels, biographies, articles, descriptive or critical analyses, and essays. Develop factors such as themes, plots, characterizations, psychological analyses, historical environments, action, and dialogue to create material. Confer with clients, editors, publishers, or producers to discuss changes or revisions to written material. Conduct research to obtain factual information and authentic detail, using sources such as newspaper accounts, diaries, and interviews. Write narrative, dramatic, lyric, or other types of poetry for publication. Attend book launches and publicity events or conduct public readings. Write words to fit musical compositions, including lyrics for operas, musical plays, and choral works. Adapt text to accommodate musical requirements of composers and singers. Teach writing classes. Write humorous material for publication or for performances such as comedy routines, gags, and comedy shows. Collaborate with other writers on specific projects.

Drama/Theater Arts

Personality Type: Artistic–Enterprising–Social

Useful Facts About the Major

Focuses on the general study of dramatic works and their performance.

Related CIP Program: 50.0501 Drama and Dramatics/Theatre Arts, General

Specializations in the Major: Acting; design and technology; directing.

Typical Sequence of College Courses: English composition, foreign language, history of theater, acting technique, dramatic literature, performance techniques, theater technology (e.g., set/costume/lighting), theater practicum.

Typical Sequence of High School Courses: English, foreign language, literature, public speaking.

Career Snapshot

Drama is one of the most ancient art forms and continues to entertain audiences today. As in all performing arts, there are better opportunities for teachers than for performers. Teaching at the postsecondary level usually requires a master's degree. The technical aspects of theater—set design, lighting, costume design, and makeup—also offer jobs for nonperformers. The academic program includes many opportunities to learn through student performances.

Useful Averages for the Related Jobs

- **Annual Earnings:** $56,310
- **Growth:** 16.4%
- **Self-Employed:** 30.4%
- **Part-Time:** 23.3%
- **Verbal Skill Rating:** 66.0
- **Math Skill Rating:** 35.9

Other Details About the Related Jobs

Total Annual Job Openings: 22,000

Interest Area: 03 Arts and Communication

Skills—Management of personnel resources; speaking; time management; monitoring; active listening; social perceptiveness. **Values**—Authority; creativity; ability utilization; autonomy; recognition; responsibility. **Work Conditions**—Indoors, environmentally controlled; sitting.

Related Jobs

1. Actors

Personality Type: Artistic–Enterprising–Social

Earnings: No data available
Growth: 16.1%
Annual Openings: 11,000

Most Common Education/Training Level: Long-term on-the-job training

Play parts in stage, television, radio, video, or motion picture productions for entertainment, information, or instruction. Interpret serious or comic role by speech, gesture, and body movement to entertain or inform audience. May dance and sing. Study and rehearse roles from scripts to interpret, learn, and memorize lines, stunts, and cues as directed. Work closely with directors, other actors, and playwrights to find the interpretation most suited to the role. Learn about characters in scripts and their relationships to each other to develop role interpretations. Collaborate with other actors as part of

Artistic

an ensemble. Perform humorous and serious interpretations of emotions, actions, and situations, using body movements, facial expressions, and gestures. Attend auditions and casting calls to audition for roles. Portray and interpret roles, using speech, gestures, and body movements to entertain, inform, or instruct radio, film, television, or live audiences. Work with other crewmembers responsible for lighting, costumes, makeup, and props. Sing or dance during dramatic or comedic performances. Read from scripts or books to narrate action or to inform or entertain audiences, utilizing few or no stage props. Promote productions, using means such as interviews about plays or movies. Write original or adapted material for dramas, comedies, puppet shows, narration, or other performances. Prepare and perform action stunts for motion picture, television, or stage productions. Tell jokes; perform comic dances, songs, and skits; impersonate mannerisms and voices of others; contort face; and use other devices to amuse audiences. Introduce performances and performers to stimulate excitement and coordinate smooth transition of acts during events. Manipulate strings, wires, rods, or fingers to animate puppets or dummies in synchronization with talking, singing, or recorded programs. Dress in comical clown costumes and makeup and perform comedy routines to entertain audiences. Perform original and stock tricks of illusion to entertain and mystify audiences, occasionally including audience members as participants. Construct puppets and ventriloquist dummies and sew accessory clothing, using hand tools and machines.

2. Producers and Directors

Personality Type: Artistic–Enterprising–Social

Earnings: $56,310
Growth: 16.6%
Annual Openings: 11,000

Most Common Education/Training Level: Work experience plus degree

Job Specializations

Directors—Stage, Motion Pictures, Television, and Radio. Interpret script, conduct rehearsals, and direct activities of cast and technical crew for stage, motion pictures, television, or radio programs. Direct live broadcasts, films and recordings, or non-broadcast programming for public entertainment or education. Supervise and coordinate the work of camera, lighting, design, and sound crew members. Study and research scripts to determine how they should be directed. Cut and edit film or tape to integrate component parts into desired sequences. Collaborate with film and sound editors during the post-production process as films are edited and soundtracks are added. Confer with technical directors, managers, crew members, and writers to discuss details of production, such as photography, script, music, sets, and costumes. Plan details such as framing, composition, camera movement, sound, and actor movement for each shot or scene. Communicate to actors the approach, characterization, and movement needed for each scene in such a way that rehearsals and takes are minimized. Establish pace of programs and sequences of scenes according to time requirements and cast and set accessibility. Choose settings and locations for films and determine how scenes will be shot in these settings. Identify and approve equipment and elements required for productions, such as scenery, lights, props, costumes, choreography, and music. Compile scripts, program notes, and other material related to productions. Perform producers' duties such as securing financial backing, establishing and administering budgets, and recruiting cast and crew. Select plays or scripts for production and determine how material should be interpreted and performed. Compile cue words and phrases; cue announcers, cast members, and technicians during performances. Consult with writers, producers, or actors about script changes or "workshop" scripts, through rehearsal with writers and actors, to create final drafts. Collaborate with producers to hire crew members such as art directors, cinematographers, and costumer designers. Review film daily to check on work in progress and to plan for future filming. Interpret stage-set diagrams to determine stage layouts and supervise placement of equipment and scenery. Hold auditions for parts or negotiate contracts with actors determined suitable for specific roles, working in conjunction with producers.

Producers. Plan and coordinate various aspects of radio, television, stage, or motion picture production, such as selecting script; coordinating writing, directing, and editing; and arranging financing. Coordinate the activities of writers, directors, managers, and other personnel throughout the production process. Monitor post-production processes to ensure accurate completion of all details. Perform management activities such as budgeting, scheduling, planning, and marketing. Determine production size, content, and budget, establishing details such as production schedules and management policies. Compose and edit scripts or provide screenwriters with story outlines from which scripts can be written. Conduct meetings with staff to discuss production progress and to ensure production objectives are attained. Resolve personnel problems that arise during the production process by acting as liaisons between dissenting parties when necessary. Produce shows for special occasions, such as holidays or testimonials. Edit and write news stories from information collected by reporters. Write and submit proposals to bid on contracts for projects. Hire directors, principal cast members, and key production staff members. Arrange financing for productions. Select plays, scripts, books, or ideas to be produced. Review film, recordings, or rehearsals to ensure conformance to production and broadcast standards. Perform administrative duties such as preparing operational reports, distributing rehearsal call sheets and script copies, and arranging for rehearsal quarters. Obtain and distribute costumes, props, music, and studio equipment needed to complete productions. Negotiate contracts with artistic personnel, often in accordance with collective bargaining agreements. Maintain knowledge of minimum wages and working conditions established by unions or associations of actors and technicians. Plan and coordinate the production of musical recordings, selecting music and directing performers. Negotiate with parties, including independent producers and the distributors and broadcasters who will be handling completed productions. Develop marketing plans for finished products, collaborating with sales associates to supervise product distribution. Determine and direct the content of radio programming.

Program Directors. Direct and coordinate activities of personnel engaged in preparation of radio or television station program schedules and programs such as sports or news. Plan and schedule programming and event coverage based on broadcast length; time availability; and other factors such as community needs, ratings data, and viewer demographics. Monitor and review programming to ensure that schedules are met, guidelines are adhered to, and performances are

Artistic

of adequate quality. Direct and coordinate activities of personnel engaged in broadcast news, sports, or programming. Check completed program logs for accuracy and conformance with FCC rules and regulations and resolve program log inaccuracies. Establish work schedules and assign work to staff members. Coordinate activities between departments such as news and programming. Perform personnel duties such as hiring staff and evaluating work performance. Evaluate new and existing programming for suitability and to assess the need for changes, using information such as audience surveys and feedback. Develop budgets for programming and broadcasting activities and monitor expenditures to ensure that they remain within budgetary limits. Confer with directors and production staff to discuss issues such as production and casting problems, budgets, policies, and news coverage. Select, acquire, and maintain programs, music, films, and other needed materials and obtain legal clearances for their use as necessary. Monitor network transmissions for advisories concerning daily program schedules, program content, special feeds, or program changes. Develop promotions for current programs and specials. Prepare copy and edit tape so that material is ready for broadcasting. Develop ideas for programs and features that a station could produce. Participate in the planning and execution of fundraising activities. Review information about programs and schedules to ensure accuracy and provide such information to local media outlets as necessary. Read news, read or record public service and promotional announcements, and otherwise participate as a member of an on-air shift as required. Operate and maintain on-air and production audio equipment. Direct setup of remote facilities and install or cancel programs at remote stations.

Talent Directors. Audition and interview performers to select most appropriate talent for parts in stage, television, radio, or motion picture productions. Review performer information such as photos, resumes, voice tapes, videos, and union membership to decide whom to audition for parts. Read scripts and confer with producers to determine the types and numbers of performers required for a given production. Select performers for roles or submit lists of suitable performers to producers or directors for final selection. Serve as liaisons between directors, actors, and agents. Audition and interview performers to match their attributes to specific roles or to increase the pool of available acting talent. Maintain talent files that include information such as performers' specialties, past performances, and availability. Prepare actors for auditions by providing scripts and information about roles and casting requirements. Attend or view productions to maintain knowledge of available actors. Negotiate contract agreements with performers, with agents, or between performers and agents or production companies. Contact agents and actors to provide notification of audition and performance opportunities and to set up audition times. Hire and supervise workers who help locate people with specified attributes and talents. Arrange for or design screen tests or auditions for prospective performers. Locate performers or extras for crowd and background scenes and stand-ins or photo doubles for actors by direct contact or through agents.

Technical Directors/Managers. Coordinate activities of technical departments, such as taping, editing, engineering, and maintenance, to produce radio or television programs. Direct technical aspects of newscasts and other productions, checking and switching between video sources and taking responsibility for the on-air product, including camera shots and graphics. Test equipment to ensure proper operation. Monitor broadcasts to ensure that programs conform to station or network policies and regulations. Observe pictures through monitors and direct camera and video staff concerning shading and composition. Act as liaisons between engineering and production departments. Supervise and assign duties to workers engaged in technical control and production of radio and television programs. Schedule use of studio and editing facilities for producers and engineering and maintenance staff. Confer with operations directors to formulate and maintain fair and attainable technical policies for programs. Operate equipment to produce programs or broadcast live programs from remote loca-

tions. Train workers in use of equipment such as switchers, cameras, monitors, microphones, and lights. Switch between video sources in a studio or on multi-camera remotes, using equipment such as switchers, video slide projectors, and video effects generators. Set up and execute video transitions and special effects such as fades, dissolves, cuts, keys, and supers, using computers to manipulate pictures as necessary. Collaborate with promotions directors to produce on-air station promotions. Discuss filter options, lens choices, and the visual effects of objects being filmed with photography directors and video operators. Follow instructions from production managers and directors during productions, such as commands for camera cuts, effects, graphics, and takes.

English

Personality Type: Artistic

Useful Facts About the Major

Focuses on the English language, including its history, structure, and related communications skills, and the literature and culture of English-speaking peoples.

Related CIP Program: 23.0101 English Language and Literature, General

Specializations in the Major: Creative writing; English education; language; literature.

Typical Sequence of College Courses: English composition, introduction to literary study, foreign language, survey of British literature, survey of American literature, a major writer (e.g., Shakespeare, Romantic poets), a genre (e.g., drama, short story, poetry), creative writing, history of the English language, comparative literature.

Typical Sequence of High School Courses: English, foreign language, literature, history, public speaking, social science.

Career Snapshot

English majors not only learn about a great literary tradition, but they also develop first-rate writing and critical-thinking skills that can be valuable in a variety of careers. Besides teaching, many of them go into business, law, and library science, usually with an appropriate master's or law degree. They are said to make excellent trainees in computer programming. In a wide range of careers, their humanistic skills often allow them to advance higher than those who prepare through more specifically career-oriented curricula.

Useful Averages for the Related Jobs

- **Annual Earnings:** $43,702
- **Growth:** 12.8%
- **Self-Employed:** 36.6%
- **Part-Time:** 30.7%
- **Verbal Skill Rating:** 77.6
- **Math Skill Rating:** 38.1

Other Details About the Related Jobs

Total Annual Job Openings: 34,000

Interest Area: 03 Arts and Communication

Skills—Instructing; writing; learning strategies; social perceptiveness; persuasion; reading comprehension. **Values**—Authority; social service; creativity; achievement; ability utilization; autonomy. **Work Conditions**—Indoors, environmentally controlled; sitting.

Related Jobs

1. Editors

Personality Type: Artistic–Enterprising–Social

Earnings: $46,990
Growth: 14.8%
Annual Openings: 16,000

Most Common Education/Training Level: Bachelor's degree

Perform variety of editorial duties, such as laying out, indexing, and revising content of written materials, in preparation for final publication. Prepare, rewrite, and edit copy to improve readability or supervise others who do this work. Read copy or proof to detect and correct errors in spelling, punctuation, and syntax. Allocate print space for story text, photos, and illustrations according to space parameters and copy significance, using knowledge of layout principles. Plan the contents of publications according to the publication's style, editorial policy, and publishing requirements. Verify facts, dates, and statistics, using standard reference sources. Review and approve proofs submitted by composing room prior to publication production. Develop story or content ideas, considering reader or audience appeal. Oversee publication production, including artwork, layout, computer typesetting, and printing, ensuring adherence to deadlines and budget requirements. Confer with management and editorial staff members regarding placement and emphasis of developing news stories. Assign topics, events, and stories to individual writers or reporters for coverage. Read, evaluate, and edit manuscripts or other materials submitted for publication and confer with authors regarding changes in content, style or organization, or publication. Monitor news-gathering operations to ensure utilization of all news sources, such as press releases, telephone contacts, radio, television, wire services, and other reporters. Meet frequently with artists, typesetters, layout personnel, marketing directors, and production managers to discuss projects and resolve problems. Supervise and coordinate work of reporters and other editors. Make manuscript acceptance or revision recommendations to the publisher. Select local, state, national, and international news items received from wire services based on assessment of items' significance and interest value. Interview and hire writers and reporters or negotiate contracts, royalties, and payments for authors or freelancers. Direct the policies and departments of newspapers, magazines, and other publishing establishments. Arrange for copyright permissions. Read material to determine index items and arrange them alphabeti-

cally or topically, indicating page or chapter location.

2. Reporters and Correspondents

Personality Type:
Artistic–Investigative–Enterprising

Earnings: $33,470
Growth: 4.9%
Annual Openings: 4,000

Most Common Education/Training Level:
Work experience plus degree

Collect and analyze facts about newsworthy events by interview, investigation, or observation. Report and write stories for newspaper, news magazine, radio, or television. Report and write news stories for publication or broadcast, describing the background and details of events. Arrange interviews with people who can provide information about a particular story. Review copy and correct errors in content, grammar, and punctuation, following prescribed editorial style and formatting guidelines. Review and evaluate notes taken about event aspects to isolate pertinent facts and details. Determine a story's emphasis, length, and format and organize material accordingly. Research and analyze background information related to stories in order to be able to provide complete and accurate information. Gather information about events through research; interviews; experience; and attendance at political, news, sports, artistic, social, and other functions. Investigate breaking news developments such as disasters, crimes, and human interest stories. Research and report on specialized fields such as medicine, science and technology, politics, foreign affairs, sports, arts, consumer affairs, business, religion, crime, or education. Check reference materials such as books, news files, and public records to obtain

Artistic

relevant facts. Receive assignments or evaluate leads and tips to develop story ideas. Discuss issues with editors in order to establish priorities and positions. Revise work to meet editorial approval or to fit time or space requirements. Photograph or videotape news events or request that a photographer be assigned to provide such coverage. Develop ideas and material for columns or commentaries by analyzing and interpreting news, current issues, and personal experiences. Transmit news stories or reporting information from remote locations, using equipment such as satellite phones, telephones, fax machines, or modems. Present live or recorded commentary via broadcast media. Conduct taped or filmed interviews or narratives. Edit or assist in editing videos for broadcast. Write columns, editorials, commentaries, or reviews that interpret events or offer opinions. Write reviews of literary, musical, and other artwork based on knowledge, judgment, and experience.

3. Writers and Authors

Personality Type: Artistic–Enterprising–Social

Earnings: $48,640
Growth: 17.7%
Annual Openings: 14,000

Most Common Education/Training Level: Bachelor's degree

Job Specializations

Copy Writers. Write advertising copy for use by publication or broadcast media to promote sale of goods and services. Write advertising copy for use by publication, broadcast, or Internet media to promote the sale of goods and services. Present drafts and ideas to clients. Discuss with the client the product, advertising themes and methods, and any changes that should be made in advertising copy. Consult with sales, media,

and marketing representatives to obtain information on product or service and discuss style and length of advertising copy. Vary language and tone of messages based on product and medium. Edit or rewrite existing copy as necessary and submit copy for approval by supervisor. Write to customers in their terms and on their level so that the advertiser's sales message is more readily received. Write articles; bulletins; sales letters; speeches; and other related informative, marketing, and promotional material. Invent names for products and write the slogans that appear on packaging, brochures, and other promotional material. Review advertising trends, consumer surveys, and other data regarding marketing of goods and services to determine the best way to promote products. Develop advertising campaigns for a wide range of clients, working with an advertising agency's creative director and art director to determine the best way to present advertising information. Conduct research and interviews to determine which of a product's selling features should be promoted.

Poets, Lyricists, and Creative Writers. Create original written works, such as scripts, essays, prose, poetry, or song lyrics, for publication or performance. Revise written material to meet personal standards and to satisfy needs of clients, publishers, directors, or producers. Choose subject matter and suitable form to express personal feelings and experiences or ideas or to narrate stories or events. Plan project arrangements or outlines and organize material accordingly. Prepare works in appropriate format for publication and send them to publishers or producers. Follow appropriate procedures to get copyrights for completed work. Write fiction or nonfiction prose such as short stories, novels, biographies, articles, descriptive or critical analyses, and essays. Develop factors such as themes, plots, characterizations, psychological analyses, historical environments, action, and dialogue to create material. Confer with clients, editors, publishers, or producers to discuss changes or revisions to written material. Conduct research to obtain factual information and authentic detail, using sources such as newspaper accounts, diaries, and interviews. Write narrative, dramatic, lyric, or other types of poetry for publication. Attend book launches and publicity events or conduct public readings. Write words to fit musical compositions, including lyrics for operas, musical plays, and choral works. Adapt text to accommodate musical requirements of composers and singers. Teach writing classes. Write humorous material for publication or for performances such as comedy routines, gags, and comedy shows. Collaborate with other writers on specific projects.

Artistic

Film/Cinema Studies

Personality Type: Artistic–Enterprising–Social

Useful Facts About the Major

Film/Cinema Studies focuses on the study of the history, development, theory, and criticism of the film/video arts, as well as the basic principles of filmmaking and film production.

Related CIP Programs: 50.0602 Cinematography and Film/Video Production; 50.0601 Film/Cinema Studies

Specializations in the Major: Criticism; directing/producing; editing; screenwriting.

Typical Sequence of College Courses: English composition, foreign language, world history in the modern era, introduction to psychology, film as a narrative art, history of film, film styles and genres, major film directors, literature and media, film theory and criticism, gender and film, seminar (reporting on research).

Typical Sequence of High School Courses: English, foreign language, literature, history, photography.

Career Snapshot

Film is one of the newest art forms and still straddles the borderline between popular culture and high art. The American film and video industry continues to grow as it increasingly dominates the world market, but there is keen competition for creative jobs in this field. Some graduates of film programs become critics or work in industrial or educational film production. Students can usually tailor the academic program to emphasize the aspect of film that interests them; therefore, they may do a lot of writing about film or a lot of hands-on work producing film.

Useful Averages for the Related Jobs

- **Annual Earnings:** $51,199
- **Growth:** 16.4%
- **Self-Employed:** 26.6%
- **Part-Time:** 26.0%
- **Verbal Skill Rating:** 64.6
- **Math Skill Rating:** 39.0

Other Details About the Related Jobs

Total Annual Job Openings: 18,000

Interest Area: 03 Arts and Communication

Skills—Management of personnel resources; time management; speaking; monitoring; coordination; active listening. **Values**—Authority; creativity; responsibility; autonomy; recognition; ability utilization. **Work Conditions**—Indoors, environmentally controlled; sitting.

Related Jobs

1. Camera Operators, Television, Video, and Motion Picture

Personality Type:
Artistic–Realistic–Enterprising

Earnings: $40,060
Growth: 14.2%
Annual Openings: 4,000

Most Common Education/Training Level:
Moderate-term on-the-job training

Operate television, video, or motion picture camera to photograph images or scenes for

various purposes, such as TV broadcasts, advertising, video production, or motion pictures. Operate television or motion picture cameras to record scenes for television broadcasts, advertising, or motion pictures. Compose and frame each shot, applying the technical aspects of light, lenses, film, filters, and camera settings to achieve the effects sought by directors. Operate zoom lenses, changing images according to specifications and rehearsal instructions. Use cameras in any of several different camera mounts, such as stationary, track-mounted, or crane-mounted. Test, clean, and maintain equipment to ensure proper working condition. Adjust positions and controls of cameras, printers, and related equipment to change focus, exposure, and lighting. Gather and edit raw footage on location to send to television affiliates for broadcast, using electronic news-gathering or film-production equipment. Confer with directors, sound and lighting technicians, electricians, and other crew members to discuss assignments and determine filming sequences, desired effects, camera movements, and lighting requirements. Observe sets or locations for potential problems and to determine filming and lighting requirements. Instruct camera operators regarding camera setups, angles, distances, movement, and variables and cues for starting and stopping filming. Select and assemble cameras, accessories, equipment, and film stock to be used during filming, using knowledge of filming techniques, requirements, and computations. Label and record contents of exposed film and note details on report forms. Read charts and compute ratios to determine variables such as lighting, shutter angles, filter factors, and camera distances. Set up cameras, optical printers, and related equipment to produce photographs and special effects. View films to resolve problems of exposure control, subject and camera movement, changes in subject dis-

tance, and related variables. Reload camera magazines with fresh raw film stock. Read and analyze work orders and specifications to determine locations of subject material, work procedures, sequences of operations, and machine setups. Receive raw film stock and maintain film inventories.

2. Film and Video Editors

Personality Type:
Artistic–Enterprising–Investigative

Earnings: $46,670
Growth: 18.6%
Annual Openings: 3,000

Most Common Education/Training Level:
Bachelor's degree

Edit motion picture soundtracks, film, and video. Cut shot sequences to different angles at specific points in scenes, making each individual cut as fluid and seamless as possible. Study scripts to become familiar with production concepts and requirements. Edit films and videotapes to insert music, dialogue, and sound effects; to arrange films into sequences; and to correct errors, using editing equipment. Select and combine the most effective shots of each scene to form a logical and smoothly running story. Mark frames where a particular shot or piece of sound is to begin or end. Determine the specific audio and visual effects and music necessary to complete films. Verify key numbers and time codes on materials. Organize and string together raw footage into a continuous whole according to scripts or the instructions of directors and producers. Review assembled films or edited videotapes on screens or monitors to determine if corrections are necessary. Program computerized graphic effects. Review footage sequence by sequence to become familiar with it before assembling it into a final product. Set up

Artistic

and operate computer editing systems, electronic titling systems, video switching equipment, and digital video effects units to produce a final product. Record needed sounds or obtain them from sound effects libraries. Confer with producers and directors concerning layout or editing approaches needed to increase dramatic or entertainment value of productions. Manipulate plot, score, sound, and graphics to make the parts into a continuous whole, working closely with people in audio, visual, music, optical, or special effects departments. Supervise and coordinate activities of workers engaged in film editing, assembling, and recording activities. Trim film segments to specified lengths and reassemble segments in sequences that present stories with maximum effect. Develop post-production models for films. Piece sounds together to develop film soundtracks. Conduct film screenings for directors and members of production staffs. Collaborate with music editors to select appropriate passages of music and develop production scores. Discuss the sound requirements of pictures with sound effects editors.

3. Producers and Directors

Personality Type: Artistic–Enterprising–Social

Earnings: $56,310
Growth: 16.6%
Annual Openings: 11,000

Most Common Education/Training Level: Work experience plus degree

Job Specializations

Directors—Stage, Motion Pictures, Television, and Radio. Interpret script, conduct rehearsals, and direct activities of cast and technical crew for stage, motion pictures, television, or radio programs. Direct live broadcasts, films and recordings, or non-broadcast programming for public entertainment or education. Supervise and coordinate the work of camera, lighting, design, and sound crew members. Study and research scripts to determine how they should be directed. Cut and edit film or tape to integrate component parts into desired sequences. Collaborate with film and sound editors during the post-production process as films are edited and soundtracks are added. Confer with technical directors, managers, crew members, and writers to discuss details of production, such as photography, script, music, sets, and costumes. Plan details such as framing, composition, camera movement, sound, and actor movement for each shot or scene. Communicate to actors the approach, characterization, and movement needed for each scene in such a way that rehearsals and takes are minimized. Establish pace of programs and sequences of scenes according to time requirements and cast and set accessibility. Choose settings and locations for films and determine how scenes will be shot in these settings. Identify and approve equipment and elements required for productions, such as scenery, lights, props, costumes, choreography, and music. Compile scripts, program notes, and other material related to productions. Perform producers' duties such as securing financial backing, establishing and administering budgets, and recruiting cast and crew. Select plays or scripts for production and determine how material should be interpreted and performed. Compile cue words and phrases; cue announcers, cast members, and technicians during performances. Consult with writers, producers, or actors about script changes or "workshop" scripts, through rehearsal with writers and actors, to create final drafts. Collaborate with producers to hire crew members such as art directors, cinematographers, and costumer designers. Review film daily to check on work in progress and to plan for future filming. Interpret stage-set diagrams to determine stage layouts and supervise placement of equipment and scenery. Hold auditions for parts or negotiate contracts with actors determined suitable for specific roles, working in conjunction with producers.

Producers. Plan and coordinate various aspects of radio, television, stage, or motion picture production, such as selecting script; coordinating writing, directing, and editing; and arranging financing. Coordinate the activities of writers, directors, managers, and other personnel throughout the production process. Monitor post-production processes to ensure accurate completion of all details. Perform management activities such as budgeting, scheduling, planning, and marketing. Determine production size, content, and budget, establishing details such as production schedules and management policies. Compose and edit scripts or provide screenwriters with story outlines from which scripts can be written. Conduct meetings with staff to discuss production progress and to ensure production objectives are attained. Resolve personnel problems that arise during the production process by acting as liaisons between dissenting parties when necessary. Produce shows for special occasions, such as holidays or testimonials. Edit and write news stories from information collected by reporters. Write and submit proposals to bid on contracts for projects. Hire directors, principal cast members, and key production staff members. Arrange financing for productions. Select plays, scripts, books, or ideas to be produced. Review film, recordings, or rehearsals to ensure conformance to production and broadcast standards. Perform administrative duties such as preparing operational reports, distributing rehearsal call sheets and script copies, and arranging for rehearsal quarters. Obtain and distribute costumes, props, music, and studio equipment needed to com-

plete productions. Negotiate contracts with artistic personnel, often in accordance with collective bargaining agreements. Maintain knowledge of minimum wages and working conditions established by unions or associations of actors and technicians. Plan and coordinate the production of musical recordings, selecting music and directing performers. Negotiate with parties, including independent producers and the distributors and broadcasters who will be handling completed productions. Develop marketing plans for finished products, collaborating with sales associates to supervise product distribution. Determine and direct the content of radio programming.

Program Directors. Direct and coordinate activities of personnel engaged in preparation of radio or television station program schedules and programs such as sports or news. Plan and schedule programming and event coverage based on broadcast length; time availability; and other factors such as community needs, ratings data, and viewer demographics. Monitor and review programming to ensure that schedules are met, guidelines are adhered to, and performances are of adequate quality. Direct and coordinate activities of personnel engaged in broadcast news, sports, or programming. Check completed program logs for accuracy and conformance with FCC rules and regulations and resolve program log inaccuracies. Establish work schedules and assign work to staff members. Coordinate activities between departments such as news and programming. Perform personnel duties such as hiring staff and evaluating work performance. Evaluate new and existing programming for suitability and to assess the need for changes, using information such as audience surveys and feedback. Develop budgets for programming and broadcasting activities and monitor expenditures to ensure that they remain within

Artistic

budgetary limits. Confer with directors and production staff to discuss issues such as production and casting problems, budgets, policies, and news coverage. Select, acquire, and maintain programs, music, films, and other needed materials and obtain legal clearances for their use as necessary. Monitor network transmissions for advisories concerning daily program schedules, program content, special feeds, or program changes. Develop promotions for current programs and specials. Prepare copy and edit tape so that material is ready for broadcasting. Develop ideas for programs and features that a station could produce. Participate in the planning and execution of fundraising activities. Review information about programs and schedules to ensure accuracy and provide such information to local media outlets as necessary. Read news, read or record public service and promotional announcements, and otherwise participate as a member of an on-air shift as required. Operate and maintain on-air and production audio equipment. Direct setup of remote facilities and install or cancel programs at remote stations.

Talent Directors. Audition and interview performers to select most appropriate talent for parts in stage, television, radio, or motion picture productions. Review performer information such as photos, resumes, voice tapes, videos, and union membership to decide whom to audition for parts. Read scripts and confer with producers to determine the types and numbers of performers required for a given production. Select performers for roles or submit lists of suitable performers to producers or directors for final selection. Serve as liaisons between directors, actors, and agents. Audition and interview performers to match their attributes to specific roles or to increase the pool of available acting talent. Maintain talent files that include information such as performers' specialties, past per-

formances, and availability. Prepare actors for auditions by providing scripts and information about roles and casting requirements. Attend or view productions to maintain knowledge of available actors. Negotiate contract agreements with performers, with agents, or between performers and agents or production companies. Contact agents and actors to provide notification of audition and performance opportunities and to set up audition times. Hire and supervise workers who help locate people with specified attributes and talents. Arrange for or design screen tests or auditions for prospective performers. Locate performers or extras for crowd and background scenes and stand-ins or photo doubles for actors by direct contact or through agents.

Technical Directors/Managers. Coordinate activities of technical departments, such as taping, editing, engineering, and maintenance, to produce radio or television programs. Direct technical aspects of newscasts and other productions, checking and switching between video sources and taking responsibility for the on-air product, including camera shots and graphics. Test equipment to ensure proper operation. Monitor broadcasts to ensure that programs conform to station or network policies and regulations. Observe pictures through monitors and direct camera and video staff concerning shading and composition. Act as liaisons between engineering and production departments. Supervise and assign duties to workers engaged in technical control and production of radio and television programs. Schedule use of studio and editing facilities for producers and engineering and maintenance staff. Confer with operations directors to formulate and maintain fair and attainable technical policies for programs. Operate equipment to produce programs or broadcast live programs from remote locations. Train workers in use of equipment such as switchers, cameras, monitors, microphones, and lights. Switch between video sources in a studio or on multi-camera remotes, using equipment such as switchers, video slide projectors, and video effects generators. Set up and execute video transitions and special effects such as fades, dissolves, cuts, keys, and supers, using computers to manipulate pictures as necessary. Collaborate with promotions directors to produce on-air station promotions. Discuss filter options, lens choices, and the visual effects of objects being filmed with photography directors and video operators. Follow instructions from production managers and directors during productions, such as commands for camera cuts, effects, graphics, and takes.

Artistic

Industrial Design

Personality Type: Artistic

Useful Facts About the Major

Prepares individuals to use artistic techniques to effectively communicate ideas and information to business and consumer audiences via the creation of effective forms, shapes, and packaging for manufactured products.

Related CIP Program: 50.0404 Industrial Design

Specializations in the Major: Computer modeling; product design.

Typical Sequence of College Courses: English composition, college algebra, basic drawing, oral communication, introduction to economics, art history: Renaissance to modern, general physics, introduction to marketing, introduction to graphic design, visual thinking and problem solving, presentation graphics, industrial design materials and processes, human factors in design (ergonomics), computer modeling, history of industrial design, professional practices for industrial design, senior design project.

Typical Sequence of High School Courses: Algebra, geometry, trigonometry, pre-calculus, English, public speaking, art, computer science, mechanical drawing, photography.

Career Snapshot

Industrial designers develop every conceivable kind of manufactured product, from cars to computers to children's toys. They need to understand the technology that will make the product work, the human context in which the product will be used—such as the way it will be held in the hand—as well as the marketplace in which the product will compete. Therefore, this field requires students to learn a combination of technical, creative, and business skills. Knowledge of computer-assisted design (CAD) has become essential, and skill with this tool can help in a field that is often keenly competitive and can suffer from outsourcing of work to foreign design firms.

Useful Averages for the Related Jobs

- **Annual Earnings:** $42,091
- **Growth:** 14.6%
- **Self-Employed:** 26.4%
- **Part-Time:** 32.0%
- **Verbal Skill Rating:** 64.5
- **Math Skill Rating:** 53.1

Other Details About the Related Jobs

Total Annual Job Openings: 42,000

Interest Area: 03 Arts and Communication

Skills—Persuasion; operations analysis; writing; time management; instructing; complex problem solving. **Values**—Creativity; ability utilization; achievement; recognition; working conditions; autonomy. **Work Conditions**—Indoors, environmentally controlled; sitting.

Related Jobs

1. Commercial and Industrial Designers
Personality Type:
Artistic–Realistic–Enterprising

Earnings: $54,560
Growth: 10.8%
Annual Openings: 7,000

Most Common Education/Training Level:
Bachelor's degree

Develop and design manufactured products, such as cars, home appliances, and children's toys. Combine artistic talent with research on product use, marketing, and materials to create the most functional and appealing product design. Prepare sketches of ideas, detailed drawings, illustrations, artwork, or blueprints, using drafting instruments, paints and brushes, or computer-aided design equipment. Direct and coordinate the fabrication of models or samples and the drafting of working drawings and specification sheets from sketches. Modify and refine designs, using working models, to conform with customer specifications, production limitations, or changes in design trends. Coordinate the look and function of product lines. Confer with engineering, marketing, production, or sales departments, or with customers, to establish and evaluate design concepts for manufactured products. Present designs and reports to customers or design committees for approval and discuss need for modification. Evaluate feasibility of design ideas based on factors such as appearance, safety, function, serviceability, budget, production costs/methods, and market characteristics. Read publications, attend showings, and study competing products and design styles and motifs to obtain perspective and generate design concepts. Research production specifications, costs, production materials, and manufacturing methods and provide cost estimates and itemized production requirements. Design graphic material for use as ornamentation, illustration, or advertising on manufactured materials and packaging or containers. Develop manufacturing procedures and monitor the manufacture of their designs in a factory to improve operations and product quality. Supervise assistants' work throughout the design process. Fabricate models or samples in paper, wood, glass, fabric, plastic, metal, or other materials, using hand or power tools. Investigate product characteristics such as the product's safety and handling qualities; its market appeal; how efficiently it can be produced; and ways of distributing, using, and maintaining it. Develop industrial standards and regulatory guidelines. Participate in new product planning or market research, including studying the potential need for new products. Advise corporations on issues involving corporate image projects or problems.

2. Graphic Designers

Personality Type:
Artistic–Enterprising–Realistic

Earnings: $39,900
Growth: 15.2%
Annual Openings: 35,000

Most Common Education/Training Level:
Bachelor's degree

Design or create graphics to meet specific commercial or promotional needs, such as packaging, displays, or logos. May use a variety of media to achieve artistic or decorative effects. Create designs, concepts, and sample layouts based on knowledge of layout principles and esthetic design concepts. Determine size and arrangement of illustrative material and copy and select style and size of type. Use computer software to generate new images. Mark up, paste, and assemble final layouts to prepare layouts for printer. Draw and print charts, graphs, illustrations, and other artwork, using computer. Review final layouts and suggest improvements as needed. Confer with clients to discuss and determine layout design. Develop graphics and layouts for product illustrations, company logos, and Internet Web sites. Key information into computer equipment to create layouts for client

Artistic

or supervisor. Prepare illustrations or rough sketches of material, discussing them with clients or supervisors and making necessary changes. Study illustrations and photographs to plan presentation of materials, products, or services. Prepare notes and instructions for workers who assemble and prepare final layouts for printing. Develop negatives and prints to produce layout photographs, using negative- and print-developing equipment and tools. Photograph layouts, using camera, to make layout prints for supervisors or clients. Produce still and animated graphics for on-air and taped portions of television news broadcasts, using electronic video equipment.

Journalism and Mass Communications

Personality Type: Artistic

Useful Facts About the Major

Focuses on the theory and practice of gathering, processing, and delivering news and prepares individuals to be professional print journalists, news editors, and news managers.

Related CIP Program: 09.0401 Journalism

Specializations in the Major: Media management; news editing and editorializing; news reporting; photojournalism; radio and television news.

Typical Sequence of College Courses: English composition, oral communication, American government, introduction to economics, foreign language, introduction to psychology, introduction to mass communication, writing for mass media, news writing and reporting, copy editing, mass communication law, communication ethics, feature writing, photojournalism, media management, visual design for media.

Typical Sequence of High School Courses: English, algebra, foreign language, art, literature, public speaking, social science.

Career Snapshot

Journalism is a good preparation not only for news reporting and writing, but also for advertising and (with specialized coursework) news media production. Competition for entry-level journalism jobs can be keen, especially for prestigious newspapers and media outlets. Expect to start in a smaller operation and move around to increasingly bigger employers as you build your career. Although some workers are losing jobs as media outlets merge, new media technologies (such as Web-based magazines) have created some new job openings.

Useful Averages for the Related Jobs

- **Annual Earnings:** $43,942
- **Growth:** 12.7%
- **Self-Employed:** 34.6%
- **Part-Time:** 30.4%
- **Verbal Skill Rating:** 75.9
- **Math Skill Rating:** 37.4

Other Details About the Related Jobs

Total Annual Job Openings: 38,000

Interest Area: 03 Arts and Communication; 07 Government and Public Administration

Skills—Writing; reading comprehension; active listening; persuasion; critical thinking; speaking. **Values**—Creativity; recognition; ability utilization; achievement; responsibility; autonomy. **Work Conditions**—Indoors, environmentally controlled; sitting.

Related Jobs

1. Broadcast News Analysts

Personality Type: Artistic–Social–Enterprising

Earnings: $46,710
Growth: 4.3%
Annual Openings: 1,000

Most Common Education/Training Level: Work experience plus degree

Artistic

Analyze, interpret, and broadcast news received from various sources. Analyze and interpret news and information received from various sources in order to be able to broadcast the information. Write commentaries, columns, or scripts, using computers. Examine news items of local, national, and international significance to determine topics to address or obtain assignments from editorial staff members. Coordinate and serve as an anchor on news broadcast programs. Edit news material to ensure that it fits within available time or space. Select material most pertinent to presentation and organize this material into appropriate formats. Gather information and develop perspectives about news subjects through research, interviews, observation, and experience. Present news stories and introduce in-depth videotaped segments or live transmissions from on-the-scene reporters.

2. Court Reporters

Personality Type: Artistic–Conventional–Social

Earnings: $45,610
Growth: 14.8%
Annual Openings: 3,000

Most Common Education/Training Level:
Postsecondary vocational training

Use verbatim methods and equipment to capture, store, retrieve, and transcribe pretrial and trial proceedings or other information. Includes stenocaptioners who operate computerized stenographic captioning equipment to provide captions of live or prerecorded broadcasts for hearing-impaired viewers. Take notes in shorthand or use a stenotype or shorthand machine that prints letters on a paper tape. Provide transcripts of proceedings upon request of judges, lawyers, or the public. Record verbatim proceedings of courts, legislative assemblies, committee meetings, and other proceedings,

using computerized recording equipment, electronic stenograph machines, or stenomasks. Transcribe recorded proceedings in accordance with established formats. Ask speakers to clarify inaudible statements. File a legible transcript of records of a court case with the court clerk's office. File and store shorthand notes of court session. Respond to requests during court sessions to read portions of the proceedings already recorded. Record depositions and other proceedings for attorneys. Verify accuracy of transcripts by checking copies against original records of proceedings and accuracy of rulings by checking with judges. Record symbols on computer disks or CD-ROM; then translate and display them as text in computer-aided transcription process.

3. Editors

Personality Type: Artistic–Enterprising–Social

Earnings: $46,990
Growth: 14.8%
Annual Openings: 16,000

Most Common Education/Training Level:
Bachelor's degree

Perform variety of editorial duties, such as laying out, indexing, and revising content of written materials, in preparation for final publication. Prepare, rewrite, and edit copy to improve readability or supervise others who do this work. Read copy or proof to detect and correct errors in spelling, punctuation, and syntax. Allocate print space for story text, photos, and illustrations according to space parameters and copy significance, using knowledge of layout principles. Plan the contents of publications according to the publication's style, editorial policy, and publishing requirements. Verify facts, dates, and statistics, using standard reference sources. Review and approve proofs submitted by composing room prior to publication production. Develop story or content ideas, considering reader or audience appeal. Oversee publication production, including artwork, layout, computer typesetting, and printing, ensuring adherence to deadlines and budget requirements. Confer with management and editorial staff members regarding placement and emphasis of developing news stories. Assign topics, events, and stories to individual writers or reporters for coverage. Read, evaluate, and edit manuscripts or other materials submitted for publication and confer with authors regarding changes in content, style or organization, or publication. Monitor news-gathering operations to ensure utilization of all news sources, such as press releases, telephone contacts, radio, television, wire services, and other reporters. Meet frequently with artists, typesetters, layout personnel, marketing directors, and production managers to discuss projects and resolve problems. Supervise and coordinate work of reporters and other editors. Make manuscript acceptance or revision recommendations to the publisher. Select local, state, national, and international news items received from wire services based on assessment of items' significance and interest value. Interview and hire writers and reporters or negotiate contracts, royalties, and payments for authors or freelancers. Direct the policies and departments of newspapers, magazines, and other publishing establishments. Arrange for copyright permissions. Read material to determine index items and arrange them alphabetically or topically, indicating page or chapter location.

4. Reporters and Correspondents

Personality Type:
Artistic–Investigative–Enterprising

Earnings: $33,470
Growth: 4.9%
Annual Openings: 4,000

Most Common Education/Training Level:
Work experience plus degree

Collect and analyze facts about newsworthy events by interview, investigation, or observation. Report and write stories for newspaper, news magazine, radio, or television. Report and write news stories for publication or broadcast, describing the background and details of events. Arrange interviews with people who can provide information about a particular story. Review copy and correct errors in content, grammar, and punctuation, following prescribed editorial style and formatting guidelines. Review and evaluate notes taken about event aspects to isolate pertinent facts and details. Determine a story's emphasis, length, and format and organize material accordingly. Research and analyze background information related to stories in order to be able to provide complete and accurate information. Gather information about events through research; interviews; experience; and attendance at political, news, sports, artistic, social, and other functions. Investigate breaking news developments such as disasters, crimes, and human interest stories. Research and report on specialized fields such as medicine, science and technology, politics, foreign affairs, sports, arts, consumer affairs, business, religion, crime, or education. Check reference materials such as books, news files, and public records to obtain relevant facts. Receive assignments or evaluate leads and tips to develop story ideas. Discuss issues with editors in order to establish priorities and positions. Revise work to meet editorial approval or to fit time or space requirements. Photograph or videotape news events or request

Artistic

that a photographer be assigned to provide such coverage. Develop ideas and material for columns or commentaries by analyzing and interpreting news, current issues, and personal experiences. Transmit news stories or reporting information from remote locations, using equipment such as satellite phones, telephones, fax machines, or modems. Present live or recorded commentary via broadcast media. Conduct taped or filmed interviews or narratives. Edit or assist in editing videos for broadcast. Write columns, editorials, commentaries, or reviews that interpret events or offer opinions. Write reviews of literary, musical, and other artwork based on knowledge, judgment, and experience.

5. Writers and Authors

Personality Type: Artistic–Enterprising–Social

Earnings: $48,640
Growth: 17.7%
Annual Openings: 14,000

Most Common Education/Training Level: Bachelor's degree

Job Specializations

Copy Writers. Write advertising copy for use by publication or broadcast media to promote sale of goods and services. Write advertising copy for use by publication, broadcast, or Internet media to promote the sale of goods and services. Present drafts and ideas to clients. Discuss with the client the product, advertising themes and methods, and any changes that should be made in advertising copy. Consult with sales, media, and marketing representatives to obtain information on product or service and discuss style and length of advertising copy. Vary language and tone of messages based on product and medium. Edit or rewrite existing copy as necessary and submit copy for approval by supervisor.

Write to customers in their terms and on their level so that the advertiser's sales message is more readily received. Write articles; bulletins; sales letters; speeches; and other related informative, marketing, and promotional material. Invent names for products and write the slogans that appear on packaging, brochures, and other promotional material. Review advertising trends, consumer surveys, and other data regarding marketing of goods and services to determine the best way to promote products. Develop advertising campaigns for a wide range of clients, working with an advertising agency's creative director and art director to determine the best way to present advertising information. Conduct research and interviews to determine which of a product's selling features should be promoted.

Poets, Lyricists and Creative Writers. Create original written works, such as scripts, essays, prose, poetry, or song lyrics, for publication or performance. Revise written material to meet personal standards and to satisfy needs of clients, publishers, directors, or producers. Choose subject matter and suitable form to express personal feelings and experiences or ideas or to narrate stories or events. Plan project arrangements or outlines and organize material accordingly. Prepare works in appropriate format for publication and send them to publishers or producers. Follow appropriate procedures to get copyrights for completed work. Write fiction or nonfiction prose such as short stories, novels, biographies, articles, descriptive or critical analyses, and essays. Develop factors such as themes, plots, characterizations, psychological analyses, historical environments, action, and dialogue to create material. Confer with clients, editors, publishers, or producers to discuss changes or revisions to written material. Conduct research to obtain factual information and authentic detail, using sources such as newspaper accounts, diaries, and interviews. Write narrative, dramatic, lyric, or other types of poetry for publication. Attend book launches and publicity events or conduct public readings. Write words to fit musical compositions, including lyrics for operas, musical plays, and choral works. Adapt text to accommodate musical requirements of composers and singers. Teach writing classes. Write humorous material for publication or for performances such as comedy routines, gags, and comedy shows. Collaborate with other writers on specific projects.

Artistic

Social Majors

African-American Studies

Personality Type: Social–Investigative–Artistic

Useful Facts About the Major

Focuses on the history, sociology, politics, culture, and economics of the North American peoples descended from the African diaspora, focusing on the United States, Canada, and the Caribbean, but also including reference to Latin American elements of the diaspora.

Related CIP Program: 05.0201 African-American/Black Studies

Specializations in the Major: Behavioral and social inquiry; history and culture; literature, language, and the arts.

Typical Sequence of College Courses: English composition, foreign language, American history, introduction to African-American studies, African-American literature, African-American history, African Diaspora studies, research methods in African-American studies, seminar (reporting on research).

Typical Sequence of High School Courses: English, algebra, foreign language, history, literature, public speaking, social science.

Career Snapshot

African-American studies draws on a number of disciplines, including history, sociology, literature, linguistics, and political science. Usually you can shape the program to emphasize whichever appeals most to you. Graduates frequently pursue higher degrees as a means of establishing a career in a field such as college teaching or the law.

Useful Averages for the Related Jobs

- **Annual Earnings:** $57,770
- **Growth:** 32.2%
- **Self-Employed:** 0.4%
- **Part-Time:** 24.8%
- **Verbal Skill Rating:** 83.9
- **Math Skill Rating:** 61.9

Other Details About the Related Jobs

Total Annual Job Openings: 329,000

Interest Area: 05 Education and Training

Skills—Writing; critical thinking; instructing; persuasion; active learning; learning strategies. **Values**—Authority; social service; creativity; achievement; social status; ability utilization. **Work Conditions**—Indoors, environmentally controlled; sitting.

Related Jobs

1. Area, Ethnic, and Cultural Studies Teachers, Postsecondary

Personality Type: Social–Investigative–Artistic

Earnings: $56,380
Growth: 32.2%
Annual Openings: 329,000 for all postsecondary teaching jobs

Most Common Education/Training Level: Master's degree

Teach courses pertaining to the culture and development of an area (e.g., Latin America), an ethnic group, or any other group (e.g.,

women's studies, urban affairs). Keep abreast of developments in their field by reading current literature, talking with colleagues, and participating in professional conferences. Conduct research in a particular field of knowledge and publish findings in professional journals, books, and/or electronic media. Evaluate and grade students' classwork, assignments, and papers. Prepare course materials such as syllabi, homework assignments, and handouts. Prepare and deliver lectures to undergraduate and/or graduate students on topics such as race and ethnic relations, gender studies, and cross-cultural perspectives. Initiate, facilitate, and moderate classroom discussions. Compile, administer, and grade examinations or assign this work to others. Maintain regularly scheduled office hours in order to advise and assist students. Plan, evaluate, and revise curricula, course content, and course materials and methods of instruction. Maintain student attendance records, grades, and other required records. Advise students on academic and vocational curricula and on career issues. Supervise undergraduate and/or graduate teaching, internship, and research work. Select and obtain materials and supplies such as textbooks. Collaborate with colleagues to address teaching and research issues. Serve on academic or administrative committees that deal with institutional policies, departmental matters, and academic issues. Compile bibliographies of specialized materials for outside reading assignments. Write grant proposals to procure external research funding. Participate in campus and community events. Participate in student recruitment, registration, and placement activities. Act as advisers to student organizations. Incorporate experiential/site visit components into courses. Perform administrative duties such as serving as department head. Provide professional consulting services to government and/or industry.

2. Graduate Teaching Assistants

Personality Type:
Social–Investigative–Conventional

Earnings: $27,840
Growth: 32.2%
Annual Openings: 329,000 for all postsecondary teaching jobs

Most Common Education/Training Level: Master's degree

Assist department chairperson, faculty members, or other professional staff members in college or university by performing teaching or teaching-related duties, such as teaching lower-level courses, developing teaching materials, preparing and giving examinations, and grading examinations or papers. Graduate assistants must be enrolled in a graduate school program. Graduate assistants who primarily perform non-teaching duties, such as laboratory research, should be reported in the occupational category related to the work performed. Lead discussion sections, tutorials, and laboratory sections. Evaluate and grade examinations, assignments, and papers and record grades. Return assignments to students in accordance with established deadlines. Schedule and maintain regular office hours to meet with students. Inform students of the procedures for completing and submitting class work such as lab reports. Prepare and proctor examinations. Notify instructors of errors or problems with assignments. Meet with supervisors to discuss students' grades and to complete required grade-related paperwork. Copy and distribute classroom materials. Demonstrate use of laboratory equipment and enforce laboratory rules. Teach undergraduate-level courses. Complete laboratory projects prior to assigning them to students so that any needed modifications can be made. Develop teaching materials such as syllabi,

Social

visual aids, answer keys, supplementary notes, and course Web sites. Provide assistance to faculty members or staff with laboratory or field research. Arrange for supervisors to conduct teaching observations; meet with supervisors to receive feedback about teaching performance. Attend lectures given by the instructor whom they are assisting. Order or obtain materials needed for classes. Provide instructors with assistance in the use of audiovisual equipment. Assist faculty members or staff with student conferences.

American Studies

Personality Type: Social–Investigative–Artistic

Useful Facts About the Major

Focuses on the history, society, politics, culture, and economics of the United States and its Pre-Columbian and colonial predecessors, including the flow of immigrants from other societies.

Related CIP Program: 05.0102
American/United States Studies/Civilization

Specializations in the Major: History and political science; literature, language, and the arts; popular culture.

Typical Sequence of College Courses: English composition, American history, American government, American literature, American popular culture, seminar (reporting on research).

Typical Sequence of High School Courses: English, algebra, foreign language, history, literature, public speaking, social science.

Career Snapshot

American studies is an interdisciplinary major that allows you to concentrate on the aspect of American culture that is of greatest interest to you—for example, history, the arts, or social and ethnic groups. Many, perhaps most, graduates use this major as a springboard to postgraduate or professional training that prepares for a career in college teaching, business, law, the arts, politics, or some other field.

Useful Averages for the Related Jobs

- **Annual Earnings:** $57,770
- **Growth:** 32.2%
- **Self-Employed:** 0.4%
- **Part-Time:** 24.8%
- **Verbal Skill Rating:** 83.9
- **Math Skill Rating:** 61.9

Other Details About the Related Jobs

Total Annual Job Openings: 329,000

Interest Area: 05 Education and Training

Skills—Writing; critical thinking; instructing; persuasion; active learning; learning strategies. **Values**—Authority; social service; creativity; achievement; social status; ability utilization. **Work Conditions**—Indoors, environmentally controlled; sitting.

Related Jobs

1. Area, Ethnic, and Cultural Studies Teachers, Postsecondary

Personality Type: Social–Investigative–Artistic

Earnings: $56,380
Growth: 32.2%
Annual Openings: 329,000 for all postsecondary teaching jobs

Most Common Education/Training Level: Master's degree

Teach courses pertaining to the culture and development of an area (e.g., Latin America), an ethnic group, or any other group (e.g., women's studies, urban affairs). Keep abreast of developments in their field by reading current

Social

literature, talking with colleagues, and participating in professional conferences. Conduct research in a particular field of knowledge and publish findings in professional journals, books, and/or electronic media. Evaluate and grade students' classwork, assignments, and papers. Prepare course materials such as syllabi, homework assignments, and handouts. Prepare and deliver lectures to undergraduate and/or graduate students on topics such as race and ethnic relations, gender studies, and cross-cultural perspectives. Initiate, facilitate, and moderate classroom discussions. Compile, administer, and grade examinations or assign this work to others. Maintain regularly scheduled office hours in order to advise and assist students. Plan, evaluate, and revise curricula, course content, and course materials and methods of instruction. Maintain student attendance records, grades, and other required records. Advise students on academic and vocational curricula and on career issues. Supervise undergraduate and/or graduate teaching, internship, and research work. Select and obtain materials and supplies such as textbooks. Collaborate with colleagues to address teaching and research issues. Serve on academic or administrative committees that deal with institutional policies, departmental matters, and academic issues. Compile bibliographies of specialized materials for outside reading assignments. Write grant proposals to procure external research funding. Participate in campus and community events. Participate in student recruitment, registration, and placement activities. Act as advisers to student organizations. Incorporate experiential/site visit components into courses. Perform administrative duties such as serving as department head. Provide professional consulting services to government and/or industry.

2. Graduate Teaching Assistants

Personality Type:
Social–Investigative–Conventional

Earnings: $27,840
Growth: 32.2%
Annual Openings: 329,000 for all postsecondary teaching jobs

Most Common Education/Training Level: Master's degree

Assist department chairperson, faculty members, or other professional staff members in college or university by performing teaching or teaching-related duties, such as teaching lower-level courses, developing teaching materials, preparing and giving examinations, and grading examinations or papers. Graduate assistants must be enrolled in a graduate school program. Graduate assistants who primarily perform non-teaching duties, such as laboratory research, should be reported in the occupational category related to the work performed. Lead discussion sections, tutorials, and laboratory sections. Evaluate and grade examinations, assignments, and papers and record grades. Return assignments to students in accordance with established deadlines. Schedule and maintain regular office hours to meet with students. Inform students of the procedures for completing and submitting class work such as lab reports. Prepare and proctor examinations. Notify instructors of errors or problems with assignments. Meet with supervisors to discuss students' grades and to complete required grade-related paperwork. Copy and distribute classroom materials. Demonstrate use of laboratory equipment and enforce laboratory rules. Teach undergraduate-level courses. Complete laboratory projects prior to assigning them to students so that any needed modifications can be made. Develop teaching materials such as syllabi, visual aids, answer keys, supplementary notes, and course Web sites. Provide assistance to faculty members or staff with laboratory or field research. Arrange for supervisors to conduct teaching observations; meet with supervisors to receive feedback about teaching performance. Attend lectures given by the instructor whom they are assisting. Order or obtain materials needed for classes. Provide instructors with assistance in the use of audiovisual equipment. Assist faculty members or staff with student conferences.

Social

Area Studies

Personality Type: Social–Investigative–Artistic

Useful Facts About the Major

Focuses on the history, society, politics, culture, and economics of one or more of the peoples of a geographical region, such as Africa, the United States, Asia, the Caribbean, Latin America, the Middle East, and so forth.

Related CIP Programs: 05.0101 African Studies; 05.0102 American/United States Studies/Civilization; 05.0103 Asian Studies/Civilization; 05.0116 Balkans Studies; 05.0117 Baltic Studies; 05.0115 Canadian Studies; 05.0119 Caribbean Studies; 05.0105 Central/Middle and Eastern European Studies; 05.0123 Chinese Studies; 05.0121 Commonwealth Studies; 05.0104 East Asian Studies; 05.0106 European Studies/Civilization; 05.0124 French Studies; 05.0125 German Studies; 05.0126 Italian Studies; 05.0127 Japanese Studies; 05.0128 Korean Studies; 05.0107 Latin American Studies; 05.0108 Near and Middle Eastern Studies; 05.0109 Pacific Area/Pacific Rim Studies; 05.0129 Polish Studies; 05.0122 Regional Studies (U.S., Canadian, Foreign); 05.0110 Russian Studies; 05.0111 Scandinavian Studies; 05.0118 Slavic Studies; 05.0112 South Asian Studies; 05.0113 Southeast Asian Studies; 05.0130 Spanish and Iberian Studies; 05.0131 Tibetan Studies; 05.0132 Ukraine Studies; 05.0120 Ural-Altaic and Central Asian Studies; 05.0114 Western European Studies

Specializations in the Major: Economics and trade; history and culture; language and literature; political science.

Typical Sequence of College Courses: English composition, foreign language, foreign literature and culture, comparative governments, introduction to economics, international economics, seminar (reporting on research).

Typical Sequence of High School Courses: English, foreign language, history, literature, social science, algebra.

Career Snapshot

Certain very popular area studies—African-American studies, American studies, and women's studies—are described elsewhere in this book. But many colleges offer other area studies majors, usually defined in terms of a region of the world: East Asian studies, European studies, Latin American studies, and so on. These are interdisciplinary majors that may involve some combination of linguistics, literature, history, sociology, political science, economic development, or other disciplines. Usually you can emphasize whichever aspects interest you most. Graduates of area studies may go into a business or government career where knowledge of a foreign culture is an advantage. Many get higher degrees to prepare for a career in law or college teaching.

Useful Averages for the Related Jobs

- **Annual Earnings:** $57,770
- **Growth:** 32.2%
- **Self-Employed:** 0.4%
- **Part-Time:** 24.8%
- **Verbal Skill Rating:** 83.9
- **Math Skill Rating:** 61.9

Other Details About the Related Jobs

Total Annual Job Openings: 329,000

Interest Area: 05 Education and Training

Skills—Writing; critical thinking; instructing; persuasion; active learning; learning strategies. **Values**—Authority; social service; creativity; achievement; social status; ability utilization. **Work Conditions**—Indoors, environmentally controlled; sitting.

Related Jobs

1. Area, Ethnic, and Cultural Studies Teachers, Postsecondary

Personality Type: Social–Investigative–Artistic

Earnings: $56,380
Growth: 32.2%
Annual Openings: 329,000 for all postsecondary teaching jobs

Most Common Education/Training Level: Master's degree

Teach courses pertaining to the culture and development of an area (e.g., Latin America), an ethnic group, or any other group (e.g., women's studies, urban affairs). Keep abreast of developments in their field by reading current literature, talking with colleagues, and participating in professional conferences. Conduct research in a particular field of knowledge and publish findings in professional journals, books, and/or electronic media. Evaluate and grade students' classwork, assignments, and papers. Prepare course materials such as syllabi, homework assignments, and handouts. Prepare and deliver lectures to undergraduate and/or graduate students on topics such as race and ethnic relations, gender studies, and cross-cultural perspectives. Initiate, facilitate, and moderate classroom discussions. Compile, administer, and grade examinations or assign this work to others. Maintain regularly scheduled office hours in order to advise and assist students. Plan, evaluate, and revise curricula, course content, and course materials and methods of instruction. Maintain student attendance records, grades, and other required records. Advise students on academic and vocational curricula and on career issues. Supervise undergraduate and/or graduate teaching, internship, and research work. Select and obtain materials and supplies such as textbooks. Collaborate with colleagues to address teaching and research issues. Serve on academic or administrative committees that deal with institutional policies, departmental matters, and academic issues. Compile bibliographies of specialized materials for outside reading assignments. Write grant proposals to procure external research funding. Participate in campus and community events. Participate in student recruitment, registration, and placement activities. Act as advisers to student organizations. Incorporate experiential/site visit components into courses. Perform administrative duties such as serving as department head. Provide professional consulting services to government and/or industry.

2. Graduate Teaching Assistants

Personality Type:
Social–Investigative–Conventional

Earnings: $27,840
Growth: 32.2%
Annual Openings: 329,000 for all postsecondary teaching jobs

Most Common Education/Training Level: Master's degree

Social

Assist department chairperson, faculty members, or other professional staff members in college or university by performing teaching or teaching-related duties, such as teaching lower-level courses, developing teaching materials, preparing and giving examinations, and grading examinations or papers. **Graduate assistants must be enrolled in a graduate school program. Graduate assistants who primarily perform non-teaching duties, such as laboratory research, should be reported in the occupational category related to the work performed.** Lead discussion sections, tutorials, and laboratory sections. Evaluate and grade examinations, assignments, and papers and record grades. Return assignments to students in accordance with established deadlines. Schedule and maintain regular office hours to meet with students. Inform students of the procedures for completing and submitting class work such as lab reports. Prepare and proctor examinations. Notify instructors of errors or problems with assignments. Meet with supervisors to discuss students' grades and to complete required grade-related paperwork. Copy and distribute classroom materials. Demonstrate use of laboratory equipment and enforce laboratory rules. Teach undergraduate-level courses. Complete laboratory projects prior to assigning them to students so that any needed modifications can be made. Develop teaching materials such as syllabi, visual aids, answer keys, supplementary notes, and course Web sites. Provide assistance to faculty members or staff with laboratory or field research. Arrange for supervisors to conduct teaching observations; meet with supervisors to receive feedback about teaching performance. Attend lectures given by the instructor whom they are assisting. Order or obtain materials needed for classes. Provide instructors with assistance in the use of audiovisual equipment. Assist faculty members or staff with student conferences.

Early Childhood Education

Personality Type: Social–Artistic

Useful Facts About the Major

Prepares individuals to teach students in formal settings prior to beginning regular elementary school, usually ranging in age from three to six years (or grade one), depending on the school system or state regulations; includes preparation to teach all relevant subject matter.

Related CIP Programs: 13.1210 Early Childhood Education and Teaching; 13.1209 Kindergarten/Preschool Education and Teaching

Specializations in the Major: Art education; bilingual education; music education; reading readiness.

Typical Sequence of College Courses: Introduction to psychology, English composition, oral communication, history and philosophy of education, human growth and development, teaching methods, educational alternatives for exceptional students, educational psychology, reading assessment and teaching, mathematics education, art education, music education, physical education, health education, science education, children's literature, student teaching.

Typical Sequence of High School Courses: English, algebra, geometry, trigonometry, science, foreign language, public speaking.

Career Snapshot

Because very young children do not think exactly the same way as we do, an important part of an early childhood education major is learning effective educational techniques for this age group. As in any other teaching major, a bachelor's degree is the minimum requirement for employment, and a master's degree is often needed for job security and a pay raise. Although enrollments of very young students are expected to decline for some time, jobs will open to replace teachers who are retiring. Best opportunities are expected in high-growth regions of the country and in inner-city and rural schools.

Useful Averages for the Related Jobs

- Annual Earnings: $29,250
- Growth: 29.8%
- Self-Employed: 1.4%
- Part-Time: 27.0%
- Verbal Skill Rating: 63.6
- Math Skill Rating: 39.6

Other Details About the Related Jobs

Total Annual Job Openings: 105,000

Interest Area: 05 Education and Training

Skills—Learning strategies; social perceptiveness; writing; monitoring; instructing; negotiation. Values—Social service; authority; creativity; responsibility; achievement; autonomy. Work Conditions—Exposed to disease or infections; spend time kneeling, crouching, stooping, or crawling.

Related Jobs

1. Kindergarten Teachers, Except Special Education

Personality Type: Social–Artistic–Investigative

Social

Earnings: $43,580
Growth: 22.4%
Annual Openings: 28,000

Most Common Education/Training Level:
Bachelor's degree

Teach elemental natural and social science, personal hygiene, music, art, and literature to children from 4 to 6 years old. Promote physical, mental, and social development. May be required to hold state certification. Teach basic skills such as color, shape, number, and letter recognition; personal hygiene; and social skills. Establish and enforce rules for behavior and policies and procedures to maintain order among students. Observe and evaluate children's performance, behavior, social development, and physical health. Instruct students individually and in groups, adapting teaching methods to meet students' varying needs and interests. Read books to entire classes or to small groups. Demonstrate activities to children. Provide a variety of materials and resources for children to explore, manipulate, and use, both in learning activities and in imaginative play. Plan and conduct activities for a balanced program of instruction, demonstration, and work time that provides students with opportunities to observe, question, and investigate. Confer with parents or guardians, other teachers, counselors, and administrators to resolve students' behavioral and academic problems. Prepare children for later grades by encouraging them to explore learning opportunities and to persevere with challenging tasks. Establish clear objectives for all lessons, units, and projects and communicate those objectives to children. Prepare and implement remedial programs for students requiring extra help. Meet with parents and guardians to discuss their children's progress and to determine their priorities for their children and their resource needs. Prepare objectives and outlines for courses of study, following curriculum guidelines or requirements of states and schools. Organize and lead activities designed to promote physical, mental, and social development, such as games, arts and crafts, music, and storytelling. Guide and counsel students with adjustment or academic problems or special academic interests. Identify children showing signs of emotional, developmental, or health-related problems and discuss them with supervisors, parents or guardians, and child development specialists. Instruct and monitor students in the use and care of equipment and materials to prevent injuries and damage. Assimilate arriving children to the school environment by greeting them, helping them remove outerwear, and selecting activities of interest to them.

2. Preschool Teachers, Except Special Education

Personality Type: Social–Artistic–Conventional

Earnings: $22,680
Growth: 33.1%
Annual Openings: 77,000

Most Common Education/Training Level:
Postsecondary vocational training

Instruct children (normally up to 5 years of age) in activities designed to promote social, physical, and intellectual growth needed for primary school in preschool, day care center, or other child development facility. May be required to hold state certification. Provide a variety of materials and resources for children to explore, manipulate, and use, both in learning activities and in imaginative play. Attend to children's basic needs by feeding them, dressing them, and changing their diapers. Establish and enforce rules for behavior and procedures for maintaining order. Read books to entire classes or to small groups. Teach basic skills such as color, shape, number, and letter recognition; personal hygiene; and social skills. Organize and lead activities designed to promote physical, mental, and social development, such as games, arts and crafts, music, storytelling, and field trips. Observe and evaluate children's performance, behavior, social development, and physical health. Meet with parents and guardians to discuss their children's progress and needs, determine their priorities for their children, and suggest ways that they can promote learning and development. Identify children showing signs of emotional, developmental, or health-related problems and discuss them with supervisors, parents or guardians, and child development specialists. Enforce all administration policies and rules governing students. Prepare materials and classrooms for class activities. Serve meals and snacks in accordance with nutritional guide-lines. Teach proper eating habits and personal hygiene. Assimilate arriving children to the school environment by greeting them, helping them remove outerwear, and selecting activities of interest to them. Adapt teaching methods and instructional materials to meet students' varying needs and interests. Establish clear objectives for all lessons, units, and projects and communicate those objectives to children. Demonstrate activities to children. Arrange indoor and outdoor space to facilitate creative play, motor-skill activities, and safety. Plan and conduct activities for a balanced program of instruction, demonstration, and work time that provides students with opportunities to observe, question, and investigate. Maintain accurate and complete student records as required by laws, district policies, and administrative regulations.

Social

Graduate Study for College Teaching

Personality Type: Social–Investigative

Useful Facts About the Major

Focuses on an academic subject at an advanced level to prepare students to teach courses in a postsecondary institution such as a college, university, professional school, or adult school.

Related CIP Programs: No data available; a large number of CIP programs may be studied at the graduate level.

Specializations in the Major: Any of the subjects that are taught in postsecondary institutions: agricultural sciences; anthropology and archeology; architecture; area, ethnic, and cultural studies; art, drama, and music; atmospheric, earth, marine, and space sciences; biological science; business; chemistry; communications; computer science; criminal justice and law enforcement; economics; education; engineering; English language and literature; environmental science; foreign language and literature; forestry and conservation science; geography; graduate teaching assistants; health specialties; history; home economics; law; library science; mathematical science; nursing instructors and; philosophy and religion; physics; political science; psychology; recreation and fitness studies; social sciences; social work; sociology; vocational education; others.

Typical Sequence of College Courses: Courses appropriate for a bachelor's program in an undergraduate major, followed by graduate courses in a related major, including seminars (where research is presented to the class) and

research methods and concluding with an original research project and a dissertation describing it.

Typical Sequence of High School Courses: Biology, chemistry, algebra, geometry, trigonometry, computer science, English, public speaking. Also advanced courses in science, social science, or humanities.

Career Snapshot

Focuses on an academic subject at an advanced level to prepare students to teach courses in a postsecondary institution such as a college, university, professional school, or adult school.

Useful Averages for the Related Jobs

- **Annual Earnings:** $57,770
- **Growth:** 32.2%
- **Self-Employed:** 0.4%
- **Part-Time:** 24.8%
- **Verbal Skill Rating:** 83.9
- **Math Skill Rating:** 61.9

Other Details About the Related Jobs

Total Annual Job Openings: 329,000

Interest Area: 05 Education and Training

Skills—Instructing; reading comprehension; critical thinking; writing; learning strategies; active learning. **Values**—Achievement; ability utilization; authority; autonomy; responsibility; working conditions. **Work Conditions**—Indoors, environmentally controlled; sitting or standing.

Related Jobs

1. Agricultural Sciences Teachers, Postsecondary

Personality Type: Investigative–Social–Artistic

Earnings: $75,140
Growth: 32.2%
Annual Openings: 329,000 for all postsecondary teaching jobs

Most Common Education/Training Level: Master's degree

Teach courses in the agricultural sciences. Includes teachers of agronomy, dairy sciences, fisheries management, horticultural sciences, poultry sciences, range management, and agricultural soil conservation. Includes both teachers primarily engaged in teaching and those who do a combination of both teaching and research.

2. Anthropology and Archeology Teachers, Postsecondary

Personality Type: Social–Investigative–Artistic

Earnings: $62,820
Growth: 32.2%
Annual Openings: 329,000 for all postsecondary teaching jobs

Most Common Education/Training Level: Master's degree

Teach courses in anthropology or archeology. Includes both teachers primarily engaged in teaching and those who do a combination of both teaching and research.

3. Architecture Teachers, Postsecondary

Personality Type: No data available

Earnings: $64,620
Growth: 32.2%
Annual Openings: 329,000 for all postsecondary teaching jobs

Most Common Education/Training Level: Master's degree

Teach courses in architecture and architectural design, such as architectural environmental design, interior architecture/design, and landscape architecture. Includes both teachers primarily engaged in teaching and those who do a combination of both teaching and research.

4. Area, Ethnic, and Cultural Studies Teachers, Postsecondary

Personality Type: Social–Investigative–Artistic

Earnings: $56,380
Growth: 32.2%
Annual Openings: 329,000 for all postsecondary teaching jobs

Most Common Education/Training Level: Master's degree

Teach courses pertaining to the culture and development of an area (e.g., Latin America), an ethnic group, or any other group (e.g., women's studies, urban affairs). Includes both teachers primarily engaged in teaching and those who do a combination of both teaching and research.

5. Art, Drama, and Music Teachers, Postsecondary

Personality Type: Artistic–Social–Investigative

Earnings: $53,160
Growth: 32.2%
Annual Openings: 329,000 for all postsecondary teaching jobs

Social

Most Common Education/Training Level: Master's degree

Teach courses in drama; music; and the arts, including fine and applied art, such as painting and sculpture, or design and crafts.

6. Atmospheric, Earth, Marine, and Space Sciences Teachers, Postsecondary

Personality Type: No data available

Earnings: $69,300
Growth: 32.2%
Annual Openings: 329,000 for all postsecondary teaching jobs

Most Common Education/Training Level: Master's degree

Teach courses in the physical sciences, except chemistry and physics. Includes both teachers primarily engaged in teaching and those who do a combination of both teaching and research.

7. Biological Science Teachers, Postsecondary

Personality Type: Investigative–Social–Artistic

Earnings: $69,210
Growth: 32.2%
Annual Openings: 329,000 for all postsecondary teaching jobs

Most Common Education/Training Level: Master's degree

Teach courses in biological sciences. Includes both teachers primarily engaged in teaching and those who do a combination of both teaching and research.

8. Business Teachers, Postsecondary

Personality Type: No data available

Earnings: $62,040
Growth: 32.2%
Annual Openings: 329,000 for all postsecondary teaching jobs

Most Common Education/Training Level: Master's degree

Teach courses in business administration and management, such as accounting, finance, human resources, labor relations, marketing, and operations research. Includes both teachers primarily engaged in teaching and those who do a combination of both teaching and research.

9. Chemistry Teachers, Postsecondary

Personality Type: Investigative–Social–Realistic

Earnings: $61,220
Growth: 32.2%
Annual Openings: 329,000 for all postsecondary teaching jobs

Most Common Education/Training Level: Master's degree

Teach courses pertaining to the chemical and physical properties and compositional changes of substances. Work may include instruction in the methods of qualitative and quantitative chemical analysis. Includes both teachers primarily engaged in teaching and those who do a combination of both teaching and research.

10. Communications Teachers, Postsecondary

Personality Type: No data available

Earnings: $53,110
Growth: 32.2%
Annual Openings: 329,000 for all postsecondary teaching jobs

Most Common Education/Training Level: Master's degree

Teach courses in communications, such as organizational communications, public relations, radio/television broadcasting, and journalism. Includes both teachers primarily engaged in teaching and those who do a combination of both teaching and research.

11. Computer Science Teachers, Postsecondary

Personality Type: Investigative–Conventional–Realistic

Earnings: $57,620
Growth: 32.2%
Annual Openings: 329,000 for all postsecondary teaching jobs

Most Common Education/Training Level: Master's degree

Teach courses in computer science. May specialize in a field of computer science, such as the design and function of computers or operations and research analysis. Includes both teachers primarily engaged in teaching and those who do a combination of both teaching and research.

12. Criminal Justice and Law Enforcement Teachers, Postsecondary

Personality Type: No data available

Earnings: $49,730
Growth: 32.2%
Annual Openings: 329,000 for all postsecondary teaching jobs

Most Common Education/Training Level: Master's degree

Teach courses in criminal justice, corrections, and law enforcement administration.

13. Economics Teachers, Postsecondary

Personality Type: Social–Investigative–Artistic

Earnings: $71,850
Growth: 32.2%
Annual Openings: 329,000 for all postsecondary teaching jobs

Most Common Education/Training Level: Master's degree

Teach courses in economics. Includes both teachers primarily engaged in teaching and those who do a combination of both teaching and research.

14. Education Teachers, Postsecondary

Personality Type: No data available

Earnings: $52,800
Growth: 32.2%
Annual Openings: 329,000 for all postsecondary teaching jobs

Most Common Education/Training Level: Master's degree

Teach courses pertaining to education, such as counseling, curriculum, guidance, instruction, teacher education, and teaching English as a second language.

15. Engineering Teachers, Postsecondary

Personality Type: Investigative–Realistic–Social

Earnings: $76,670
Growth: 32.2%
Annual Openings: 329,000 for all postsecondary teaching jobs

Social

Most Common Education/Training Level: Master's degree

Teach courses pertaining to the application of physical laws and principles of engineering for the development of machines, materials, instruments, processes, and services. Includes teachers of subjects such as chemical, civil, electrical, industrial, mechanical, mineral, and petroleum engineering. Includes both teachers primarily engaged in teaching and those who do a combination of both teaching and research.

16. English Language and Literature Teachers, Postsecondary

Personality Type: Artistic–Social–Investigative

Earnings: $51,730
Growth: 32.2%
Annual Openings: 329,000 for all postsecondary teaching jobs

Most Common Education/Training Level: Master's degree

Teach courses in English language and literature, including linguistics and comparative literature.

17. Environmental Science Teachers, Postsecondary

Personality Type: No data available

Earnings: $64,780
Growth: 32.2%
Annual Openings: 329,000 for all postsecondary teaching jobs

Most Common Education/Training Level: Master's degree

Teach courses in environmental science. Includes both teachers primarily engaged in

teaching and those who do a combination of both teaching and research.

18. Foreign Language and Literature Teachers, Postsecondary

Personality Type: Artistic–Social–Investigative

Earnings: $51,900
Growth: 32.2%
Annual Openings: 329,000 for all postsecondary teaching jobs

Most Common Education/Training Level: Master's degree

Teach courses in foreign (i.e., other than English) languages and literature.

19. Forestry and Conservation Science Teachers, Postsecondary

Personality Type: Investigative–Social–Artistic

Earnings: $64,430
Growth: 32.2%
Annual Openings: 329,000 for all postsecondary teaching jobs

Most Common Education/Training Level: Master's degree

Teach courses in environmental and conservation science. Includes both teachers primarily engaged in teaching and those who do a combination of both teaching and research.

20. Geography Teachers, Postsecondary

Personality Type: No data available

Earnings: $59,000
Growth: 32.2%
Annual Openings: 329,000 for all postsecondary teaching jobs

Most Common Education/Training Level: Master's degree

Teach courses in geography. Includes both teachers primarily engaged in teaching and those who do a combination of both teaching and research.

21. Graduate Teaching Assistants

Personality Type:
Social–Investigative–Conventional

Earnings: $27,840
Growth: 32.2%
Annual Openings: 329,000 for all postsecondary teaching jobs

Most Common Education/Training Level:
Master's degree

Assist department chairperson, faculty members, or other professional staff members in college or university by performing teaching or teaching-related duties, such as teaching lower-level courses, developing teaching materials, preparing and giving examinations, and grading examinations or papers. Graduate assistants must be enrolled in a graduate school program. Graduate assistants who primarily perform non-teaching duties, such as laboratory research, should be reported in the occupational category related to the work performed.

22. Health Specialties Teachers, Postsecondary

Personality Type: Investigative–Social–Artistic

Earnings: $77,190
Growth: 32.2%
Annual Openings: 329,000 for all postsecondary teaching jobs

Most Common Education/Training Level:
Master's degree

Teach courses in health specialties, such as veterinary medicine, dentistry, pharmacy, therapy, laboratory technology, and public health.

Includes both teachers primarily engaged in teaching and those who do a combination of both teaching and research.

23. History Teachers, Postsecondary

Personality Type: Social–Investigative–Artistic

Earnings: $57,390
Growth: 32.2%
Annual Openings: 329,000 for all postsecondary teaching jobs

Most Common Education/Training Level:
Master's degree

Teach courses in human history and historiography.

24. Home Economics Teachers, Postsecondary

Personality Type: No data available

Earnings: $55,310
Growth: 32.2%
Annual Openings: 329,000 for all postsecondary teaching jobs

Most Common Education/Training Level:
Master's degree

Teach courses in child care, family relations, finance, nutrition, and related subjects as pertaining to home management.

25. Law Teachers, Postsecondary

Personality Type: No data available

Earnings: $87,240
Growth: 32.2%
Annual Openings: 329,000 for all postsecondary teaching jobs

Most Common Education/Training Level:
First professional degree

Teach courses in law.

Social

26. Library Science Teachers, Postsecondary

Personality Type: No data available

Earnings: $54,570
Growth: 32.2%
Annual Openings: 329,000 for all postsecondary teaching jobs

Most Common Education/Training Level: Master's degree

Teach courses in library science.

27. Mathematical Science Teachers, Postsecondary

Personality Type: Investigative–Conventional–Social

Earnings: $56,420
Growth: 32.2%
Annual Openings: 329,000 for all postsecondary teaching jobs

Most Common Education/Training Level: Master's degree

Teach courses pertaining to mathematical concepts, statistics, and actuarial science and to the application of original and standardized mathematical techniques in solving specific problems and situations.

28. Nursing Instructors and Teachers, Postsecondary

Personality Type: Social–Investigative–Artistic

Earnings: $55,280
Growth: 32.2%
Annual Openings: 329,000 for all postsecondary teaching jobs

Most Common Education/Training Level: Master's degree

Demonstrate and teach patient care in classroom and clinical units to nursing students. Includes both teachers primarily engaged in teaching and those who do a combination of both teaching and research.

29. Philosophy and Religion Teachers, Postsecondary

Personality Type: No data available

Earnings: $54,880
Growth: 32.2%
Annual Openings: 329,000 for all postsecondary teaching jobs

Most Common Education/Training Level: Master's degree

Teach courses in philosophy, religion, and theology.

30. Physics Teachers, Postsecondary

Personality Type: Investigative–Social–Realistic

Earnings: $68,170
Growth: 32.2%
Annual Openings: 329,000 for all postsecondary teaching jobs

Most Common Education/Training Level: Master's degree

Teach courses pertaining to the laws of matter and energy. Includes both teachers primarily engaged in teaching and those who do a combination of both teaching and research.

31. Political Science Teachers, Postsecondary

Personality Type: Social–Investigative–Artistic

Earnings: $61,820
Growth: 32.2%

Annual Openings: 329,000 for all postsecondary teaching jobs

Most Common Education/Training Level: Master's degree

Teach courses in political science, international affairs, and international relations. Includes both teachers primarily engaged in teaching and those who do a combination of both teaching and research.

32. Postsecondary Teachers, All Other

Personality Type: No data available

Earnings: $63,930
Growth: 32.2%
Annual Openings: 329,000 for all postsecondary teaching jobs

Most Common Education/Training Level: Master's degree

All postsecondary teachers not listed separately.

33. Psychology Teachers, Postsecondary

Personality Type: Social–Investigative–Artistic

Earnings: $58,670
Growth: 32.2%
Annual Openings: 329,000 for all postsecondary teaching jobs

Most Common Education/Training Level: Master's degree

Teach courses in psychology, such as child, clinical, and developmental psychology, and psychological counseling. Includes both teachers primarily engaged in teaching and those who do a combination of both teaching and research.

34. Recreation and Fitness Studies Teachers, Postsecondary

Personality Type: No data available

Earnings: $49,270
Growth: 32.2%
Annual Openings: 329,000 for all postsecondary teaching jobs

Most Common Education/Training Level: Master's degree

Teach courses pertaining to recreation, leisure, and fitness studies, including exercise physiology and facilities management.

35. Social Sciences Teachers, Postsecondary, All Other

Personality Type: No data available

Earnings: $61,210
Growth: 32.2%
Annual Openings: 329,000 for all postsecondary teaching jobs

Most Common Education/Training Level: Master's degree

All postsecondary social sciences teachers not listed separately.

36. Social Work Teachers, Postsecondary

Personality Type: No data available

Earnings: $54,340
Growth: 32.2%
Annual Openings: 329,000 for all postsecondary teaching jobs

Social

Most Common Education/Training Level:
Master's degree

Teach courses in social work.

37. Sociology Teachers, Postsecondary

Personality Type: Social–Investigative–Artistic

Earnings: $56,620
Growth: 32.2%
Annual Openings: 329,000 for all
postsecondary teaching jobs

Most Common Education/Training Level:
Master's degree

Teach courses in sociology. Includes both teachers primarily engaged in teaching and those who do a combination of both teaching and research.

38. Vocational Education Teachers, Postsecondary

Personality Type: Social–Realistic–Enterprising

Earnings: $43,900
Growth: 32.2%
Annual Openings: 329,000 for all
postsecondary teaching jobs

Most Common Education/Training Level:
Work experience in a related occupation

Teach or instruct vocational or occupational subjects at the postsecondary level (but at less than the baccalaureate) to students who have graduated or left high school. Includes correspondence school instructors; industrial, commercial, and government training instructors; and adult education teachers and instructors who prepare persons to operate industrial machinery and equipment and transportation and communications equipment. Teaching may take place in public or private schools whose primary business is education or in a school associated with an organization whose primary business is other than education.

Humanities

Personality Type: Social–Investigative–Artistic

Useful Facts About the Major

Focuses on combined studies and research in the humanities subjects as distinguished from the social and physical sciences, emphasizing languages, literatures, art, music, philosophy, and religion.

Related CIP Program: 24.0103 Humanities/Humanistic Studies

Specializations in the Major: History; language; literature; peace and justice studies; philosophy; religion; the arts.

Typical Sequence of College Courses: Foreign language, major thinkers and issues in philosophy, literature, art and culture, European history and civilization, writing, seminar (reporting on research).

Typical Sequence of High School Courses: English, algebra, foreign language, history, literature, public speaking, social science.

Career Snapshot

Humanities (sometimes called liberal arts) is an interdisciplinary major that covers a wide range of the arts and other non-scientific modes of thought, such as history, philosophy, religious studies, and language. Graduates of this major usually have strong skills for communicating and critical thinking, and they often advance further in the business world than those who hold more business-focused degrees. Some pursue careers in teaching, media, or the arts. Others get professional degrees in the law or medicine.

Useful Averages for the Related Jobs

- **Annual Earnings:** $57,770
- **Growth:** 32.2%
- **Self-Employed:** 0.4%
- **Part-Time:** 24.8%
- **Verbal Skill Rating:** 83.9
- **Math Skill Rating:** 61.9

Other Details About the Related Jobs

Total Annual Job Openings: 329,000

Interest Area: 05 Education and Training

Skills—Instructing; learning strategies; writing; social perceptiveness; speaking; reading comprehension. **Values**—Authority; social service; creativity; achievement; co-workers; ability utilization. **Work Conditions**—Indoors, environmentally controlled; sitting.

Related Jobs

1. Anthropology and Archeology Teachers, Postsecondary

Personality Type: Social–Investigative–Artistic

Earnings: $62,820
Growth: 32.2%
Annual Openings: 329,000 for all postsecondary teaching jobs

Most Common Education/Training Level: Master's degree

Teach courses in anthropology or archeology. Includes both teachers primarily engaged in teaching and those who do a combination of both teaching and research. Conduct research in a particular field of knowledge and publish findings in professional journals, books, and

Social

electronic media. Keep abreast of developments in their field by reading current literature, talking with colleagues, and participating in professional conferences. Prepare and deliver lectures to undergraduate and graduate students on topics such as research methods, urban anthropology, and language and culture. Evaluate and grade students' classwork, assignments, and papers. Initiate, facilitate, and moderate classroom discussions. Write grant proposals to procure external research funding. Supervise undergraduate and/or graduate teaching, internship, and research work. Prepare course materials such as syllabi, homework assignments, and handouts. Compile, administer, and grade examinations or assign this work to others. Supervise students' laboratory work or fieldwork. Plan, evaluate, and revise curricula, course content, and course materials and methods of instruction. Advise students on academic and vocational curricula, career issues, and laboratory and field research. Maintain student attendance records, grades, and other required records. Maintain regularly scheduled office hours in order to advise and assist students. Collaborate with colleagues to address teaching and research issues. Compile bibliographies of specialized materials for outside reading assignments. Perform administrative duties such as serving as department head. Select and obtain materials and supplies such as textbooks and laboratory equipment. Serve on academic or administrative committees that deal with institutional policies, departmental matters, and academic issues. Participate in student recruitment, registration, and placement activities. Participate in campus and community events. Provide professional consulting services to government and industry. Act as advisers to student organizations.

2. Area, Ethnic, and Cultural Studies Teachers, Postsecondary

Personality Type: Social–Investigative–Artistic

Earnings: $56,380
Growth: 32.2%
Annual Openings: 329,000 for all postsecondary teaching jobs

Most Common Education/Training Level: Master's degree

Teach courses pertaining to the culture and development of an area (e.g., Latin America), an ethnic group, or any other group (e.g., women's studies, urban affairs). Includes both teachers primarily engaged in teaching and those who do a combination of both teaching and research. Keep abreast of developments in their field by reading current literature, talking with colleagues, and participating in professional conferences. Conduct research in a particular field of knowledge and publish findings in professional journals, books, and/or electronic media. Evaluate and grade students' classwork, assignments, and papers. Prepare course materials such as syllabi, homework assignments, and handouts. Prepare and deliver lectures to undergraduate and/or graduate students on topics such as race and ethnic relations, gender studies, and cross-cultural perspectives. Initiate, facilitate, and moderate classroom discussions. Compile, administer, and grade examinations or assign this work to others. Maintain regularly scheduled office hours in order to advise and assist students. Plan, evaluate, and revise curricula, course content, and course materials and methods of instruction. Maintain student attendance records, grades, and other required records. Advise students on academic and vocational curricula and on career issues. Supervise undergraduate and/or graduate teaching, internship, and research work. Select and obtain materials and supplies such as textbooks. Collaborate with colleagues to address teaching and research issues. Serve on academic or administrative committees that deal with institutional policies, departmental matters, and academic issues. Compile bibliographies of specialized materials for outside reading assignments. Write grant proposals to procure external research funding. Participate in campus and community events. Participate in student recruitment, registration, and placement activities. Act as advisers to student organizations. Incorporate experiential/site visit components into courses. Perform administrative duties such as serving as department head. Provide professional consulting services to government and/or industry.

3. Art, Drama, and Music Teachers, Postsecondary

Personality Type: Artistic–Social–Investigative

Earnings: $53,160
Growth: 32.2%
Annual Openings: 329,000 for all postsecondary teaching jobs

Most Common Education/Training Level: Master's degree

Teach courses in drama; music; and the arts, including fine and applied art, such as painting and sculpture, or design and crafts. Evaluate and grade students' classwork, performances, projects, assignments, and papers. Explain and demonstrate artistic techniques. Prepare students for performances, exams, or assessments. Prepare and deliver lectures to undergraduate or graduate students on topics such as acting techniques, fundamentals of music, and art history.

Organize performance groups and direct their rehearsals. Prepare course materials such as syllabi, homework assignments, and handouts. Initiate, facilitate, and moderate classroom discussions. Keep abreast of developments in their field by reading current literature, talking with colleagues, and participating in professional conferences. Advise students on academic and vocational curricula and on career issues. Maintain student attendance records, grades, and other required records. Conduct research in a particular field of knowledge and publish findings in professional journals, books, or electronic media. Supervise undergraduate and/or graduate teaching, internship, and research work. Plan, evaluate, and revise curricula, course content, and course materials and methods of instruction. Maintain regularly scheduled office hours to advise and assist students. Compile, administer, and grade examinations or assign this work to others. Participate in student recruitment, registration, and placement activities. Select and obtain materials and supplies such as textbooks and performance pieces. Collaborate with colleagues to address teaching and research issues. Serve on academic or administrative committees that deal with institutional policies, departmental matters, and academic issues. Participate in campus and community events. Keep students informed of community events such as plays and concerts. Compile bibliographies of specialized materials for outside reading assignments. Display students' work in schools, galleries, and exhibitions. Perform administrative duties such as serving as department head. Act as advisers to student organizations. Write grant proposals to procure external research funding. Provide professional consulting services to government or industry.

Social

4. Communications Teachers, Postsecondary

Personality Type: No data available

Earnings: $53,110
Growth: 32.2%
Annual Openings: 329,000 for all postsecondary teaching jobs

Most Common Education/Training Level: Master's degree

Teach courses in communications, such as organizational communications, public relations, radio/television broadcasting, and journalism. Includes both teachers primarily engaged in teaching and those who do a combination of both teaching and research. Evaluate and grade students' classwork, assignments, and papers. Prepare course materials such as syllabi, homework assignments, and handouts. Initiate, facilitate, and moderate classroom discussions. Prepare and deliver lectures to undergraduate or graduate students on topics such as public speaking, media criticism, and oral traditions. Compile, administer, and grade examinations or assign this work to others. Maintain student attendance records, grades, and other required records. Plan, evaluate, and revise curricula, course content, and course materials and methods of instruction. Maintain regularly scheduled office hours to advise and assist students. Keep abreast of developments in their field by reading current literature, talking with colleagues, and participating in professional conferences. Advise students on academic and vocational curricula and on career issues. Supervise undergraduate or graduate teaching, internship, and research work. Select and obtain materials and supplies such as textbooks. Collaborate with colleagues to address teaching and research issues. Conduct research in a particular field of knowledge and publish findings in professional journals, books, or electronic media. Participate in student recruitment, registration, and placement activities. Serve on academic or administrative committees that deal with institutional policies, departmental matters, and academic issues. Compile bibliographies of specialized materials for outside reading assignments. Act as advisers to student organizations. Participate in campus and community events. Perform administrative duties such as serving as department head. Write grant proposals to procure external research funding. Provide professional consulting services to government or industry.

5. Economics Teachers, Postsecondary

Personality Type: Social–Investigative–Artistic

Earnings: $71,850
Growth: 32.2%
Annual Openings: 329,000 for all postsecondary teaching jobs

Most Common Education/Training Level: Master's degree

Teach courses in economics. Includes both teachers primarily engaged in teaching and those who do a combination of both teaching and research. Prepare and deliver lectures to undergraduate and/or graduate students on topics such as econometrics, price theory, and macroeconomics. Prepare course materials such as syllabi, homework assignments, and handouts. Evaluate and grade students' classwork, assignments, and papers. Compile, administer, and grade examinations or assign this work to others. Keep abreast of developments in their field by reading current literature, talking with colleagues, and participating in professional conferences. Maintain student attendance records, grades, and other required records. Initiate, facilitate, and moderate classroom discussions. Maintain regularly scheduled office hours in order to advise and assist students. Select and obtain materials and supplies such as textbooks. Plan, evaluate, and revise curricula, course content, and course materials and methods of instruction. Conduct research in a particular field of knowledge and publish findings in professional journals, books, and/or electronic media. Supervise undergraduate and/or graduate teaching, internship, and research work. Advise students on academic and vocational curricula and on career issues. Serve on academic or administrative committees that deal with institutional policies, departmental matters, and academic issues. Collaborate with colleagues to address teaching and research issues. Compile bibliographies of specialized materials for outside reading assignments. Participate in student recruitment, registration, and placement activities. Perform administrative duties such as serving as department head. Write grant proposals to procure external research funding. Participate in campus and community events. Provide professional consulting services to government and/or industry. Act as advisers to student organizations.

6. Education Teachers, Postsecondary

Personality Type: No data available

Earnings: $52,800
Growth: 32.2%
Annual Openings: 329,000 for all postsecondary teaching jobs

Most Common Education/Training Level: Master's degree

Teach courses pertaining to education, such as counseling, curriculum, guidance, instruction, teacher education, and teaching English as a second language. Prepare course materials such as syllabi, homework assignments, and handouts. Prepare and deliver lectures to undergraduate and/or graduate students on topics such as children's literature, learning and development, and reading instruction. Initiate, facilitate, and moderate classroom discussions. Evaluate and grade students' classwork, assignments, and papers. Plan, evaluate, and revise curricula, course content, and course materials and methods of instruction. Supervise students' fieldwork, internship, and research work. Keep abreast of developments in their field by reading current literature, talking with colleagues, and participating in professional conferences. Advise students on academic and vocational curricula and on career issues. Maintain regularly scheduled office hours to advise and assist students. Maintain student attendance records, grades, and other required records. Collaborate with colleagues to address teaching and research issues. Compile, administer, and grade examinations or assign this work to others. Conduct research in a particular field of knowledge and publish findings in professional journals, books, or electronic media. Select and obtain materials and supplies such as textbooks. Participate in student recruitment, registration, and placement activities. Advise and instruct teachers employed in school systems by providing activities such as in-service seminars. Serve on academic or administrative committees that deal with institutional policies, departmental matters, and academic issues. Compile bibliographies of specialized materials for outside reading assignments. Write grant proposals to procure external research funding. Participate in campus and community events. Perform administrative duties such as serving as department head. Act as advisers to student organizations. Provide professional consulting services to government and/or industry.

Social

7. English Language and Literature Teachers, Postsecondary

Personality Type: Artistic–Social–Investigative

Earnings: $51,730
Growth: 32.2%
Annual Openings: 329,000 for all postsecondary teaching jobs

Most Common Education/Training Level: Master's degree

Teach courses in English language and literature, including linguistics and comparative literature. Initiate, facilitate, and moderate classroom discussions. Evaluate and grade students' classwork, assignments, and papers. Prepare course materials such as syllabi, homework assignments, and handouts. Prepare and deliver lectures to undergraduate and graduate students on topics such as poetry, novel structure, and translation and adaptation. Maintain student attendance records, grades, and other required records. Plan, evaluate, and revise curricula, course content, and course materials and methods of instruction. Compile, administer, and grade examinations or assign this work to others. Maintain regularly scheduled office hours in order to advise and assist students. Keep abreast of developments in their field by reading current literature, talking with colleagues, and participating in professional conferences. Select and obtain materials and supplies such as textbooks. Advise students on academic and vocational curricula and on career issues. Conduct research in a particular field of knowledge and publish findings in professional journals, books, or electronic media. Collaborate with colleagues to address teaching and research issues. Serve on academic or administrative committees that deal with institutional policies, departmental matters, and academic issues. Participate in campus and community events. Participate in student recruitment, registration, and placement activities. Compile bibliographies of specialized materials for outside reading assignments. Supervise undergraduate and/or graduate teaching, internship, and research work. Provide assistance to students in college writing centers. Perform administrative duties such as serving as department head. Recruit, train, and supervise student writing instructors. Act as advisers to student organizations. Write grant proposals to procure external research funding. Provide professional consulting services to government or industry.

8. Foreign Language and Literature Teachers, Postsecondary

Personality Type: Artistic–Social–Investigative

Earnings: $51,900
Growth: 32.2%
Annual Openings: 329,000 for all postsecondary teaching jobs

Most Common Education/Training Level: Master's degree

Teach courses in foreign (i.e., other than English) languages and literature. Evaluate and grade students' classwork, assignments, and papers. Prepare course materials such as syllabi, homework assignments, and handouts. Initiate, facilitate, and moderate classroom discussions. Maintain student attendance records, grades, and other required records. Compile, administer, and grade examinations or assign this work to others. Plan, evaluate, and revise curricula, course content, and course materials and methods of instruction. Prepare and deliver lectures to undergraduate and graduate students on topics such as how to speak and write a foreign language and the cultural aspects of areas where a particular language is used. Maintain regularly scheduled office hours to advise and assist students. Select and obtain materials and supplies such as textbooks. Keep abreast of developments in their field by reading current literature, talking with colleagues, and participating in professional organizations and activities. Advise students on academic and vocational curricula and on career issues. Conduct research in a particular field of knowledge and publish findings in scholarly journals, books, and/or electronic media. Collaborate with colleagues to address teaching and research issues. Serve on academic or administrative committees that deal with institutional policies, departmental matters, and academic issues. Participate in student recruitment, registration, and placement activities. Compile bibliographies of specialized materials for outside reading assignments. Participate in campus and community events. Act as advisers to student organizations. Perform administrative duties such as serving as department head. Supervise undergraduate and graduate teaching, internship, and research work. Write grant proposals to procure external research funding. Provide professional consulting services to government or industry.

9. Geography Teachers, Postsecondary

Personality Type: No data available

Earnings: $59,000
Growth: 32.2%
Annual Openings: 329,000 for all postsecondary teaching jobs

Most Common Education/Training Level: Master's degree

Teach courses in geography. Includes both teachers primarily engaged in teaching and those who do a combination of both teaching and research. Prepare and deliver lectures to undergraduate and/or graduate students on topics such as urbanization, environmental systems, and cultural geography. Evaluate and grade students' classwork, assignments, and papers. Compile, administer, and grade examinations or assign this work to others. Initiate, facilitate, and moderate classroom discussions. Maintain student attendance records, grades, and other required records. Prepare course materials such as syllabi, homework assignments, and handouts. Keep abreast of developments in their field by reading current literature, talking with colleagues, and participating in professional conferences. Supervise undergraduate and/or graduate teaching, internship, and research work. Plan, evaluate, and revise curricula, course content, and course materials and methods of instruction. Maintain regularly scheduled office hours to advise and assist students. Supervise students' laboratory work and fieldwork. Conduct research in a particular field of knowledge and publish findings in professional journals, books, and electronic media. Collaborate with colleagues to address teaching and research issues. Select and obtain materials and supplies such as textbooks. Advise students on academic and vocational curricula and on career issues. Serve on academic or administrative committees that deal with institutional policies, departmental matters, and academic issues. Participate in student recruitment, registration, and placement activities. Participate in campus and community events. Compile bibliographies of specialized materials for outside reading assignments. Perform administrative duties such as serving as department head. Write grant proposals to procure external research funding. Maintain geographic information systems laboratories, performing duties such as updating software. Perform spatial analysis and modeling, using geographic information system techniques. Act as advisers to student organizations. Provide professional consulting services to government and industry.

Social

10. Graduate Teaching Assistants

Personality Type:
Social–Investigative–Conventional

Earnings: $27,840
Growth: 32.2%
Annual Openings: 329,000 for all
postsecondary teaching jobs

Most Common Education/Training Level:
Master's degree

Assist department chairperson, faculty members, or other professional staff members in college or university by performing teaching or teaching-related duties, such as teaching lower-level courses, developing teaching materials, preparing and giving examinations, and grading examinations or papers. Graduate assistants must be enrolled in a graduate school program. Graduate assistants who primarily perform non-teaching duties, such as laboratory research, should be reported in the occupational category related to the work performed. Lead discussion sections, tutorials, and laboratory sections. Evaluate and grade examinations, assignments, and papers and record grades. Return assignments to students in accordance with established deadlines. Schedule and maintain regular office hours to meet with students. Inform students of the procedures for completing and submitting class work such as lab reports. Prepare and proctor examinations. Notify instructors of errors or problems with assignments. Meet with supervisors to discuss students' grades and to complete required grade-related paperwork. Copy and distribute classroom materials. Demonstrate use of laboratory equipment and enforce laboratory rules. Teach undergraduate-level courses. Complete laboratory projects prior to assigning them to students so that any needed modifications can be made. Develop teaching materials such as syllabi, visu-al aids, answer keys, supplementary notes, and course Web sites. Provide assistance to faculty members or staff with laboratory or field research. Arrange for supervisors to conduct teaching observations; meet with supervisors to receive feedback about teaching performance. Attend lectures given by the instructor whom they are assisting. Order or obtain materials needed for classes. Provide instructors with assistance in the use of audiovisual equipment. Assist faculty members or staff with student conferences.

11. History Teachers, Postsecondary

Personality Type: Social–Investigative–Artistic

Earnings: $57,390
Growth: 32.2%
Annual Openings: 329,000 for all
postsecondary teaching jobs

Most Common Education/Training Level:
Master's degree

Teach courses in human history and historiography. Prepare and deliver lectures to undergraduate and/or graduate students on topics such as ancient history, postwar civilizations, and the history of third-world countries. Evaluate and grade students' classwork, assignments, and papers. Prepare course materials such as syllabi, homework assignments, and handouts. Compile, administer, and grade examinations or assign this work to others. Initiate, facilitate, and moderate classroom discussions. Keep abreast of developments in their field by reading current literature, talking with colleagues, and participating in professional conferences. Plan, evaluate, and revise curricula, course content, and course materials and methods of instruction. Maintain student attendance records, grades, and other required records. Maintain regularly scheduled office hours to advise and assist students. Conduct research in a particular field of knowledge and publish findings in professional journals, books, or electronic media. Select and obtain materials and supplies such as textbooks. Advise students on academic and vocational curricula and on career issues. Collaborate with colleagues to address teaching and research issues. Serve on academic or administrative committees that deal with institutional policies, departmental matters, and academic issues. Participate in campus and community events. Act as advisers to student organizations. Participate in student recruitment, registration, and placement activities. Compile bibliographies of specialized materials for outside reading assignments. Supervise undergraduate and graduate teaching, internship, and research work. Perform administrative duties such as serving as department head. Write grant proposals to procure external research funding. Provide professional consulting services to government, educational institutions, and industry.

12. Library Science Teachers, Postsecondary

Personality Type: No data available

Earnings: $54,570
Growth: 32.2%
Annual Openings: 329,000 for all postsecondary teaching jobs

Most Common Education/Training Level: Master's degree

Teach courses in library science. Prepare course materials such as syllabi, homework assignments, and handouts. Prepare and deliver lectures to undergraduate or graduate students on topics such as collection development, archival methods, and indexing and abstracting. Evaluate and grade students' classwork, assignments, and papers. Keep abreast of developments in their field by reading current literature, talking with colleagues, and participating in professional conferences. Initiate, facilitate, and moderate classroom discussions. Plan, evaluate, and revise curricula, course content, and course materials and methods of instruction. Conduct research in a particular field of knowledge and publish findings in professional journals, books, and/or electronic media. Maintain student attendance records, grades, and other required records. Collaborate with colleagues to address teaching and research issues. Advise students on academic and vocational curricula and on career issues. Compile, administer, and grade examinations or assign this work to others. Supervise undergraduate or graduate teaching, internship, and research work. Maintain regularly scheduled office hours in order to advise and assist students. Write grant proposals to procure external research funding. Select and obtain materials and supplies such as textbooks. Serve on academic or administrative committees that deal with institutional policies, departmental matters, and academic issues. Compile bibliographies of specialized materials for outside reading assignments. Participate in student recruitment, registration, and placement activities. Perform administrative duties such as serving as department head. Participate in campus and community events. Act as advisers to student organizations. Provide professional consulting services to government and/or industry.

13. Philosophy and Religion Teachers, Postsecondary

Personality Type: No data available

Earnings: $54,880
Growth: 32.2%
Annual Openings: 329,000 for all postsecondary teaching jobs

Social

Most Common Education/Training Level:
Master's degree

Teach courses in philosophy, religion, and theology. Evaluate and grade students' classwork, assignments, and papers. Initiate, facilitate, and moderate classroom discussions. Prepare and deliver lectures to undergraduate and graduate students on topics such as ethics, logic, and contemporary religious thought. Prepare course materials such as syllabi, homework assignments, and handouts. Compile, administer, and grade examinations or assign this work to others. Keep abreast of developments in their field by reading current literature, talking with colleagues, and participating in professional conferences. Maintain student attendance records, grades, and other required records. Plan, evaluate, and revise curricula, course content, and course materials and methods of instruction. Maintain regularly scheduled office hours to advise and assist students. Select and obtain materials and supplies such as textbooks. Advise students on academic and vocational curricula and on career issues. Conduct research in a particular field of knowledge and publish findings in professional journals, books, or electronic media. Perform administrative duties such as serving as department head. Serve on academic or administrative committees that deal with institutional policies, departmental matters, and academic issues. Collaborate with colleagues to address teaching and research issues. Participate in campus and community events. Participate in student recruitment, registration, and placement activities. Compile bibliographies of specialized materials for outside reading assignments. Supervise undergraduate and graduate teaching, internship, and research work. Act as advisers to student organizations. Write grant proposals to procure external research funding. Provide professional consulting services to government or industry.

14. Political Science Teachers, Postsecondary

Personality Type: Social–Investigative–Artistic

Earnings: $61,820
Growth: 32.2%
Annual Openings: 329,000 for all postsecondary teaching jobs

Most Common Education/Training Level:
Master's degree

Teach courses in political science, international affairs, and international relations. Includes both teachers primarily engaged in teaching and those who do a combination of both teaching and research. Initiate, facilitate, and moderate classroom discussions. Prepare and deliver lectures to undergraduate or graduate students on topics such as classical political thought, international relations, and democracy and citizenship. Evaluate and grade students' classwork, assignments, and papers. Compile, administer, and grade examinations or assign this work to others. Prepare course materials such as syllabi, homework assignments, and handouts. Keep abreast of developments in their field by reading current literature, talking with colleagues, and participating in professional conferences. Plan, evaluate, and revise curricula, course content, and course materials and methods of instruction. Maintain student attendance records, grades, and other required records. Maintain regularly scheduled office hours in order to advise and assist students. Advise students on academic and vocational curricula and on career issues. Select and obtain materials and supplies such as textbooks. Conduct research in a particular field of knowledge and publish findings in professional journals, books, and electronic media. Supervise undergraduate and graduate teaching, internship, and research work. Collaborate with colleagues to address teaching and research issues. Serve on academic or administrative committees that deal with institutional policies, departmental matters, and academic issues. Participate in student recruitment, registration, and placement activities. Participate in campus and community events. Compile bibliographies of specialized materials for outside reading assignments. Act as advisers to student organizations. Perform administrative duties such as serving as department head. Write grant proposals to procure external research funding. Provide professional consulting services to government and industry.

15. Psychology Teachers, Postsecondary

Personality Type: Social–Investigative–Artistic

Earnings: $58,670
Growth: 32.2%
Annual Openings: 329,000 for all postsecondary teaching jobs

Most Common Education/Training Level: Master's degree

Teach courses in psychology, such as child, clinical, and developmental psychology and psychological counseling. Includes both teachers primarily engaged in teaching and those who do a combination of both teaching and research. Prepare and deliver lectures to undergraduate and/or graduate students on topics such as abnormal psychology, cognitive processes, and work motivation. Evaluate and grade students' classwork, laboratory work, assignments, and papers. Initiate, facilitate, and moderate classroom discussions. Compile, administer, and grade examinations or assign this work to others. Keep abreast of developments in their field by reading current literature, talking with colleagues, and participating in professional conferences. Prepare course materials such as syllabi, homework assignments, and handouts. Plan,

evaluate, and revise curricula, course content, and course materials and methods of instruction. Maintain student attendance records, grades, and other required records. Supervise undergraduate and/or graduate teaching, internship, and research work. Maintain regularly scheduled office hours to advise and assist students. Conduct research in a particular field of knowledge and publish findings in professional journals, books, and electronic media. Advise students on academic and vocational curricula and on career issues. Select and obtain materials and supplies such as textbooks. Collaborate with colleagues to address teaching and research issues. Serve on academic or administrative committees that deal with institutional policies, departmental matters, and academic issues. Compile bibliographies of specialized materials for outside reading assignments. Participate in student recruitment, registration, and placement activities. Supervise students' laboratory work. Perform administrative duties such as serving as department head. Act as advisers to student organizations. Write grant proposals to procure external research funding. Participate in campus and community events. Provide professional consulting services to government and industry.

16. Sociology Teachers, Postsecondary

Personality Type: Social–Investigative–Artistic

Earnings: $56,620
Growth: 32.2%
Annual Openings: 329,000 for all postsecondary teaching jobs

Most Common Education/Training Level: Master's degree

Teach courses in sociology. Includes both teachers primarily engaged in teaching and those who do a combination of both teaching and research. Evaluate and grade students'

Social

classwork, assignments, and papers. Prepare and deliver lectures to undergraduate and graduate students on topics such as race and ethnic relations, measurement and data collection, and workplace social relations. Initiate, facilitate, and moderate classroom discussions. Prepare course materials such as syllabi, homework assignments, and handouts. Compile, administer, and grade examinations or assign this work to others. Keep abreast of developments in their field by reading current literature, talking with colleagues, and participating in professional conferences. Maintain student attendance records, grades, and other required records. Maintain regularly scheduled office hours in order to advise and assist students. Plan, evaluate, and revise curricula, course content, and course materials and methods of instruction. Advise students on academic and vocational curricula and on career issues. Collaborate with colleagues to address teaching and research issues. Conduct research in a particular field of knowledge and publish findings in professional journals, books, or electronic media. Select and obtain materials and supplies such as textbooks and laboratory equipment. Supervise undergraduate and graduate teaching, internship, and research work. Serve on academic or administrative committees that deal with institutional policies, departmental matters, and academic issues. Participate in student recruitment, registration, and placement activities. Perform administrative duties such as serving as department head. Supervise students' laboratory work and fieldwork. Write grant proposals to procure external research funding. Act as advisers to student organizations. Compile bibliographies of specialized materials for outside reading assignments. Participate in campus and community events. Provide professional consulting services to government and industry.

Nursing (R.N. Training)

Personality Type: Social–Investigative

Useful Facts About the Major

Prepares individuals in the knowledge, techniques, and procedures for promoting health and providing care for sick, disabled, infirm, or other individuals or groups.

Related CIP Program: 51.1601 Nursing/ Registered Nurse (RN, ASN, BSN, MSN)

Specializations in the Major: Community health nursing; mental health nursing; nursing administration; pediatric nursing.

Typical Sequence of College Courses: English composition, introduction to psychology, college algebra, introduction to sociology, oral communication, general chemistry, general biology, human anatomy and physiology, general microbiology, ethics in health care, patient examination and evaluation, pharmacology, reproductive health nursing, pediatric nursing, adult health nursing, mental health nursing, nursing leadership and management, community health nursing, clinical nursing experience.

Typical Sequence of High School Courses: English, algebra, geometry, trigonometry, biology, computer science, public speaking, chemistry, foreign language.

Career Snapshot

The study of nursing includes a combination of classroom and clinical work. Students learn what science tells us about the origins and treatment of disease, how to care effectively for the physical and emotional needs of sick and injured people, and how to teach people to maintain health.

Nurses work in a variety of health-care settings, including physicians' offices, patients' homes, schools and companies, and in desk jobs for HMOs. The employment outlook is excellent in all specialties.

Useful Averages for the Related Job

- **Annual Earnings:** $57,280
- **Growth:** 29.4%
- **Self-Employed:** 0.7%
- **Part-Time:** 30.1%
- **Verbal Skill Rating:** 72.1
- **Math Skill Rating:** 57.4

Other Details About the Related Job

Total Annual Job Openings: 229,000

Interest Area: 08 Health Science

Skills—Social perceptiveness; service orientation; science; time management; monitoring; reading comprehension. **Values**—Social service; co-workers; ability utilization; achievement; activity; social status. **Work Conditions**—Exposed to disease or infections; common protective or safety equipment.

Related Job

Registered Nurses

Personality Type: Social–Investigative–Realistic

Earnings: $57,280
Growth: 29.4%
Annual Openings: 229,000

Most Common Education/Training Level: Associate degree

Social

Assess patient health problems and needs, develop and implement nursing care plans, and maintain medical records. Administer nursing care to ill, injured, convalescent, or disabled patients. May advise patients on health maintenance and disease prevention or provide case management. Licensing or registration required. Includes advance practice nurses, such as nurse practitioners, clinical nurse specialists, certified nurse midwives, and certified registered nurse anesthetists. Advanced practice nursing is practiced by RNs who have specialized formal, post-basic education and who function in highly autonomous and specialized roles. Maintain accurate, detailed reports and records. Monitor, record, and report symptoms and changes in patients' conditions. Record patients' medical information and vital signs. Modify patient treatment plans as indicated by patients' responses and conditions. Consult and coordinate with health-care team members to assess, plan, implement, and evaluate patient care plans. Order, interpret, and evaluate diagnostic tests to identify and assess patient's condition. Monitor all aspects of patient care, including diet and physical activity. Direct and supervise less-skilled nursing or health-care personnel or supervise a particular unit. Prepare patients for, and assist with, examinations and treatments. Observe nurses and visit patients to ensure proper nursing care. Assess the needs of individuals, families, or communities, including assessment of individuals' home or work environments, to identify potential health or safety problems. Instruct individuals, families, and other groups on topics such as health education, disease prevention, and childbirth; develop health improvement programs. Prepare rooms, sterile instruments, equipment, and supplies and ensure that stock of supplies is maintained. Inform physician of patient's condition during anesthesia. Deliver infants and provide prenatal and postpartum care and treatment under obstetrician's supervision. Administer local, inhalation, intravenous, and other anesthetics. Provide health care, first aid, immunizations, and assistance in convalescence and rehabilitation in locations such as schools, hospitals, and industry. Conduct specified laboratory tests. Perform physical examinations, make tentative diagnoses, and treat patients en route to hospitals or at disaster site triage centers. Hand items to surgeons during operations. Prescribe or recommend drugs; medical devices; or other forms of treatment, such as physical therapy, inhalation therapy, or related therapeutic procedures. Direct and coordinate infection control programs, advising and consulting with specified personnel about necessary precautions. Perform administrative and managerial functions, such as taking responsibility for a unit's staff, budget, planning, and long-range goals.

Occupational Therapy

Personality Type: Social–Realistic

Useful Facts About the Major

Prepares individuals to assist patients limited by physical, cognitive, psychosocial, mental, developmental, and learning disabilities, as well as adverse environmental conditions, to maximize their independence and maintain optimum health through a planned mix of acquired skills, performance motivation, environmental adaptations, assistive technologies, and physical agents.

Related CIP Program: 51.2306 Occupational Therapy/Therapist

Specializations in the Major: Geriatric OT; pediatric OT; prosthetics.

Typical Sequence of College Courses: English composition, statistics for business and social sciences, general chemistry, general biology, human anatomy and physiology, introduction to psychology, human growth and development, introduction to computer science, abnormal psychology, fundamentals of medical science, neuroscience for therapy, occupational therapy for developmental problems, occupational therapy for physiological diagnoses, occupational therapy for psychosocial diagnoses, administration of occupational therapy services, research methods in occupational therapy, methods of facilitating therapeutic adaptation, occupational therapy fieldwork experience, seminar (reporting on research).

Typical Sequence of High School Courses: English, algebra, geometry, trigonometry, chemistry, physics, biology, foreign language, computer science.

Career Snapshot

Occupational therapists help people cope with disabilities and lead more productive and enjoyable lives. Some therapists enter the field with a bachelor's degree in occupational therapy; others get a master's after a bachelor's in another field. They learn about the nature of various kinds of disabilities—developmental, emotional, and so on—and how to help people overcome them or compensate for them in their daily lives. The long-range outlook for jobs is considered quite good, although in the short run it may be affected by cutbacks in Medicare coverage of therapies.

Useful Averages for the Related Job

- **Annual Earnings:** $60,470
- **Growth:** 33.6%
- **Self-Employed:** 6.0%
- **Part-Time:** 39.4%
- **Verbal Skill Rating:** 75.6
- **Math Skill Rating:** 45.4

Other Details About the Related Job

Total Annual Job Openings: 7,000

Interest Area: 08 Health Science

Skills—Science; writing; reading comprehension; instructing; learning strategies; complex problem solving. **Values**—Social service; authority; achievement; creativity; ability utilization; co-workers. **Work Conditions**—Indoors; exposed to disease or infections; environmentally controlled.

Social

Related Job

Occupational Therapists

Personality Type: Social–Realistic–Investigative

Earnings: $60,470
Growth: 33.6%
Annual Openings: 7,000

Most Common Education/Training Level: Master's degree

Assess, plan, organize, and participate in rehabilitative programs that help restore vocational, homemaking, and daily living skills, as well as general independence, to disabled persons. Complete and maintain necessary records. Evaluate patients' progress and prepare reports that detail progress. Test and evaluate patients' physical and mental abilities and analyze medical data to determine realistic rehabilitation goals for patients. Select activities that will help individuals learn work and life-management skills within limits of their mental and physical capabilities. Plan, organize, and conduct occupational therapy programs in hospital, institutional, or community settings to help rehabilitate those impaired because of illness, injury, or psychological or developmental problems. Recommend changes in patients' work or living environments consistent with their needs and capabilities. Consult with rehabilitation team to select activity programs and coordinate occupational therapy with other therapeutic activities. Help clients improve decisionmaking, abstract reasoning, memory, sequencing, coordination, and perceptual skills, using computer programs. Develop and participate in health promotion programs, group activities, or discussions to promote client health, facilitate social adjustment, alleviate stress, and prevent physical or mental disability. Provide training and supervision in therapy techniques and objectives for students and nurses and other medical staff. Design and create, or requisition, special supplies and equipment, such as splints, braces, and computer-aided adaptive equipment. Plan and implement programs and social activities to help patients learn work and school skills and adjust to handicaps. Lay out materials such as puzzles, scissors, and eating utensils for use in therapy; clean and repair these tools after therapy sessions. Advise on health risks in the workplace and on health-related transition to retirement. Conduct research in occupational therapy. Provide patients with assistance in locating and holding jobs.

Physical Therapy

Personality Type: Social–Realistic–Investigative

Useful Facts About the Major

Prepares individuals to alleviate physical and functional impairments and limitations caused by injury or disease through the design and implementation of therapeutic interventions to promote fitness and health.

Related CIP Program: 51.2308 Physical Therapy/Therapist

Specializations in the Major: Geriatric physical therapy; neurological physical therapy; orthopedics; physical therapy education; sports medicine.

Typical Sequence of College Courses: English composition, statistics for business and social sciences, general chemistry, general biology, human anatomy and physiology, introduction to psychology, human growth and development, introduction to computer science, abnormal psychology, fundamentals of medical science, neuroanatomy, neuroscience for therapy, cardiopulmonary system, musculoskeletal system, clinical orthopedics, clinical applications of neurophysiology, therapeutic exercise techniques, physical and electrical agents in physical therapy, medical considerations in physical therapy, psychomotor development throughout the lifespan, psychosocial aspects of physical disability, research in physical therapy practice, research in physical therapy practice.

Typical Sequence of High School Courses: English, algebra, geometry, trigonometry, chemistry, physics, biology, foreign language, computer science.

Career Snapshot

Physical therapists help people overcome pain and limited movement caused by disease or injury and help them avoid further disabilities. They review patients' medical records and the prescriptions of physicians, evaluate patients' mobility, and then guide patients through appropriate exercise routines and apply therapeutic agents such as heat and electrical stimulation. They need to be knowledgeable about many disabling conditions and therapeutic techniques. The master's program is currently the standard requirement for entry into this field, but it will be replaced by the doctorate by 2020. Entry to master's programs is extremely competitive. The short-term job outlook has been hurt by cutbacks in Medicare coverage of therapy; however, the long-term outlook is expected to be good because of the aging of the population.

Useful Averages for the Related Job

- **Annual Earnings:** $66,200
- **Growth:** 36.7%
- **Self-Employed:** 4.5%
- **Part-Time:** 21.4%
- **Verbal Skill Rating:** 78.4
- **Math Skill Rating:** 35.6

Other Details About the Related Job

Total Annual Job Openings: 13,000

Interest Area: 08 Health Science

Skills—Science; reading comprehension; instructing; writing; learning strategies; complex problem solving. **Values**—Social service; authority; achievement; ability utilization; co-workers; social status. **Work Conditions**—Indoors;

Social

exposed to disease or infections; environmentally controlled.

Related Job

Physical Therapists

Personality Type: Social–Realistic–Investigative

Earnings: $66,200
Growth: 36.7%
Annual Openings: 13,000

Most Common Education/Training Level:
Master's degree

Assess, plan, organize, and participate in rehabilitative programs that improve mobility, relieve pain, increase strength, and decrease or prevent deformity of patients suffering from disease or injury. Plan, prepare, and carry out individually designed programs of physical treatment to maintain, improve, or restore physical functioning; alleviate pain; and prevent physical dysfunction in patients. Perform and document an initial exam, evaluating data to identify problems and determine a diagnosis prior to intervention. Evaluate effects of treatment at various stages and adjust treatments to achieve maximum benefit. Administer manual exercises, massage, or traction to help relieve pain, increase patient strength, or decrease or prevent deformity or crippling. Instruct patient and family in treatment procedures to be continued at home. Confer with the patient, medical practitioners, and appropriate others to plan, implement, and assess the intervention program. Review physician's referral and patient's medical records to help determine diagnosis and physical therapy treatment required. Obtain patients' informed consent to proposed interventions. Record prognosis, treatment, response, and progress in patient's chart or enter information into computer. Discharge patient from physical therapy when goals or projected outcomes have been attained and provide for appropriate follow-up care or referrals. Test and measure patient's strength, motor development and function, sensory perception, functional capacity, and respiratory and circulatory efficiency and record data. Identify and document goals, anticipated progress, and plans for reevaluation. Provide information to the patient about the proposed intervention, its material risks and expected benefits, and any reasonable alternatives. Inform patients when diagnosis reveals findings outside physical therapy and refer to appropriate practitioners. Direct, supervise, assess, and communicate with supportive personnel. Administer treatment involving application of physical agents, using equipment, moist packs, ultraviolet and infrared lamps, and ultrasound machines. Teach physical therapy students as well as those in other health professions. Evaluate, fit, and adjust prosthetic and orthotic devices and recommend modification to orthotist. Provide educational information about physical therapy and physical therapists, injury prevention, ergonomics, and ways to promote health.

Women's Studies

Personality Type: Social–Investigative–Artistic

Useful Facts About the Major

Focuses on the history, sociology, politics, culture, and economics of women and the development of modern feminism in relation to the roles played by women in different periods and locations in North America and the world.

Related CIP Program: 05.0207 Women's Studies

Specializations in the Major: Feminist theory; history of feminism; women's issues in art and culture; women's political issues.

Typical Sequence of College Courses: English composition, foreign language, American history, introduction to women's studies, women of color, theories of feminism, historical and philosophical origins of feminism, feminism from a global perspective, seminar (reporting on research).

Typical Sequence of High School Courses: English, algebra, foreign language, history, literature, public speaking, social science.

Career Snapshot

Women's studies is an interdisciplinary major that looks at the experience of women from the perspectives of history, literature, psychology, and sociology, among others. Graduates of this major may go into business fields where understanding of women's issues can be helpful—for example, advertising or human resources management. With further education, they may also find careers in fields where they can affect the lives of women, such as social work, law, public health, or public administration.

Useful Averages for the Related Jobs

- **Annual Earnings:** $57,770
- **Growth:** 32.2%
- **Self-Employed:** 0.4%
- **Part-Time:** 24.8%
- **Verbal Skill Rating:** 83.9
- **Math Skill Rating:** 61.9

Other Details About the Related Jobs

Total Annual Job Openings: 329,000

Interest Area: 05 Education and Training

Skills—Writing; critical thinking; instructing; persuasion; active learning; learning strategies. **Values**—Authority; social service; creativity; achievement; social status; ability utilization. **Work Conditions**—Indoors, environmentally controlled; sitting.

Related Jobs

1. Area, Ethnic, and Cultural Studies Teachers, Postsecondary

Personality Type: Social–Investigative–Artistic

Earnings: $56,380
Growth: 32.2%
Annual Openings: 329,000 for all postsecondary teaching jobs

Most Common Education/Training Level: Master's degree

Teach courses pertaining to the culture and development of an area (e.g., Latin America), an ethnic group, or any other group (e.g., women's studies, urban affairs). Keep abreast of developments in their field by reading current literature, talking with colleagues, and

Social

participating in professional conferences. Conduct research in a particular field of knowledge and publish findings in professional journals, books, and/or electronic media. Evaluate and grade students' classwork, assignments, and papers. Prepare course materials such as syllabi, homework assignments, and handouts. Prepare and deliver lectures to undergraduate and/or graduate students on topics such as race and ethnic relations, gender studies, and cross-cultural perspectives. Initiate, facilitate, and moderate classroom discussions. Compile, administer, and grade examinations or assign this work to others. Maintain regularly scheduled office hours in order to advise and assist students. Plan, evaluate, and revise curricula, course content, and course materials and methods of instruction. Maintain student attendance records, grades, and other required records. Advise students on academic and vocational curricula and on career issues. Supervise undergraduate and/or graduate teaching, internship, and research work. Select and obtain materials and supplies such as textbooks. Collaborate with colleagues to address teaching and research issues. Serve on academic or administrative committees that deal with institutional policies, departmental matters, and academic issues. Compile bibliographies of specialized materials for outside reading assignments. Write grant proposals to procure external research funding. Participate in campus and community events. Participate in student recruitment, registration, and placement activities. Act as advisers to student organizations. Incorporate experiential/site visit components into courses. Perform administrative duties such as serving as department head. Provide professional consulting services to government and/or industry.

2. Graduate Teaching Assistants

Personality Type:
Social–Investigative–Conventional

Earnings: $27,840
Growth: 32.2%
Annual Openings: 329,000 for all postsecondary teaching jobs

Most Common Education/Training Level: Master's degree

Assist department chairperson, faculty members, or other professional staff members in college or university by performing teaching or teaching-related duties, such as teaching lower-level courses, developing teaching materials, preparing and giving examinations, and grading examinations or papers. Graduate assistants must be enrolled in a graduate school program. Graduate assistants who primarily perform non-teaching duties, such as laboratory research, should be reported in the occupational category related to the work performed. Lead discussion sections, tutorials, and laboratory sections. Evaluate and grade examinations, assignments, and papers and record grades. Return assignments to students in accordance with established deadlines. Schedule and maintain regular office hours to meet with students. Inform students of the procedures for completing and submitting class work such as lab reports. Prepare and proctor examinations. Notify instructors of errors or problems with assignments. Meet with supervisors to discuss students' grades and to complete required grade-related paperwork. Copy and distribute classroom materials. Demonstrate use of laboratory equipment and enforce laboratory rules. Teach undergraduate-level courses. Complete laboratory projects prior to assigning them to students so that any needed modifications can be made. Develop teaching materials such as syllabi, visual aids, answer keys, supplementary notes, and course Web sites. Provide assistance to faculty members or staff with laboratory or field research. Arrange for supervisors to conduct teaching observations; meet with supervisors to receive feedback about teaching performance. Attend lectures given by the instructor whom they are assisting. Order or obtain materials needed for classes. Provide instructors with assistance in the use of audiovisual equipment. Assist faculty members or staff with student conferences.

Social

Enterprising Majors

Advertising

Personality Type: Enterprising–Artistic

Useful Facts About the Major

Focuses on the creation, execution, transmission, and evaluation of commercial messages in various media intended to promote and sell products, services, and brands and that prepares individuals to function as advertising assistants, technicians, and managers.

Related CIP Program: 09.0903 Advertising

Specializations in the Major: Creative process; management.

Typical Sequence of College Courses: English composition, oral communication, statistics for business and social sciences, introduction to marketing, introduction to advertising, communications theory, advertising message strategy, communication ethics, advertising media, advertising copy and layout, advertising account planning and research, advertising campaign management, mass communication law, introduction to communication research.

Typical Sequence of High School Courses: English, algebra, foreign language, art, literature, public speaking, social science.

Career Snapshot

Advertising is a combination of writing, art, and business. Graduates with a bachelor's degree in advertising often go on to jobs in advertising agencies, mostly in large cities. They may start as copywriters and advance to management.

Competition can be keen because the industry is considered glamorous. A knowledge of how to advertise on the Internet can be an advantage.

Useful Averages for the Related Jobs

- **Annual Earnings:** $48,594
- **Growth:** 17.1%
- **Self-Employed:** 6.0%
- **Part-Time:** 24.4%
- **Verbal Skill Rating:** 62.4
- **Math Skill Rating:** 50.9

Other Details About the Related Jobs

Total Annual Job Openings: 33,000

Interest Area: 06 Finance and Insurance; 14 Retail and Wholesale Sales and Service

Skills—Negotiation; management of financial resources; persuasion; service orientation; writing; speaking. **Values**—Creativity; working conditions; variety; ability utilization; achievement; autonomy. **Work Conditions**—Outdoors, exposed to weather.

Related Jobs

1. Advertising and Promotions Managers

Personality Type: Artistic–Enterprising–Social

Earnings: $73,060
Growth: 20.3%
Annual Openings: 9,000

Most Common Education/Training Level: Work experience plus degree

Plan and direct advertising policies and programs or produce collateral materials, such as posters, contests, coupons, or giveaways, to create extra interest in the purchase of a product or service for a department, for an entire organization, or on an account basis. Prepare budgets and submit estimates for program costs as part of campaign plan development. Plan and prepare advertising and promotional material to increase sales of products or services, working with customers, company officials, sales departments, and advertising agencies. Assist with annual budget development. Inspect layouts and advertising copy and edit scripts, audiotapes and videotapes, and other promotional material for adherence to specifications. Coordinate activities of departments, such as sales, graphic arts, media, finance, and research. Prepare and negotiate advertising and sales contracts. Identify and develop contacts for promotional campaigns and industry programs that meet identified buyer targets, such as dealers, distributors, or consumers. Gather and organize information to plan advertising campaigns. Confer with department heads or staff to discuss topics such as contracts, selection of advertising media, or product to be advertised. Confer with clients to provide marketing or technical advice. Monitor and analyze sales promotion results to determine cost-effectiveness of promotion campaigns. Read trade journals and professional literature to stay informed on trends, innovations, and changes that affect media planning. Formulate plans to extend business with established accounts and to transact business as agent for advertising accounts. Provide presentation and product demonstration support during the introduction of new products and services to field staff and customers. Direct, motivate, and monitor the mobilization of a campaign team to advance campaign goals. Plan and execute advertising policies and strategies for organizations. Track program budgets and expenses and campaign response rates to evaluate each campaign based on program objectives and industry norms. Assemble and communicate with a strong, diverse coalition of organizations or public figures, securing their cooperation, support, and action to further campaign goals. Train and direct workers engaged in developing and producing advertisements. Coordinate with the media to disseminate advertising.

2. Advertising Sales Agents

Personality Type:
Enterprising–Social–Conventional

Earnings: $42,750
Growth: 16.3%
Annual Openings: 24,000

Most Common Education/Training Level:
Moderate-term on-the-job training

Sell or solicit advertising, including graphic art, advertising space in publications, custom-made signs, or TV and radio advertising time. May obtain leases for outdoor advertising sites or persuade retailer to use sales promotion display items. Prepare and deliver sales presentations to new and existing customers to sell new advertising programs and to protect and increase existing advertising. Explain to customers how specific types of advertising will help promote their products or services in the most effective way possible. Maintain assigned account bases while developing new accounts. Process all correspondence and paperwork related to accounts. Deliver advertising or illustration proofs to customers for approval. Draw up contracts for advertising work and collect payments due. Locate and contact potential clients to offer advertising services. Provide clients with estimates of the costs of advertising products or services. Recommend appropriate sizes and formats for advertising, depending on medium being used. Inform customers of available

Enterprising

options for advertisement artwork and provide samples. Obtain and study information about clients' products, needs, problems, advertising history, and business practices to offer effective sales presentations and appropriate product assistance. Determine advertising medium to be used and prepare sample advertisements within the selected medium for presentation to customers. Consult with company officials, sales departments, and advertising agencies to develop promotional plans. Prepare promotional plans, sales literature, media kits, and sales contracts, using computer. Identify new advertising markets and propose products to serve them. Write copy as part of layout. Attend sales meetings, industry trade shows, and training seminars to gather information, promote products, expand network of contacts, and increase knowledge. Gather all relevant material for bid processes and coordinate bidding and contract approval. Arrange for commercial taping sessions and accompany clients to sessions. Write sales outlines for use by staff.

Architecture

Personality Type:
Enterprising–Realistic–Investigative

Useful Facts About the Major

Prepares individuals for the independent professional practice of architecture and to conduct research in various aspects of the field.

Related CIP Program: 04.0201 Architecture (BArch, BA/BS, MArch, MA/MS, PhD)

Specializations in the Major: Architectural engineering; design; history; theory and criticism; urban studies.

Typical Sequence of College Courses: English composition, basic drawing, art history: Renaissance to modern, calculus, introduction to computer science, general physics, history of architecture, structures, building science, visual analysis of architecture, architectural graphics, architectural design, architectural computer graphics, site analysis, introduction to urban planning.

Typical Sequence of High School Courses: English, algebra, geometry, trigonometry, pre-calculus, calculus, physics, computer science, art.

Career Snapshot

Architects design buildings and the spaces between them. They must have a combination of artistic, technical, and business skills. In order to be licensed, they must obtain a professional degree in architecture (sometimes a five-year bachelor's degree, sometimes a master's degree after a bachelor's in another field); work as an intern, typically for three years; and pass a licensing exam. About one-fifth are self-employed, and most architectural firms are quite small. Computer skills can be a big advantage for new graduates. Best internship opportunities will be for those who have interned while still in school. Demand for architectural services depends on the amount of building construction and therefore varies with economic ups and downs and by geographic region.

Useful Averages for the Related Jobs

- **Annual Earnings:** $90,798
- **Growth:** 14.5%
- **Self-Employed:** 8.4%
- **Part-Time:** 10.7%
- **Verbal Skill Rating:** 71.2
- **Math Skill Rating:** 70.3

Other Details About the Related Jobs

Total Annual Job Openings: 22,000

Interest Area: 02 Architecture and Construction; 15 Scientific Research, Engineering, and Mathematics

Skills—Operations analysis; management of financial resources; technology design; science; quality control analysis; complex problem solving. **Values**—Creativity; authority; compensation; recognition; ability utilization; autonomy. **Work Conditions**—Indoors, environmentally controlled; sitting.

Related Jobs

1. Architects, Except Landscape and Naval

Personality Type:
Artistic–Realistic–Investigative

Enterprising

Earnings: $64,150
Growth: 17.3%
Annual Openings: 7,000

Most Common Education/Training Level:
Bachelor's degree

Plan and design structures, such as private residences, office buildings, theaters, factories, and other structural property. Prepare information regarding design, structure specifications, materials, color, equipment, estimated costs, or construction time. Consult with client to determine functional and spatial requirements of structure. Direct activities of workers engaged in preparing drawings and specification documents. Plan layout of project. Prepare contract documents for building contractors. Prepare scale drawings. Integrate engineering element into unified design. Conduct periodic on-site observation of work during construction to monitor compliance with plans. Administer construction contracts. Represent client in obtaining bids and awarding construction contracts. Prepare operating and maintenance manuals, studies, and reports.

2. Engineering Managers

Personality Type:
Enterprising–Investigative–Realistic

Earnings: $105,430
Growth: 13.0%
Annual Openings: 15,000

Most Common Education/Training Level:
Work experience plus degree

Plan, direct, or coordinate activities in such fields as architecture and engineering or research and development in these fields. Confer with management, production, and marketing staff to discuss project specifications and procedures. Coordinate and direct projects, making detailed plans to accomplish goals and directing the integration of technical activities. Analyze technology, resource needs, and market demand to plan and assess the feasibility of projects. Plan and direct the installation, testing, operation, maintenance, and repair of facilities and equipment. Direct, review, and approve product design and changes. Recruit employees; assign, direct, and evaluate their work; and oversee the development and maintenance of staff competence. Prepare budgets, bids, and contracts and direct the negotiation of research contracts. Develop and implement policies, standards, and procedures for the engineering and technical work performed in the department, service, laboratory, or firm. Review and recommend or approve contracts and cost estimates. Perform administrative functions such as reviewing and writing reports, approving expenditures, enforcing rules, and making decisions about the purchase of materials or services. Present and explain proposals, reports, and findings to clients. Consult or negotiate with clients to prepare project specifications. Set scientific and technical goals within broad outlines provided by top management. Administer highway planning, construction, and maintenance. Direct the engineering of water control, treatment, and distribution projects. Plan, direct, and coordinate survey work with other staff activities, certifying survey work and writing land legal descriptions. Confer with and report to officials and the public to provide information and solicit support for projects.

Business Management

Personality Type: Enterprising–Conventional

Useful Facts About the Major

Prepares individuals to plan, organize, direct, and control the functions and processes of a firm or organization.

Related CIP Program: 52.0201 Business Administration and Management, General

Specializations in the Major: International business; management; marketing; operations.

Typical Sequence of College Courses: English composition, business writing, introduction to psychology, principles of microeconomics, principles of macroeconomics, calculus for business and social sciences, statistics for business and social sciences, introduction to management information systems, introduction to accounting, legal environment of business, principles of management and organization, operations management, strategic management, business finance, introduction to marketing, organizational behavior, human resource management, international management, organizational theory.

Typical Sequence of High School Courses: English, algebra, geometry, trigonometry, science, foreign language, computer science, public speaking.

Career Snapshot

Students of business management learn about the principles of economics, the legal and social environment in which business operates, and quantitative methods for measuring and projecting business activity. Graduates may enter the business world directly or pursue a master's degree. Some get a bachelor's degree in a non-business field and enter a master's of business administration program after getting some entry-level work experience. The outlook for graduates is generally good but varies among various business specializations and industries.

Useful Averages for the Related Jobs

- **Annual Earnings:** $83,211
- **Growth:** 16.6%
- **Self-Employed:** 11.0%
- **Part-Time:** 11.7%
- **Verbal Skill Rating:** 64.9
- **Math Skill Rating:** 57.9

Other Details About the Related Jobs

Total Annual Job Openings: 481,000

Interest Area: 02 Architecture and Construction; 04 Business and Administration; 06 Finance and Insurance; 07 Government and Public Administration; 13 Manufacturing; 14 Retail and Wholesale Sales and Service; 16 Transportation, Distribution, and Logistics

Skills—Management of financial resources; management of personnel resources; management of material resources; negotiation; monitoring; persuasion. **Values**—Authority; creativity; autonomy; responsibility; compensation; working conditions. **Work Conditions**—Indoors, environmentally controlled; sitting.

Related Jobs

1. Administrative Services Managers

Personality Type:
Enterprising–Conventional–Social

Enterprising

Earnings: $67,690
Growth: 16.9%
Annual Openings: 25,000

Most Common Education/Training Level:
Work experience plus degree

Plan, direct, or coordinate supportive services of an organization, such as recordkeeping, mail distribution, telephone operator/receptionist, and other office support services. May oversee facilities planning and maintenance and custodial operations. Monitor the facility to ensure that it remains safe, secure, and well-maintained. Direct or coordinate the supportive services department of a business, agency, or organization. Set goals and deadlines for the department. Prepare and review operational reports and schedules to ensure accuracy and efficiency. Analyze internal processes and recommend and implement procedural or policy changes to improve operations such as supply changes or the disposal of records. Acquire, distribute, and store supplies. Plan, administer, and control budgets for contracts, equipment, and supplies. Oversee construction and renovation projects to improve efficiency and to ensure that facilities meet environmental, health, and security standards and comply with government regulations. Hire and terminate clerical and administrative personnel. Oversee the maintenance and repair of machinery, equipment, and electrical and mechanical systems. Manage leasing of facility space. Participate in architectural and engineering planning and design, including space and installation management. Conduct classes to teach procedures to staff. Dispose of, or oversee the disposal of, surplus or unclaimed property.

2. Chief Executives

Personality Type:
Enterprising–Conventional–Social

Earnings: More than $145,600
Growth: 14.9%
Annual Openings: 38,000

Most Common Education/Training Level:
Work experience plus degree

Determine and formulate policies and provide the overall direction of companies or private- and public-sector organizations within the guidelines set up by a board of directors or similar governing body. Plan, direct, or coordinate operational activities at the highest level of management with the help of subordinate executives and staff managers. Direct and coordinate an organization's financial and budget activities in order to fund operations, maximize investments, and increase efficiency. Confer with board members, organization officials, and staff members to discuss issues, coordinate activities, and resolve problems. Analyze operations to evaluate performance of a company and its staff in meeting objectives and to determine areas of potential cost reduction, program improvement, or policy change. Direct, plan, and implement policies, objectives, and activities of organizations or businesses in order to ensure continuing operations, to maximize returns on investments, and to increase productivity. Prepare budgets for approval, including those for funding and implementation of programs. Direct and coordinate activities of businesses or departments concerned with production, pricing, sales, and/or distribution of products. Negotiate or approve contracts and agreements with suppliers, distributors, federal and state agencies, and other organizational entities. Review reports submitted by staff members in order to recommend approval or to suggest changes. Appoint department heads or managers and assign or delegate responsibilities to them. Direct human resources activities, including the approval of human resource plans and activities, the selection of directors and other high-level staff, and establishment and organization of major departments. Preside over or serve on boards of directors, management committees, or other governing boards. Prepare and present reports concerning activities, expenses, budgets, government statutes and rulings, and other items affecting businesses or program services. Establish departmental responsibilities and coordinate functions among departments and sites. Implement corrective action plans to solve organizational or departmental problems. Coordinate the development and implementation of budgetary control systems, recordkeeping systems, and other administrative control processes. Direct non-merchandising departments such as advertising, purchasing, credit, and accounting. Deliver speeches, write articles, and present information at meetings or conventions in order to promote services, exchange ideas, and accomplish objectives.

3. Construction Managers

Personality Type:
Enterprising–Realistic–Conventional

Earnings: $73,700
Growth: 10.4%
Annual Openings: 28,000

Most Common Education/Training Level:
Bachelor's degree

Plan, direct, coordinate, or budget, usually through subordinate supervisory personnel, activities concerned with the construction and maintenance of structures, facilities, and systems. Participate in the conceptual development of a construction project and oversee its organization, scheduling, and implementation. Confer with supervisory personnel, owners, contractors, and design professionals to discuss and resolve matters such as work procedures, complaints, and construction problems. Plan, organize, and direct activities concerned with the construction and maintenance of structures, facilities, and systems. Schedule the project in logical steps and budget time required to meet deadlines. Determine labor requirements and dispatch workers to construction sites. Inspect and review projects to monitor compliance with building and safety codes and other regulations. Prepare contracts and negotiate revisions, changes, and additions to contractual agreements with architects, consultants, clients, suppliers, and subcontractors. Interpret and explain plans and contract terms to administrative staff, workers, and clients, representing the owner or developer. Obtain all necessary permits and licenses. Direct and supervise workers. Study job specifications to determine appropriate construction methods. Select, contract, and oversee workers who complete specific pieces of the project, such as painting or plumbing. Requisition supplies and materials to complete construction projects. Prepare and submit budget estimates and progress and cost tracking reports. Take actions to deal with the results of delays, bad weather, or emergencies at construction site. Develop and implement quality control programs. Investigate damage, accidents, or delays at construction sites to ensure that proper procedures are being carried out. Evaluate construction methods and determine cost-effectiveness of plans, using computers. Direct acquisition of land for construction projects.

4. Cost Estimators

Personality Type:
Conventional–Enterprising–Social

Earnings: $52,940
Growth: 18.2%
Annual Openings: 15,000

Most Common Education/Training Level:
Work experience in a related occupation

Prepare cost estimates for product manufacturing, construction projects, or services to aid management in bidding on or determining price of product or service. May specialize according to particular service performed or type of product manufactured. Analyze blueprints and other documentation to prepare time, cost, materials, and labor estimates. Assess cost-effectiveness of products, projects, or services, tracking actual costs relative to bids as the project develops. Consult with clients, vendors, personnel in other departments, or construction foremen to discuss and formulate estimates and resolve issues. Confer with engineers, architects, owners, contractors, and subcontractors on changes and adjustments to cost estimates. Prepare estimates used by management for purposes such as planning, organizing, and scheduling work. Prepare estimates for use in selecting vendors or subcontractors. Review material and labor requirements to decide whether it is more cost-effective to produce or purchase components. Prepare cost and expenditure statements and other necessary documentation at regular intervals for the duration of the project. Prepare and maintain a directory of suppliers, contractors, and subcontractors. Set up cost-monitoring and cost-reporting systems and procedures. Establish and maintain tendering process and conduct negotiations. Conduct special studies to develop and establish standard hour and related cost data or to effect cost reduction. Visit site and record information about access, drainage and topography, and availability of services such as water and electricity.

5. General and Operations Managers

Personality Type: No data available

Earnings: $85,230
Growth: 17.0%
Annual Openings: 208,000

Most Common Education/Training Level:
Work experience plus degree

Plan, direct, or coordinate the operations of companies or public- and private-sector organizations. Duties and responsibilities include formulating policies, managing daily operations, and planning the use of materials and human resources, but are too diverse and general in nature to be classified in any one functional area of management or administration, such as personnel, purchasing, or administrative services. Includes owners and managers who head small business establishments whose duties are primarily managerial. Direct and coordinate activities of businesses or departments concerned with the production, pricing, sales, or distribution of products. Manage staff, preparing work schedules and assigning specific duties. Review financial statements, sales and activity reports, and other performance data to measure productivity and goal achievement and to determine areas needing cost reduction and program improvement. Establish and implement departmental policies, goals, objectives, and procedures, conferring with board members, organization officials, and staff members as necessary. Determine staffing requirements and interview, hire, and train new employees or oversee those personnel processes. Monitor businesses and agencies to ensure that they efficiently and effectively provide needed services while staying within budgetary limits. Oversee activities directly related to making products or providing services. Direct and coordinate organization's financial and budget activities to fund operations, maximize investments, and increase efficiency. Determine goods and services to be sold and set prices and credit terms based on forecasts of customer demand. Manage the movement of goods into and out of production facilities. Locate, select, and procure merchandise for resale, representing management in purchase negotiations. Perform sales floor work such as greeting and assisting customers, stocking shelves, and taking inventory. Develop and implement product marketing strategies, including advertising campaigns and sales promotions. Plan and direct activities such as sales promotions, coordinating with other department heads as required. Direct non-merchandising departments of businesses, such as advertising and purchasing. Recommend locations for new facilities or oversee the remodeling of current facilities. Plan store layouts and design displays.

6. Industrial Production Managers

Personality Type:
Enterprising–Conventional–Realistic

Earnings: $77,670
Growth: 0.8%
Annual Openings: 13,000

Most Common Education/Training Level:
Work experience in a related occupation

Plan, direct, or coordinate the work activities and resources necessary for manufacturing products in accordance with cost, quality, and quantity specifications. Direct and coordinate production, processing, distribution, and marketing activities of industrial organization. Develop budgets and approve expenditures for supplies, materials, and human resources, ensuring that materials, labor, and equipment are used efficiently to meet production targets. Review processing schedules and production orders to make decisions concerning inventory requirements, staffing requirements, work procedures, and duty assignments, considering budgetary limitations and time constraints.

Review operations and confer with technical or administrative staff to resolve production or processing problems. Hire, train, evaluate, and discharge staff and resolve personnel grievances. Initiate and coordinate inventory and cost control programs. Prepare and maintain production reports and personnel records. Set and monitor product standards, examining samples of raw products or directing testing during processing to ensure finished products are of prescribed quality. Develop and implement production tracking and quality control systems, analyzing production, quality control, maintenance, and other operational reports to detect production problems. Review plans and confer with research and support staff to develop new products and processes. Institute employee suggestion or involvement programs. Coordinate and recommend procedures for facility and equipment maintenance or modification, including the replacement of machines. Maintain current knowledge of the quality control field, relying on current literature pertaining to materials use, technological advances, and statistical studies. Negotiate materials prices with suppliers.

7. Management Analysts

Personality Type:
Enterprising–Investigative–Conventional

Earnings: $68,050
Growth: 20.1%
Annual Openings: 82,000

Most Common Education/Training Level:
Work experience plus degree

Conduct organizational studies and evaluations, design systems and procedures, conduct work simplifications and measurement studies, and prepare operations and procedures manuals to assist management in operating more efficiently and effectively. Includes program

Enterprising

analysts and management consultants. Gather and organize information on problems or procedures. Analyze data gathered and develop solutions or alternative methods of proceeding. Confer with personnel concerned to ensure successful functioning of newly implemented systems or procedures. Develop and implement records management program for filing, protection, and retrieval of records and assure compliance with program. Review forms and reports and confer with management and users about format, distribution, and purpose and to identify problems and improvements. Document findings of study and prepare recommendations for implementation of new systems, procedures, or organizational changes. Interview personnel and conduct on-site observation to ascertain unit functions; work performed; and methods, equipment, and personnel used. Prepare manuals and train workers in use of new forms, reports, procedures, or equipment according to organizational policy. Design, evaluate, recommend, and approve changes of forms and reports. Plan study of work problems and procedures, such as organizational change, communications, information flow, integrated production methods, inventory control, or cost analysis. Recommend purchase of storage equipment and design area layout to locate equipment in space available.

8. Sales Managers

Personality Type:
Enterprising–Conventional–Social

Earnings: $91,560
Growth: 19.7%
Annual Openings: 40,000

Most Common Education/Training Level:
Work experience plus degree

Direct the actual distribution or movement of a product or service to the customer. Coordinate sales distribution by establishing sales territories, quotas, and goals and establish training programs for sales representatives. Analyze sales statistics gathered by staff to determine sales potential and inventory requirements and monitor the preferences of customers. Resolve customer complaints regarding sales and service. Monitor customer preferences to determine focus of sales efforts. Direct and coordinate activities involving sales of manufactured products, services, commodities, real estate, or other subjects of sale. Determine price schedules and discount rates. Review operational records and reports to project sales and determine profitability. Direct, coordinate, and review activities in sales and service accounting and recordkeeping and in receiving and shipping operations. Confer or consult with department heads to plan advertising services and to secure information on equipment and customer specifications. Advise dealers and distributors on policies and operating procedures to ensure functional effectiveness of business. Prepare budgets and approve budget expenditures. Represent company at trade association meetings to promote products. Plan and direct staffing, training, and performance evaluations to develop and control sales and service programs. Visit franchised dealers to stimulate interest in establishment or expansion of leasing programs. Confer with potential customers regarding equipment needs and advise customers on types of equipment to purchase. Oversee regional and local sales managers and their staffs. Direct clerical staff to keep records of export correspondence, bid requests, and credit collections and to maintain current information on tariffs, licenses, and restrictions. Direct foreign sales and service outlets of an organization. Assess marketing potential of new and existing store locations, considering statistics and expenditures.

9. Social and Community Service Managers

Personality Type: Social–Enterprising–Artistic

Earnings: $52,070
Growth: 25.5%
Annual Openings: 17,000

Most Common Education/Training Level: Bachelor's degree

Plan, organize, or coordinate the activities of a social service program or community outreach organization. Oversee the program or organization's budget and policies regarding participant involvement, program requirements, and benefits. Work may involve directing social workers, counselors, or probation officers. Establish and maintain relationships with other agencies and organizations in community to meet community needs and to ensure that services are not duplicated. Prepare and maintain records and reports, such as budgets, personnel records, or training manuals. Direct activities of professional and technical staff members and volunteers. Evaluate the work of staff and volunteers to ensure that programs are of appropriate quality and that resources are used effectively. Establish and oversee administrative procedures to meet objectives set by boards of directors or senior management. Participate in the determination of organizational policies regarding such issues as participant eligibility, program requirements, and program benefits. Research and analyze member or community needs to determine program directions and goals. Speak to community groups to explain and interpret agency purposes, programs, and policies. Recruit, interview, and hire or sign up volunteers and staff. Represent organizations in relations with governmental and media institutions. Plan and administer budgets for programs, equipment, and support services. Analyze proposed legislation, regula-tions, or rule changes to determine how agency services could be impacted. Act as consultants to agency staff and other community programs regarding the interpretation of program-related federal, state, and county regulations and policies. Implement and evaluate staff training programs. Direct fundraising activities and the preparation of public relations materials.

10. Transportation, Storage, and Distribution Managers

Personality Type: Enterprising–Conventional–Realistic

Earnings: $73,080
Growth: 12.7%
Annual Openings: 15,000

Most Common Education/Training Level: Work experience in a related occupation

Job Specializations

Storage and Distribution Managers. Plan, direct, and coordinate the storage and distribution operations within an organization or the activities of organizations that are engaged in storing and distributing materials and products. Supervise the activities of workers engaged in receiving, storing, testing, and shipping products or materials. Plan, develop, and implement warehouse safety and security programs and activities. Review invoices, work orders, consumption reports, and demand forecasts to estimate peak delivery periods and to issue work assignments. Schedule and monitor air or surface pickup, delivery, or distribution of products or materials. Interview, select, and train warehouse and supervisory personnel. Confer with department heads to coordinate warehouse activities, such as production, sales, records control, and purchasing. Respond to customers' or shippers' questions and complaints regarding storage and distribution services. Inspect

Enterprising

physical conditions of warehouses, vehicle fleets, and equipment and order testing, maintenance, repair, or replacement as necessary. Develop and document standard and emergency operating procedures for receiving, handling, storing, shipping, or salvaging products or materials. Examine products or materials to estimate quantities or weight and type of container required for storage or transport. Negotiate with carriers, warehouse operators, and insurance company representatives for services and preferential rates. Issue shipping instructions and provide routing information to ensure that delivery times and locations are coordinated. Examine invoices and shipping manifests for conformity to tariff and customs regulations. Prepare and manage departmental budgets. Prepare or direct preparation of correspondence; reports; and operations, maintenance, and safety manuals. Arrange for necessary shipping documentation and contact customs officials to effect release of shipments. Advise sales and billing departments of transportation charges for customers' accounts. Evaluate freight costs and the inventory costs associated with transit times to ensure that costs are appropriate. Participate in setting transportation and service rates. Track and trace goods while they are en route to their destinations, expediting orders when necessary. Arrange for storage facilities when required.

Transportation Managers. Plan, direct, and coordinate the transportation operations within an organization or the activities of organizations that provide transportation services. Direct activities related to dispatching, routing, and tracking transportation vehicles such as aircraft and railroad cars. Plan, organize, and manage the work of subordinate staff to ensure that the work is accomplished in a manner consistent with organizational requirements. Direct investigations to verify and resolve customer or ship-

per complaints. Serve as contact persons for all workers within assigned territories. Implement schedule and policy changes. Collaborate with other managers and staff members to formulate and implement policies, procedures, goals, and objectives. Monitor operations to ensure that staff members comply with administrative policies and procedures, safety rules, union contracts, and government regulations. Promote safe work activities by conducting safety audits, attending company safety meetings, and meeting with individual staff members. Develop criteria, application instructions, procedural manuals, and contracts for federal and state public transportation programs. Monitor spending to ensure that expenses are consistent with approved budgets. Direct and coordinate, through subordinates, activities of operations department to obtain use of equipment, facilities, and human resources. Direct activities of staff performing repairs and maintenance to equipment, vehicles, and facilities. Conduct investigations in cooperation with government agencies to determine causes of transportation accidents and to improve safety procedures. Analyze expenditures and other financial information to develop plans, policies, and budgets for increasing profits and improving services. Negotiate and authorize contracts with equipment and materials suppliers and monitor contract fulfillment. Supervise workers assigning tariff classifications and preparing billing. Set operations policies and standards, including determination of safety procedures for the handling of dangerous goods. Recommend or authorize capital expenditures for acquisition of new equipment or property to increase efficiency and services of operations department. Prepare management recommendations, such as proposed fee and tariff increases or schedule changes.

Finance

Personality Type: Enterprising–Conventional

Useful Facts About the Major

Prepares individuals to plan, manage, and analyze the financial and monetary aspects and performance of business enterprises, banking institutions, or other organizations.

Related CIP Program: 52.0801 Finance, General

Specializations in the Major: Corporate finance; public finance; securities analysis.

Typical Sequence of College Courses: English composition, business writing, introduction to psychology, principles of microeconomics, principles of macroeconomics, calculus for business and social sciences, statistics for business and social sciences, introduction to management information systems, introduction to accounting, legal environment of business, principles of management and organization, operations management, strategic management, business finance, introduction to marketing, corporate finance, money and capital markets, investment analysis.

Typical Sequence of High School Courses: English, algebra, geometry, trigonometry, science, foreign language, computer science.

Career Snapshot

Finance is the study of how organizations acquire funds and use them in ways that maximize their value. The banking and insurance industries, as well as investment service companies, employ graduates of this field. A bachelor's degree is good preparation for entry-level jobs.

Useful Averages for the Related Jobs

- **Annual Earnings:** $70,359
- **Growth:** 13.7%
- **Self-Employed:** 7.7%
- **Part-Time:** 17.5%
- **Verbal Skill Rating:** 63.6
- **Math Skill Rating:** 60.0

Other Details About the Related Jobs

Total Annual Job Openings: 155,000

Interest Area: 04 Business and Administration; 06 Finance and Insurance

Skills—Management of financial resources; judgment and decision making; management of personnel resources; persuasion; negotiation; monitoring. **Values**—Authority; working conditions; advancement; autonomy; responsibility; ability utilization. **Work Conditions**—Indoors, environmentally controlled; sitting.

Related Jobs

1. Budget Analysts

Personality Type:
Conventional–Enterprising–Realistic

Earnings: $61,430
Growth: 13.5%
Annual Openings: 6,000

Most Common Education/Training Level: Bachelor's degree

Examine budget estimates for completeness, accuracy, and conformance with procedures and regulations. Analyze budgeting and accounting reports for the purpose of maintaining expenditure controls. Direct the

Enterprising

preparation of regular and special budget reports. Consult with managers to ensure that budget adjustments are made in accordance with program changes. Match appropriations for specific programs with appropriations for broader programs, including items for emergency funds. Provide advice and technical assistance with cost analysis, fiscal allocation, and budget preparation. Summarize budgets and submit recommendations for the approval or disapproval of funds requests. Seek new ways to improve efficiency and increase profits. Review operating budgets to analyze trends affecting budget needs. Perform cost-benefit analyses to compare operating programs, review financial requests, or explore alternative financing methods. Interpret budget directives and establish policies for carrying out directives. Compile and analyze accounting records and other data to determine the financial resources required to implement a program. Testify before examining and fund-granting authorities, clarifying and promoting the proposed budgets.

2. Credit Analysts

Personality Type:
Conventional–Enterprising–Investigative

Earnings: $52,350
Growth: 3.6%
Annual Openings: 3,000

Most Common Education/Training Level:
Bachelor's degree

Analyze current credit data and financial statements of individuals or firms to determine the degree of risk involved in extending credit or lending money. Prepare reports with this credit information for use in decision making. Evaluate customer records and recommend payment plans based on earnings, savings data, payment history, and purchase activity. Confer with

credit association and other business representatives to exchange credit information. Complete loan applications, including credit analyses and summaries of loan requests, and submit to loan committees for approval. Generate financial ratios, using computer programs, to evaluate customers' financial status. Review individual or commercial customer files to identify and select delinquent accounts for collection. Compare liquidity, profitability, and credit histories of establishments being evaluated with those of similar establishments in the same industries and geographic locations. Consult with customers to resolve complaints and verify financial and credit transactions. Analyze financial data such as income growth, quality of management, and market share to determine expected profitability of loans.

3. Financial Analysts

Personality Type:
Investigative–Conventional–Enterprising

Earnings: $66,590
Growth: 17.3%
Annual Openings: 28,000

Most Common Education/Training Level:
Bachelor's degree

Conduct quantitative analyses of information affecting investment programs of public or private institutions. Assemble spreadsheets and draw charts and graphs used to illustrate technical reports, using computer. Analyze financial information to produce forecasts of business, industry, and economic conditions for use in making investment decisions. Maintain knowledge and stay abreast of developments in the fields of industrial technology, business, finance, and economic theory. Interpret data affecting investment programs, such as price, yield, stability, future trends in investment risks, and economic influences. Monitor fundamental economic, industrial, and corporate developments through the analysis of information obtained from financial publications and services, investment banking firms, government agencies, trade publications, company sources, and personal interviews. Recommend investments and investment timing to companies, investment firm staff, or the investing public. Determine the prices at which securities should be syndicated and offered to the public. Prepare plans of action for investment based on financial analyses. Evaluate and compare the relative quality of various securities in a given industry. Present oral and written reports on general economic trends, individual corporations, and entire industries. Contact brokers and purchase investments for companies according to company policy. Collaborate with investment bankers to attract new corporate clients to securities firms.

4. Financial Managers

Personality Type:
Enterprising–Conventional–Social

Earnings: $90,970
Growth: 14.8%
Annual Openings: 63,000

Most Common Education/Training Level:
Work experience plus degree

Job Specializations

Financial Managers, Branch or Department. Direct and coordinate financial activities of workers in a branch, office, or department of an establishment, such as branch bank, brokerage firm, risk and insurance department, or credit department. Establish and maintain relationships with individual and business customers and provide assistance with problems these customers may encounter. Examine, evaluate, and process loan applications. Plan, direct, and coordinate the activities of workers in branches, offices, or departments of such establishments as branch banks, brokerage firms, risk and insurance departments, or credit departments. Oversee the flow of cash and financial instruments. Recruit staff members and oversee training programs. Network within communities to find and attract new business. Approve or reject, or coordinate the approval and rejection of, lines of credit and commercial, real estate, and personal loans. Prepare financial and regulatory reports required by laws, regulations, and boards of directors. Establish procedures for custody and control of assets, records, loan collateral, and securities in order to ensure safekeeping. Review collection reports to determine the status of collections and the amounts of outstanding balances. Prepare operational and risk reports for management analysis. Evaluate financial reporting systems, accounting and collection procedures, and investment activities and make recommendations for changes to procedures, operating systems, budgets, and other financial control functions. Plan, direct, and coordinate risk and insurance programs of establishments to control risks and losses. Submit delinquent accounts to attorneys or outside agencies for collection. Communicate with stockholders and other investors to provide information and to raise capital. Evaluate data pertaining to costs in order to plan budgets. Analyze and classify risks and investments to determine their potential impacts on companies. Review reports of securities transactions and price lists in order to analyze market conditions. Develop and analyze information to assess the current and future financial status of firms. Direct insurance negotiations, select insurance brokers and carriers, and place insurance.

Enterprising

Treasurers and Controllers. Direct financial activities, such as planning, procurement, and investments, for all or part of an organization. Prepare and file annual tax returns or prepare financial information so that outside accountants can complete tax returns. Prepare or direct preparation of financial statements, business activity reports, financial position forecasts, annual budgets, and/or reports required by regulatory agencies. Supervise employees performing financial reporting, accounting, billing, collections, payroll, and budgeting duties. Delegate authority for the receipt, disbursement, banking, protection, and custody of funds, securities, and financial instruments. Maintain current knowledge of organizational policies and procedures, federal and state policies and directives, and current accounting standards. Conduct or coordinate audits of company accounts and financial transactions to ensure compliance with state and federal requirements and statutes. Receive and record requests for disbursements; authorize disbursements in accordance with policies and procedures. Monitor financial activities and details such as reserve levels to ensure that all legal and regulatory requirements are met. Monitor and evaluate the performance of accounting and other financial staff; recommend and implement personnel actions such as promotions and dismissals. Develop and maintain relationships with banking, insurance, and non-organizational accounting personnel in order to facilitate financial activities. Coordinate and direct the financial planning, budgeting, procurement, or investment activities of all or part of an organization. Develop internal control policies, guidelines, and procedures for activities such as budget administration, cash and credit management, and accounting. Analyze the financial details of past, present, and expected operations in order to identify development opportunities and areas

where improvement is needed. Advise management on short-term and long-term financial objectives, policies, and actions. Provide direction and assistance to other organizational units regarding accounting and budgeting policies and procedures and efficient control and utilization of financial resources. Evaluate needs for procurement of funds and investment of surpluses and make appropriate recommendations.

5. Loan Officers

Personality Type:
Enterprising–Social–Conventional

Earnings: $51,760
Growth: 8.3%
Annual Openings: 38,000

Most Common Education/Training Level:
Bachelor's degree

Evaluate, authorize, or recommend approval of commercial, real estate, or credit loans. Advise borrowers on financial status and methods of payments. Includes mortgage loan officers and agents, collection analysts, loan servicing officers, and loan underwriters. Meet with applicants to obtain information for loan applications and to answer questions about the process. Approve loans within specified limits and refer loan applications outside those limits to management for approval. Analyze applicants' financial status, credit, and property evaluations to determine feasibility of granting loans. Explain to customers the different types of loans and credit options that are available, as well as the terms of those services. Obtain and compile copies of loan applicants' credit histories, corporate financial statements, and other financial information. Review and update credit and loan files. Review loan agreements to ensure that they are complete and accurate according to policy. Compute payment schedules. Stay abreast of new types of loans and other financial services and products to better meet customers' needs. Submit applications to credit analysts for verification and recommendation. Handle customer complaints and take appropriate action to resolve them. Work with clients to identify their financial goals and to find ways of reaching those goals. Confer with underwriters to aid in resolving mortgage application problems. Negotiate payment arrangements with customers who have delinquent loans. Market bank products to individuals and firms, promoting bank services that may meet customers' needs. Supervise loan personnel. Set credit policies, credit lines, procedures, and standards in conjunction with senior managers. Provide special services such as investment banking for clients with more specialized needs. Analyze potential loan markets and develop referral networks to locate prospects for loans. Prepare reports to send to customers whose accounts are delinquent and forward irreconcilable accounts for collector action. Arrange for maintenance and liquidation of delinquent properties. Interview, hire, and train new employees. Petition courts to transfer titles and deeds of collateral to banks.

6. Personal Financial Advisors

Personality Type:
Social–Enterprising–Conventional

Earnings: $66,120
Growth: 25.9%
Annual Openings: 17,000

Most Common Education/Training Level:
Bachelor's degree

Advise clients on financial plans, utilizing knowledge of tax and investment strategies, securities, insurance, pension plans, and real estate. Duties include assessing clients' assets, liabilities, cash flow, insurance coverage, tax status, and financial objectives to establish investment strategies. Prepare and interpret for clients information such as investment performance reports, financial document summaries, and income projections. Recommend strategies clients can use to achieve their financial goals and objectives, including specific recommendations in such areas as cash management, insurance coverage, and investment planning. Build and maintain client bases, keeping current client plans up to date and recruiting new clients on an ongoing basis. Devise debt liquidation plans that include payoff priorities and timelines. Implement financial planning recommendations or refer clients to someone who can assist them with plan implementation. Interview clients to determine their current income, expenses, insurance coverage, tax status, financial objectives, risk tolerance, and other information needed to develop a financial plan. Monitor financial market trends to ensure that plans are effective and to identify any necessary updates. Explain and document for clients the types of services that are to be provided and the responsibilities to be taken by the personal financial advisor. Explain to individuals and groups the details of financial assistance available to college and university students, such as loans, grants, and scholarships. Guide clients in the gathering of information such as bank account records, income tax returns, life and disability insurance records, pension plan information, and wills. Analyze financial information obtained from clients to determine strategies for meeting clients' financial objectives. Meet with clients' other advisors, including attorneys, accountants, trust officers, and investment bankers, to fully understand clients' financial goals and circumstances. Answer clients' questions about the purposes and details of financial plans and strategies. Open accounts for clients and disburse funds from account to creditors as agents for clients.

Enterprising

Authorize release of financial aid funds to students. Participate in the selection of candidates for specific financial aid awards. Research and investigate available investment opportunities to determine whether they fit into financial plans.

Health Information Systems Administration

Personality Type: Enterprising–Social

Useful Facts About the Major

Prepares individuals to plan, design, and manage systems, processes, and facilities used to collect, store, secure, retrieve, analyze, and transmit medical records and other health information used by clinical professionals and health-care organizations.

Related CIP Program: 51.0706 Health Information/Medical Records Administration/Administrator

Specializations in the Major: Information technology; management.

Typical Sequence of College Courses: English composition, introduction to computer science, college algebra, oral communication, introduction to psychology, accounting, introduction to business management, statistics for business and social sciences, epidemiology, introduction to medical terminology, financial management of health care, human resource management in health-care facilities, legal aspects of health care, American health-care systems, introduction to health records, health data and analysis, clinical classification systems, fundamentals of medical science, health data research, seminar (reporting on research).

Typical Sequence of High School Courses: Algebra, English, geometry, trigonometry, precalculus, biology, chemistry, computer science, office computer applications, public speaking, foreign language, social science.

Career Snapshot

Health information systems are needed for much more than billing patients or their HMOs. Many medical discoveries have been made when researchers have examined large collections of health information. Therefore, health information systems administrators must know about the health-care system, about various kinds of diseases and vital statistics, about the latest database technologies, and about how researchers compile data to test hypotheses. Some people enter this field with a bachelor's degree, whereas others get a bachelor's degree in another field (perhaps related to health, information systems, or management) and complete a post-graduate certification program.

Useful Averages for the Related Job

- **Annual Earnings:** $73,340
- **Growth:** 22.8%
- **Self-Employed:** 5.7%
- **Part-Time:** 11.4%
- **Verbal Skill Rating:** 76.3
- **Math Skill Rating:** 60.7

Other Details About the Related Job

Total Annual Job Openings: 33,000

Interest Area: 08 Health Science

Skills—Management of personnel resources; management of material resources; systems evaluation; management of financial resources; persuasion; service orientation. **Values**—Authority; social service; creativity; working conditions; social status; responsibility. **Work Conditions**—Exposed to disease or infections; exposed to radiation.

Enterprising

Related Job

Medical and Health Services Managers

Personality Type:
Enterprising–Social–Investigative

Earnings: $73,340
Growth: 22.8%
Annual Openings: 33,000

Most Common Education/Training Level:
Work experience plus degree

Plan, direct, or coordinate medicine and health services in hospitals, clinics, managed care organizations, public health agencies, or similar organizations. Direct, supervise, and evaluate work activities of medical, nursing, technical, clerical, service, maintenance, and other personnel. Establish objectives and evaluative or operational criteria for units they manage. Direct or conduct recruitment, hiring, and training of personnel. Develop and maintain computerized record management systems to store and process data such as personnel activities and information and to produce reports. Develop and implement organizational policies and procedures for the facility or medical unit. Conduct and administer fiscal operations, including accounting, planning budgets, authorizing expenditures, establishing rates for services, and coordinating financial reporting. Establish work schedules and assignments for staff according to workload, space, and equipment availability. Maintain communication between governing boards, medical staff, and department heads by attending board meetings and coordinating interdepartmental functioning. Monitor the use of diagnostic services, inpatient beds, facilities, and staff to ensure effective use of resources and assess the need for additional staff, equipment, and services. Maintain awareness of advances in medicine, computerized diagnostic and treatment equipment, data-processing technology, government regulations, health insurance changes, and financing options. Manage change in integrated health-care delivery systems, such as work restructuring, technological innovations, and shifts in the focus of care. Prepare activity reports to inform management of the status and implementation plans of programs, services, and quality initiatives. Plan, implement, and administer programs and services in a health-care or medical facility, including personnel administration, training, and coordination of medical, nursing, and physical plant staff. Consult with medical, business, and community groups to discuss service problems, respond to community needs, enhance public relations, coordinate activities and plans, and promote health programs. Inspect facilities and recommend building or equipment modifications to ensure emergency readiness and compliance to access, safety, and sanitation regulations.

Hospital/Health Facilities Administration

Personality Type: Enterprising–Social

Useful Facts About the Major

Prepares individuals to apply managerial principles to the administration of hospitals, clinics, nursing homes, and other health-care facilities.

Related CIP Program: 51.0702 Hospital and Health Care Facilities Administration/Management

Specializations in the Major: Health policy; hospital management; long-term care management.

Typical Sequence of College Courses: English composition, introduction to economics, college algebra, oral communication, introduction to psychology, accounting, introduction to business management, statistics for business and social sciences, American health-care systems, introduction to medical terminology, introduction to management information systems, financial management of health care, human resource management in health-care facilities, strategy and planning for health care, legal aspects of health care, health care and politics.

Typical Sequence of High School Courses: Algebra, English, geometry, trigonometry, precalculus, biology, chemistry, computer science, office computer applications, public speaking, social science, foreign language.

Career Snapshot

Hospital and health facilities administrators need to combine standard business management skills with an understanding of the American health-care system and its current issues and trends. They may be generalists who manage an entire facility, or they may specialize in running a department or some specific service of the facility. Generalists are usually expected to have a master's degree, especially in large facilities, whereas specialists or those seeking employment in small facilities may enter with a bachelor's degree. Best employment prospects are in home health agencies and practitioners' offices and clinics and for those who have experience in a specialized field, such as reimbursement.

Useful Averages for the Related Job

- **Annual Earnings:** $73,340
- **Growth:** 22.8%
- **Self-Employed:** 5.7%
- **Part-Time:** 11.4%
- **Verbal Skill Rating:** 76.3
- **Math Skill Rating:** 60.7

Other Details About the Related Job

Total Annual Job Openings: 33,000

Interest Area: 08 Health Science

Skills—Management of personnel resources; management of material resources; systems evaluation; management of financial resources; persuasion; service orientation. **Values**—Authority; social service; creativity; working conditions; social status; responsibility. **Work Conditions**—Exposed to disease or infections; exposed to radiation.

Enterprising

Related Job

Medical and Health Services Managers

Personality Type:
Enterprising–Social–Investigative

Earnings: $73,340
Growth: 22.8%
Annual Openings: 33,000

Most Common Education/Training Level:
Work experience plus degree

Plan, direct, or coordinate medicine and health services in hospitals, clinics, managed care organizations, public health agencies, or similar organizations. Direct, supervise, and evaluate work activities of medical, nursing, technical, clerical, service, maintenance, and other personnel. Establish objectives and evaluative or operational criteria for units they manage. Direct or conduct recruitment, hiring, and training of personnel. Develop and maintain computerized record management systems to store and process data such as personnel activities and information and to produce reports. Develop and implement organizational policies and procedures for the facility or medical unit. Conduct and administer fiscal operations, including accounting, planning budgets, authorizing expenditures, establishing rates for services, and coordinating financial reporting. Establish work schedules and assignments for staff according to workload, space, and equipment availability. Maintain communication between governing boards, medical staff, and department heads by attending board meetings and coordinating interdepartmental functioning. Monitor the use of diagnostic services, inpatient beds, facilities, and staff to ensure effective use of resources and assess the need for additional staff, equipment, and services. Maintain awareness of advances in medicine, computerized diagnostic and treatment equipment, data-processing technology, government regulations, health insurance changes, and financing options. Manage change in integrated health-care delivery systems, such as work restructuring, technological innovations, and shifts in the focus of care. Prepare activity reports to inform management of the status and implementation plans of programs, services, and quality initiatives. Plan, implement, and administer programs and services in a health-care or medical facility, including personnel administration, training, and coordination of medical, nursing, and physical plant staff. Consult with medical, business, and community groups to discuss service problems, respond to community needs, enhance public relations, coordinate activities and plans, and promote health programs. Inspect facilities and recommend building or equipment modifications to ensure emergency readiness and compliance to access, safety, and sanitation regulations.

Human Resources Management

Personality Type:
Enterprising–Social–Conventional

Useful Facts About the Major

Prepares individuals to manage the development of human capital in organizations and to provide related services to individuals and groups.

Related CIP Program: 52.1001 Human Resources Management/Personnel Administration, General

Specializations in the Major: Compensation/benefits; job analysis; labor relations; training.

Typical Sequence of College Courses: English composition, business writing, introduction to psychology, principles of microeconomics, principles of macroeconomics, calculus for business and social sciences, statistics for business and social sciences, introduction to management information systems, introduction to accounting, legal environment of business, principles of management and organization, operations management, strategic management, business finance, introduction to marketing, organizational theory, human resource management, compensation and benefits administration, training and development, employment law, industrial relations and labor management.

Typical Sequence of High School Courses: English, algebra, geometry, trigonometry, science, foreign language, computer science, public speaking.

Career Snapshot

Human resource managers are responsible for attracting the right employees for an organization, training them, keeping them productively employed, and sometimes severing the relationship through outplacement or retirement. Generalists often enter the field with a bachelor's degree, although specialists may find a master's degree (or perhaps a law degree) advantageous. Generalists most often find entry-level work with small organizations. There is a trend toward outsourcing many specialized functions, such as training and outplacement, to specialized service firms. Specializations that look particularly promising are training, recruiting, and compensation management.

Useful Averages for the Related Jobs

- **Annual Earnings:** $50,296
- **Growth:** 24.2%
- **Self-Employed:** 2.4%
- **Part-Time:** 22.6%
- **Verbal Skill Rating:** 67.6
- **Math Skill Rating:** 49.0

Other Details About the Related Jobs

Total Annual Job Openings: 84,000

Interest Area: 04 Business and Administration

Skills—Management of personnel resources; persuasion; service orientation; writing; social perceptiveness; negotiation. **Values**—Social service; working conditions; authority; co-workers; responsibility; autonomy. **Work Conditions**—Indoors, environmentally controlled; sitting.

Enterprising

Related Jobs

1. Compensation and Benefits Managers

Personality Type:
Enterprising–Social–Conventional

Earnings: $74,750
Growth: 21.5%
Annual Openings: 4,000

Most Common Education/Training Level:
Work experience plus degree

Plan, direct, or coordinate compensation and benefits activities and staff of an organization. Advise management on such matters as equal employment opportunity, sexual harassment, and discrimination. Direct preparation and distribution of written and verbal information to inform employees of benefits, compensation, and personnel policies. Administer, direct, and review employee benefit programs, including the integration of benefit programs following mergers and acquisitions. Plan and conduct new employee orientations to foster positive attitude toward organizational objectives. Plan, direct, supervise, and coordinate work activities of subordinates and staff relating to employment, compensation, labor relations, and employee relations. Identify and implement benefits to increase the quality of life for employees by working with brokers and researching benefits issues. Design, evaluate, and modify benefits policies to ensure that programs are current, competitive, and in compliance with legal requirements. Analyze compensation policies, government regulations, and prevailing wage rates to develop competitive compensation plan. Formulate policies, procedures, and programs for recruitment, testing, placement, classification, orientation, benefits and compensation, and labor and industrial relations. Mediate between benefits providers and employees, such as by assisting in handling employees' benefits-related questions or taking suggestions. Fulfill all reporting requirements of all relevant government rules and regulations, including the Employee Retirement Income Security Act (ERISA). Maintain records and compile statistical reports concerning personnel-related data such as hires, transfers, performance appraisals, and absenteeism rates. Analyze statistical data and reports to identify and determine causes of personnel problems and develop recommendations for improvement of organization's personnel policies and practices. Develop methods to improve employment policies, processes, and practices and recommend changes to management. Negotiate bargaining agreements. Investigate and report on industrial accidents for insurance carriers. Represent organization at personnel-related hearings and investigations.

2. Compensation, Benefits, and Job Analysis Specialists

Personality Type:
Investigative–Conventional–Enterprising

Earnings: $50,230
Growth: 20.4%
Annual Openings: 15,000

Most Common Education/Training Level:
Bachelor's degree

Conduct programs of compensation and benefits and job analysis for employer. May specialize in specific areas, such as position classification and pension programs. Evaluate job positions, determining classification, exempt or non-exempt status, and salary. Ensure company compliance with federal and state laws, including reporting requirements. Advise managers and employees on state and federal employment regulations, collective agreements, benefit and compensation policies, personnel procedures, and classification programs. Plan, develop, evaluate, improve, and communicate methods and techniques for selecting, promoting, compensating, evaluating, and training workers. Provide advice on the resolution of classification and salary complaints. Prepare occupational classifications, job descriptions, and salary scales. Assist in preparing and maintaining personnel records and handbooks. Prepare reports such as organization and flow charts and career path reports to summarize job analysis and evaluation and compensation analysis information. Administer employee insurance, pension, and savings plans, working with insurance brokers and plan carriers. Negotiate collective agreements on behalf of employers or workers and mediate labor disputes and grievances. Develop, implement, administer, and evaluate personnel and labor relations programs, including performance appraisal, affirmative action, and employment equity programs. Perform multifactor data and cost analyses that may be used in areas such as support of collective bargaining agreements. Research employee benefit and health and safety practices and recommend changes or modifications to existing policies. Analyze organizational, occupational, and industrial data to facilitate organizational functions and provide technical information to business, industry, and government. Advise staff of individuals' qualifications. Assess need for and develop job analysis instruments and materials. Review occupational data on Alien Employment Certification Applications to determine the appropriate occupational title and code; provide local offices with information about immigration and occupations. Research job and worker requirements, structural and functional relationships among jobs and occupations, and occupational trends.

3. Employment, Recruitment, and Placement Specialists

Personality Type:
Social–Enterprising–Conventional

Earnings: $42,420
Growth: 30.5%
Annual Openings: 30,000

Most Common Education/Training Level:
Bachelor's degree

Job Specializations

Employment Interviewers. Interview job applicants in employment office and refer them to prospective employers for consideration. Search application files, notify selected applicants of job openings, and refer qualified applicants to prospective employers. Contact employers to verify referral results. Record and evaluate various pertinent data. Inform applicants of job openings and details such as duties and responsibilities, compensation, benefits, schedules, working conditions, and promotion opportunities. Interview job applicants to match their qualifications with employers' needs, recording and evaluating applicant experience, education, training, and skills. Review employment applications and job orders to match applicants with job requirements, using manual or computerized file searches. Select qualified applicants or refer them to employers according to organization policy. Perform reference and background checks on applicants. Maintain records of applicants not selected for employment. Instruct job applicants in presenting a positive image by providing help with resume writing, personal appearance, and interview techniques. Refer applicants to services such as vocational counseling, literacy or language instruction, transportation assistance, vocational training, and child care. Contact employers to

Enterprising

solicit orders for job vacancies, determining their requirements and recording relevant data such as job descriptions. Conduct workshops and demonstrate the use of job listings to assist applicants with skill building. Search for and recruit applicants for open positions through campus job fairs and advertisements. Provide background information on organizations with which interviews are scheduled. Administer assessment tests to identify skill-building needs. Conduct or arrange for skill, intelligence, or psychological testing of applicants and current employees. Hire workers and place them with employers needing temporary help. Evaluate selection and testing techniques by conducting research or follow-up activities and conferring with management and supervisory personnel.

Personnel Recruiters. Seek out, interview, and screen applicants to fill existing and future job openings and promote career opportunities within an organization. Establish and maintain relationships with hiring managers to stay abreast of current and future hiring and business needs. Interview applicants to obtain information on work history, training, education, and job skills. Maintain current knowledge of Equal Employment Opportunity (EEO) and affirmative action guidelines and laws, such as the Americans with Disabilities Act (ADA). Perform searches for qualified candidates according to relevant job criteria, using computer databases, networking, Internet recruiting resources, cold calls, media, recruiting firms, and employee referrals. Prepare and maintain employment records. Contact applicants to inform them of employment possibilities, consideration, and selection. Inform potential applicants about facilities, operations, benefits, and job or career opportunities in organizations. Screen and refer applicants to hiring personnel in the organization, making hiring recommendations when

appropriate. Arrange for interviews and provide travel arrangements as necessary. Advise managers and employees on staffing policies and procedures. Review and evaluate applicant qualifications or eligibility for specified licensing according to established guidelines and designated licensing codes. Hire applicants and authorize paperwork assigning them to positions. Conduct reference and background checks on applicants. Evaluate recruitment and selection criteria to ensure conformance to professional, statistical, and testing standards, recommending revision as needed. Recruit applicants for open positions, arranging job fairs with college campus representatives. Advise management on organizing, preparing, and implementing recruiting and retention programs. Supervise personnel clerks performing filing, typing, and recordkeeping duties. Project yearly recruitment expenditures for budgetary consideration and control. Serve on selection and examination boards to evaluate applicants according to test scores, contacting promising candidates for interviews. Address civic and social groups and attend conferences to disseminate information concerning possible job openings and career opportunities.

4. Training and Development Managers

Personality Type:
Enterprising–Social–Conventional

Earnings: $80,250
Growth: 25.9%
Annual Openings: 3,000

Most Common Education/Training Level:
Work experience plus degree

Plan, direct, or coordinate the training and development activities and staff of an organization. Conduct orientation sessions and arrange on-the-job training for new hires. Evaluate instructor performance and the effectiveness of training programs, providing recommendations for improvement. Develop testing and evaluation procedures. Conduct or arrange for ongoing technical training and personal development classes for staff members. Confer with management and conduct surveys to identify training needs based on projected production processes, changes, and other factors. Develop and organize training manuals, multimedia visual aids, and other educational materials. Plan, develop, and provide training and staff development programs, using knowledge of the effectiveness of methods such as classroom training, demonstrations, on-the-job training, meetings, conferences, and workshops. Analyze training needs to develop new training programs or modify and improve existing programs. Review and evaluate training and apprenticeship programs for compliance with government standards. Train instructors and supervisors in techniques and skills for training and dealing with employees. Coordinate established courses with technical and professional courses provided by community schools and designate training procedures. Prepare training budget for department or organization.

5. Training and Development Specialists

Personality Type:
Social–Enterprising–Conventional

Earnings: $47,830
Growth: 20.8%
Annual Openings: 32,000

Most Common Education/Training Level:
Bachelor's degree

Conduct training and development programs for employees. Keep up with developments in area of expertise by reading current journals, books, and magazine articles. Present information, using a variety of instructional techniques and formats such as role playing, simulations, team exercises, group discussions, videos, and lectures. Schedule classes based on availability of classrooms, equipment, and instructors. Organize and develop, or obtain, training procedure manuals and guides and course materials such as handouts and visual materials. Offer specific training programs to help workers maintain or improve job skills. Monitor, evaluate, and record training activities and program effectiveness. Attend meetings and seminars to obtain information for use in training programs or to inform management of training program status. Coordinate recruitment and placement of training program participants. Evaluate training materials prepared by instructors, such as outlines, text, and handouts. Develop alternative training methods if expected improvements are not seen. Assess training needs through surveys; interviews with employees; focus groups; or consultation with managers, instructors, or customer representatives. Screen, hire, and assign workers to positions based on qualifications. Select and assign instructors to conduct training. Devise programs to develop executive potential among employees in lower-level positions. Design, plan, organize, and direct orientation and training for employees or customers of industrial or commercial establishment. Negotiate contracts with clients, including desired training outcomes, fees, and expenses. Supervise instructors, evaluate instructor performance, and refer instructors to classes for skill development. Monitor training costs to ensure budget is not exceeded and prepare budget reports to justify expenditures. Refer trainees to employer relations representatives, to locations offering job placement assistance, or to appropriate social services agencies if warranted.

Enterprising

Industrial and Labor Relations

Personality Type:
Enterprising–Social–Conventional

Useful Facts About the Major

Focuses on employee-management interactions and the management of issues and disputes regarding working conditions and worker benefit packages; may prepare individuals to function as labor or personnel relations specialists.

Related CIP Program: 52.1002 Labor and Industrial Relations

Specializations in the Major: Arbitration; labor law; mediation; worker compensation; worker safety.

Typical Sequence of College Courses: English composition, business writing, introduction to psychology, principles of microeconomics, principles of macroeconomics, calculus for business and social sciences, statistics for business and social sciences, introduction to management information systems, introduction to accounting, legal environment of business, business finance, introduction to marketing, organizational behavior, human resource management, industrial relations and labor management, employment law, training and development, systems of conflict resolution.

Typical Sequence of High School Courses: English, algebra, geometry, trigonometry, foreign language, computer science, public speaking, social science.

Career Snapshot

Although labor unions are not as widespread as they once were, they still play an important role in American business. The "just in time" strategy that is popular in the manufacturing and transportation industries means that a strike lasting only a few hours can seriously disrupt business. Employers are eager to settle labor disputes before they start, and this creates job opportunities for labor-relations specialists working for either the employer or the union. Other job openings are found in government agencies that deal with labor. Many of these specialists hold bachelor's degrees, but a master's degree or law degree can be helpful for jobs involving contract negotiations and mediation.

Useful Averages for the Related Jobs

- **Annual Earnings:** $49,299
- **Growth:** 26.1%
- **Self-Employed:** 2.3%
- **Part-Time:** 22.4%
- **Verbal Skill Rating:** 66.0
- **Math Skill Rating:** 46.6

Other Details About the Related Jobs

Total Annual Job Openings: 49,000

Interest Area: 04 Business and Administration

Skills—Management of personnel resources; persuasion; negotiation; service orientation; management of financial resources; social perceptiveness. **Values**—Working conditions; social service; supervision, human relations; responsibility; advancement; co-workers. **Work Conditions**—Indoors, environmentally controlled; sitting.

Related Jobs

1. Compensation and Benefits Managers

Personality Type:
Enterprising–Social–Conventional

Earnings: $74,750
Growth: 21.5%
Annual Openings: 4,000

Most Common Education/Training Level:
Work experience plus degree

Plan, direct, or coordinate compensation and benefits activities and staff of an organization. Advise management on such matters as equal employment opportunity, sexual harassment, and discrimination. Direct preparation and distribution of written and verbal information to inform employees of benefits, compensation, and personnel policies. Administer, direct, and review employee benefit programs, including the integration of benefit programs following mergers and acquisitions. Plan and conduct new employee orientations to foster positive attitude toward organizational objectives. Plan, direct, supervise, and coordinate work activities of subordinates and staff relating to employment, compensation, labor relations, and employee relations. Identify and implement benefits to increase the quality of life for employees by working with brokers and researching benefits issues. Design, evaluate, and modify benefits policies to ensure that programs are current, competitive, and in compliance with legal requirements. Analyze compensation policies, government regulations, and prevailing wage rates to develop competitive compensation plan. Formulate policies, procedures, and programs for recruitment, testing, placement, classification, orientation, benefits and compensation, and labor and industrial relations. Mediate

between benefits providers and employees, such as by assisting in handling employees' benefits-related questions or taking suggestions. Fulfill all reporting requirements of all relevant government rules and regulations, including the Employee Retirement Income Security Act (ERISA). Maintain records and compile statistical reports concerning personnel-related data such as hires, transfers, performance appraisals, and absenteeism rates. Analyze statistical data and reports to identify and determine causes of personnel problems and develop recommendations for improvement of organization's personnel policies and practices. Develop methods to improve employment policies, processes, and practices and recommend changes to management. Negotiate bargaining agreements. Investigate and report on industrial accidents for insurance carriers. Represent organization at personnel-related hearings and investigations.

2. Compensation, Benefits, and Job Analysis Specialists

Personality Type:
Investigative–Conventional–Enterprising

Earnings: $50,230
Growth: 20.4%
Annual Openings: 15,000

Most Common Education/Training Level:
Bachelor's degree

Conduct programs of compensation and benefits and job analysis for employer. May specialize in specific areas, such as position classification and pension programs. Evaluate job positions, determining classification, exempt or non-exempt status, and salary. Ensure company compliance with federal and state laws, including reporting requirements. Advise managers and employees on state and federal employment regulations, collective agreements,

Enterprising

benefit and compensation policies, personnel procedures, and classification programs. Plan, develop, evaluate, improve, and communicate methods and techniques for selecting, promoting, compensating, evaluating, and training workers. Provide advice on the resolution of classification and salary complaints. Prepare occupational classifications, job descriptions, and salary scales. Assist in preparing and maintaining personnel records and handbooks. Prepare reports such as organization and flow charts and career path reports to summarize job analysis and evaluation and compensation analysis information. Administer employee insurance, pension, and savings plans, working with insurance brokers and plan carriers. Negotiate collective agreements on behalf of employers or workers and mediate labor disputes and grievances. Develop, implement, administer, and evaluate personnel and labor relations programs, including performance appraisal, affirmative action, and employment equity programs. Perform multifactor data and cost analyses that may be used in areas such as support of collective bargaining agreements. Research employee benefit and health and safety practices and recommend changes or modifications to existing policies. Analyze organizational, occupational, and industrial data to facilitate organizational functions and provide technical information to business, industry, and government. Advise staff of individuals' qualifications. Assess need for and develop job analysis instruments and materials. Review occupational data on Alien Employment Certification Applications to determine the appropriate occupational title and code; provide local offices with information about immigration and occupations. Research job and worker requirements, structural and functional relationships among jobs and occupations, and occupational trends.

3. Employment, Recruitment, and Placement Specialists

Personality Type:
Social–Enterprising–Conventional

Earnings: $42,420
Growth: 30.5%
Annual Openings: 30,000

Most Common Education/Training Level:
Bachelor's degree

Job Specializations

Employment Interviewers. Interview job applicants in employment office and refer them to prospective employers for consideration. Search application files, notify selected applicants of job openings, and refer qualified applicants to prospective employers. Contact employers to verify referral results. Record and evaluate various pertinent data. Inform applicants of job openings and details such as duties and responsibilities, compensation, benefits, schedules, working conditions, and promotion opportunities. Interview job applicants to match their qualifications with employers' needs, recording and evaluating applicant experience, education, training, and skills. Review employment applications and job orders to match applicants with job requirements, using manual or computerized file searches. Select qualified applicants or refer them to employers according to organization policy. Perform reference and background checks on applicants. Maintain records of applicants not selected for employment. Instruct job applicants in presenting a positive image by providing help with resume writing, personal appearance, and interview techniques. Refer applicants to services such as vocational counseling, literacy or language instruction, transportation assistance, vocational training, and child care. Contact employers to solicit orders for job vacancies, determining their requirements and recording relevant data such as job descriptions. Conduct workshops and demonstrate the use of job listings to assist applicants with skill building. Search for and recruit applicants for open positions through campus job fairs and advertisements. Provide background information on organizations with which interviews are scheduled. Administer assessment tests to identify skill-building needs. Conduct or arrange for skill, intelligence, or psychological testing of applicants and current employees. Hire workers and place them with employers needing temporary help. Evaluate selection and testing techniques by conducting research or follow-up activities and conferring with management and supervisory personnel.

Personnel Recruiters. Seek out, interview, and screen applicants to fill existing and future job openings and promote career opportunities within an organization. Establish and maintain relationships with hiring managers to stay abreast of current and future hiring and business needs. Interview applicants to obtain information on work history, training, education, and job skills. Maintain current knowledge of Equal Employment Opportunity (EEO) and affirmative action guidelines and laws, such as the Americans with Disabilities Act (ADA). Perform searches for qualified candidates according to relevant job criteria, using computer databases, networking, Internet recruiting resources, cold calls, media, recruiting firms, and employee referrals. Prepare and maintain employment records. Contact applicants to inform them of employment possibilities, consideration, and selection. Inform potential applicants about facilities, operations, benefits, and job or career opportunities in organizations. Screen and refer applicants to hiring personnel in the organization, making hiring recommendations when appropriate. Arrange for interviews and provide travel arrangements as necessary. Advise managers and employees on staffing policies and procedures. Review and evaluate applicant qualifications or eligibility for specified licensing according to established guidelines and designated licensing codes. Hire applicants and authorize paperwork assigning them to positions. Conduct reference and background checks on applicants. Evaluate recruitment and selection criteria to ensure conformance to professional, statistical, and testing standards, recommending revision as needed. Recruit applicants for open positions, arranging job fairs with college campus representatives. Advise management on organizing, preparing, and implementing recruiting and retention programs. Supervise personnel clerks performing filing, typing, and recordkeeping duties. Project yearly recruitment expenditures for budgetary consideration and control. Serve on selection and examination boards to evaluate applicants according to test scores, contacting promising candidates for interviews. Address civic and social groups and attend conferences to disseminate information concerning possible job openings and career opportunities.

Enterprising

Industrial Engineering

Personality Type:
Enterprising–Investigative–Realistic

Useful Facts About the Major

Focuses on the development and application of complex mathematical or simulation models to solve problems involving operational systems where the system concerned is subject to human intervention.

Related CIP Program: 14.3701 Operations Research

Specializations in the Major: Operations research; quality control.

Typical Sequence of College Courses: English composition, technical writing, calculus, differential equations, general chemistry, introduction to computer science, general physics, statics, dynamics, numerical analysis, thermodynamics, materials engineering, engineering economics, human factors and ergonomics, engineering systems design, operations research, quality control, facilities design, simulation, analysis of industrial activities, senior design project.

Typical Sequence of High School Courses: English, algebra, geometry, trigonometry, pre-calculus, calculus, chemistry, physics, computer science.

Career Snapshot

Industrial engineers plan how an organization can most efficiently use staff, equipment, buildings, raw materials, information, and energy to output a product or service. They occupy the middle ground between management and the technology experts—for example, the mechanical or chemical engineers. Sometimes they make a career move into management positions. A bachelor's degree is good preparation for this field. The job outlook for industrial engineers is expected to be good, especially in nonmanufacturing industries, as U.S. employers attempt to boost productivity to compete in a global workplace.

Useful Averages for the Related Jobs

- **Annual Earnings:** $86,333
- **Growth:** 14.6%
- **Self-Employed:** 0.5%
- **Part-Time:** 8.4%
- **Verbal Skill Rating:** 68.9
- **Math Skill Rating:** 71.2

Other Details About the Related Jobs

Total Annual Job Openings: 28,000

Interest Area: 15 Scientific Research, Engineering, and Mathematics

Skills—Technology design; science; installation; mathematics; management of financial resources; operations analysis. **Values**—Authority; creativity; autonomy; ability utilization; social status; responsibility. **Work Conditions**—Common protective or safety equipment; hazardous equipment.

Related Jobs

1. Engineering Managers

Personality Type:
Enterprising–Investigative–Realistic

Earnings: $105,430
Growth: 13.0%
Annual Openings: 15,000

Most Common Education/Training Level:
Work experience plus degree

Plan, direct, or coordinate activities in such fields as architecture and engineering or research and development in these fields. Confer with management, production, and marketing staff to discuss project specifications and procedures. Coordinate and direct projects, making detailed plans to accomplish goals and directing the integration of technical activities. Analyze technology, resource needs, and market demand to plan and assess the feasibility of projects. Plan and direct the installation, testing, operation, maintenance, and repair of facilities and equipment. Direct, review, and approve product design and changes. Recruit employees; assign, direct, and evaluate their work; and oversee the development and maintenance of staff competence. Prepare budgets, bids, and contracts and direct the negotiation of research contracts. Develop and implement policies, standards, and procedures for the engineering and technical work performed in the department, service, laboratory, or firm. Review and recommend or approve contracts and cost estimates. Perform administrative functions such as reviewing and writing reports, approving expenditures, enforcing rules, and making decisions about the purchase of materials or services. Present and explain proposals, reports, and findings to clients. Consult or negotiate with clients to prepare project specifications. Set scientific and technical goals within broad outlines provided by top management. Administer highway planning, construction, and maintenance. Direct the engineering of water control, treatment, and distribution projects. Plan, direct, and coordinate survey work with other staff activities, certifying survey work and writing land legal descriptions. Confer with and report to officials and the public to provide information and solicit support for projects.

2. Industrial Engineers

Personality Type:
Enterprising–Investigative–Realistic

Earnings: $68,620
Growth: 16.0%
Annual Openings: 13,000

Most Common Education/Training Level:
Bachelor's degree

Design, develop, test, and evaluate integrated systems for managing industrial production processes, including human work factors, quality control, inventory control, logistics and material flow, cost analysis, and production coordination. Analyze statistical data and product specifications to determine standards and establish quality and reliability objectives of finished product. Develop manufacturing methods, labor utilization standards, and cost analysis systems to promote efficient staff and facility utilization. Recommend methods for improving utilization of personnel, material, and utilities. Plan and establish sequence of operations to fabricate and assemble parts or products and to promote efficient utilization. Apply statistical methods and perform mathematical calculations to determine manufacturing processes, staff requirements, and production standards. Coordinate quality control objectives and activities to resolve production problems, maximize product reliability, and minimize cost. Confer with vendors, staff, and management personnel regarding purchases, procedures, product specifications, manufacturing capabilities, and project status. Draft and design layout of equipment, materials, and workspace to illustrate maximum efficiency, using drafting tools and computer. Review production schedules, engineering specifications, orders, and related information to obtain knowledge of manufacturing methods, procedures, and activities.

Communicate with management and user personnel to develop production and design standards. Estimate production cost and effect of product design changes for management review, action, and control. Formulate sampling procedures and designs and develop forms and instructions for recording, evaluating, and reporting quality and reliability data. Record or oversee recording of information to ensure currency of engineering drawings and documentation of production problems. Study operations sequence, material flow, functional statements, organization charts, and project information to determine worker functions and responsibilities. Direct workers engaged in product measurement, inspection, and testing activities to ensure quality control and reliability. Implement methods and procedures for disposition of discrepant material and defective or damaged parts and assess cost and responsibility.

International Business

Personality Type: Enterprising–Conventional

Useful Facts About the Major

Prepares individuals to manage international businesses and/or business operations.

Related CIP Program: 52.1101 International Business/Trade/Commerce

Specializations in the Major: A particular aspect of business; a particular part of the world.

Typical Sequence of College Courses: English composition, business writing, introduction to psychology, foreign language, principles of microeconomics, principles of macroeconomics, calculus for business and social sciences, statistics for business and social sciences, introduction to management information systems, introduction to accounting, international management, legal environment of business, principles of management and organization, operations management, international economics, business finance, introduction to marketing, organizational behavior, human resource management, international finance.

Typical Sequence of High School Courses: English, algebra, geometry, trigonometry, science, foreign language, geography, computer science, public speaking.

Career Snapshot

The global economy demands businesspeople who are knowledgeable about other cultures. This major prepares you to work in businesses here and abroad and in the government agencies that deal with them. In addition to studying standard business subjects, you'll probably study or intern abroad to become proficient in a foreign language and gain a global perspective. The work usually requires a lot of travel and a sensitivity to cultural differences.

Useful Averages for the Related Jobs

- **Annual Earnings:** $94,442
- **Growth:** 16.7%
- **Self-Employed:** 3.7%
- **Part-Time:** 6.3%
- **Verbal Skill Rating:** 68.0
- **Math Skill Rating:** 60.1

Other Details About the Related Jobs

Total Annual Job Openings: 246,000

Interest Area: 04 Business and Administration

Skills—Management of financial resources; management of personnel resources; management of material resources; negotiation; monitoring; persuasion. **Values**—Authority; social status; working conditions; creativity; autonomy; responsibility. **Work Conditions**—Indoors, environmentally controlled.

Related Jobs

1. Chief Executives

Personality Type:
Enterprising–Conventional–Social

Earnings: More than $145,600
Growth: 14.9%
Annual Openings: 38,000

Most Common Education/Training Level: Work experience plus degree

Determine and formulate policies and provide the overall direction of companies or

Enterprising

private- and public-sector organizations within the guidelines set up by a board of directors or similar governing body. **Plan, direct, or coordinate operational activities at the highest level of management with the help of subordinate executives and staff managers.** Direct and coordinate an organization's financial and budget activities in order to fund operations, maximize investments, and increase efficiency. Confer with board members, organization officials, and staff members to discuss issues, coordinate activities, and resolve problems. Analyze operations to evaluate performance of a company and its staff in meeting objectives and to determine areas of potential cost reduction, program improvement, or policy change. Direct, plan, and implement policies, objectives, and activities of organizations or businesses in order to ensure continuing operations, to maximize returns on investments, and to increase productivity. Prepare budgets for approval, including those for funding and implementation of programs. Direct and coordinate activities of businesses or departments concerned with production, pricing, sales, and/or distribution of products. Negotiate or approve contracts and agreements with suppliers, distributors, federal and state agencies, and other organizational entities. Review reports submitted by staff members in order to recommend approval or to suggest changes. Appoint department heads or managers and assign or delegate responsibilities to them. Direct human resources activities, including the approval of human resource plans and activities, the selection of directors and other high-level staff, and establishment and organization of major departments. Preside over or serve on boards of directors, management committees, or other governing boards. Prepare and present reports concerning activities, expenses, budgets, government statutes and rulings, and other items affecting businesses or program services.

Establish departmental responsibilities and coordinate functions among departments and sites. Implement corrective action plans to solve organizational or departmental problems. Coordinate the development and implementation of budgetary control systems, recordkeeping systems, and other administrative control processes. Direct non-merchandising departments such as advertising, purchasing, credit, and accounting. Deliver speeches, write articles, and present information at meetings or conventions in order to promote services, exchange ideas, and accomplish objectives.

2. General and Operations Managers

Personality Type: No data available

Earnings: $85,230
Growth: 17.0%
Annual Openings: 208,000

Most Common Education/Training Level: Work experience plus degree

Plan, direct, or coordinate the operations of companies or public- and private-sector organizations. Duties and responsibilities include formulating policies, managing daily operations, and planning the use of materials and human resources, but are too diverse and general in nature to be classified in any one functional area of management or administration, such as personnel, purchasing, or administrative services. Includes owners and managers who head small business establishments whose duties are primarily managerial. Direct and coordinate activities of businesses or departments concerned with the production, pricing, sales, or distribution of products. Manage staff, preparing work schedules and assigning specific duties. Review financial statements, sales and activity reports, and other performance data to measure productivity and goal achievement and to determine areas needing cost reduction and program improvement. Establish and implement departmental policies, goals, objectives, and procedures, conferring with board members, organization officials, and staff members as necessary. Determine staffing requirements and interview, hire, and train new employees or oversee those personnel processes. Monitor businesses and agencies to ensure that they efficiently and effectively provide needed services while staying within budgetary limits. Oversee activities directly related to making products or providing services. Direct and coordinate organization's financial and budget activities to fund operations, maximize investments, and increase efficiency. Determine goods and services to be sold and set prices and credit terms based on forecasts of customer demand. Manage the movement of goods into and out of production facilities. Locate, select, and procure merchandise for resale, representing management in purchase negotiations. Perform sales floor work such as greeting and assisting customers, stocking shelves, and taking inventory. Develop and implement product marketing strategies, including advertising campaigns and sales promotions. Plan and direct activities such as sales promotions, coordinating with other department heads as required. Direct non-merchandising departments of businesses, such as advertising and purchasing. Recommend locations for new facilities or oversee the remodeling of current facilities. Plan store layouts and design displays.

Enterprising

International Relations

Personality Type: Enterprising–Conventional

Useful Facts About the Major

Focuses on the systematic study of international politics and institutions and the conduct of diplomacy and foreign policy.

Related CIP Program: 45.0901 International Relations and Affairs

Specializations in the Major: A regional specialization; development; diplomacy; global security; international political economy; U.S. foreign policy.

Typical Sequence of College Courses: English composition, world history to the early modern era, world history in the modern era, introduction to political science, introduction to international relations, foreign language, introduction to economics, microeconomic theory, macroeconomic theory, comparative governments, world regional geography, history of a non-Western civilization, international economics, American foreign policy, seminar (reporting on research).

Typical Sequence of High School Courses: Algebra, English, foreign language, social science, trigonometry, history.

Career Snapshot

The study of international relations is a multidisciplinary effort that draws on political science, economics, sociology, and history, among other disciplines. It attempts to find meaning in the ways people, private groups, and governments relate to one another politically and eco-

nomically. The traditional focus on sovereign states is opening up to include attention to other actors on the world stage, including nongovernmental organizations; international organizations; multinational corporations; and groups representing a religion, ethnic group, or ideology. Now that American business is opening to the world more than ever before, this major is gaining in importance. Graduates often go on to law or business school, graduate school in the social sciences, the U.S. Foreign Service, or employment in businesses or organizations with an international focus.

Useful Averages for the Related Jobs

- **Annual Earnings:** $144,875
- **Growth:** 14.8%
- **Self-Employed:** 16.1%
- **Part-Time:** 13.9%
- **Verbal Skill Rating:** 81.1
- **Math Skill Rating:** 59.5

Other Details About the Related Jobs

Total Annual Job Openings: 38,000

Interest Area: 04 Business and Administration; 15 Scientific Research, Engineering, and Mathematics

Skills—Management of financial resources; management of material resources; judgment and decision making; management of personnel resources; negotiation; systems evaluation. **Values**—Authority; social status; working conditions; creativity; autonomy; responsibility. **Work Conditions**—Sitting.

Related Jobs

1. Chief Executives

Personality Type:
Enterprising–Conventional–Social

Earnings: More than $145,600
Growth: 14.9%
Annual Openings: 38,000

Most Common Education/Training Level:
Work experience plus degree

Determine and formulate policies and provide the overall direction of companies or private- and public-sector organizations within the guidelines set up by a board of directors or similar governing body. Plan, direct, or coordinate operational activities at the highest level of management with the help of subordinate executives and staff managers. Direct and coordinate an organization's financial and budget activities in order to fund operations, maximize investments, and increase efficiency. Confer with board members, organization officials, and staff members to discuss issues, coordinate activities, and resolve problems. Analyze operations to evaluate performance of a company and its staff in meeting objectives and to determine areas of potential cost reduction, program improvement, or policy change. Direct, plan, and implement policies, objectives, and activities of organizations or businesses in order to ensure continuing operations, to maximize returns on investments, and to increase productivity. Prepare budgets for approval, including those for funding and implementation of programs. Direct and coordinate activities of businesses or departments concerned with production, pricing, sales, and/or distribution of products. Negotiate or approve contracts and agreements with suppliers, distributors, federal and state agencies, and other organizational enti-

ties. Review reports submitted by staff members in order to recommend approval or to suggest changes. Appoint department heads or managers and assign or delegate responsibilities to them. Direct human resources activities, including the approval of human resource plans and activities, the selection of directors and other high-level staff, and establishment and organization of major departments. Preside over or serve on boards of directors, management committees, or other governing boards. Prepare and present reports concerning activities, expenses, budgets, government statutes and rulings, and other items affecting businesses or program services. Establish departmental responsibilities and coordinate functions among departments and sites. Implement corrective action plans to solve organizational or departmental problems. Coordinate the development and implementation of budgetary control systems, recordkeeping systems, and other administrative control processes. Direct non-merchandising departments such as advertising, purchasing, credit, and accounting. Deliver speeches, write articles, and present information at meetings or conventions in order to promote services, exchange ideas, and accomplish objectives.

2. Political Scientists

Personality Type:
Investigative–Artistic–Enterprising

Earnings: $90,140
Growth: 7.3%
Annual Openings: Fewer than 500

Most Common Education/Training Level:
Master's degree

Study the origin, development, and operation of political systems. Research a wide range of subjects, such as relations between the United States and foreign countries, the beliefs and

Enterprising

institutions of foreign nations, or the politics of small towns or a major metropolis. May study topics such as public opinion, political decision making, and ideology. May analyze the structure and operation of governments, as well as various political entities. May conduct public opinion surveys, analyze election results, or analyze public documents. Teach political science. Disseminate research results through academic publications, written reports, or public presentations. Identify issues for research and analysis. Develop and test theories, using information from interviews, newspapers, periodicals, case law, historical papers, polls, and/or statistical sources. Maintain current knowledge of government policy decisions. Collect, analyze, and interpret data such as election results and public opinion surveys; report on findings, recommendations, and conclusions. Interpret and analyze policies; public issues; legislation; and the operations of governments, businesses, and organizations. Evaluate programs and policies and make related recommendations to institutions and organizations. Write drafts of legislative proposals and prepare speeches, correspondence, and policy papers for governmental use. Forecast political, economic, and social trends. Consult with and advise government officials, civic bodies, research agencies, the media, political parties, and others concerned with political issues. Provide media commentary and/or criticism related to public policy and political issues and events.

Landscape Architecture

Personality Type:
Enterprising–Realistic–Investigative

Useful Facts About the Major

Prepares individuals for the independent professional practice of landscape architecture and research in various aspects of the field.

Related CIP Program: 04.0601 Landscape Architecture (BS, BSLA, BLA, MSLA, MLA, PhD)

Specializations in the Major: Arid lands; ecotourism; historical and cultural landscapes; international studies; small town and urban revitalization; urban design.

Typical Sequence of College Courses: English composition, calculus, basic drawing, general biology, introduction to soil science, architectural graphics, ecology, history of landscape architecture, landscape architectural design, site analysis, introduction to horticulture, land surveying, landscape structures and materials, architectural computer graphics, land planning, professional practice of landscape architecture, senior design project.

Typical Sequence of High School Courses: English, algebra, geometry, trigonometry, precalculus, calculus, physics, computer science, art, biology.

Career Snapshot

Landscape architects must have a good flair for design, ability to work with a variety of construction techniques and technologies, and knowledge of the characteristics of many plants, plus business sense. A bachelor's degree is the usual entry route; some people enter the field with a master's degree after a bachelor's in another field. Job opportunities are expected to be good, and an internship is a very helpful credential. About 25 percent of landscape architects are self-employed.

Useful Averages for the Related Jobs

- **Annual Earnings:** $100,030
- **Growth:** 13.7%
- **Self-Employed:** 3.2%
- **Part-Time:** 5.1%
- **Verbal Skill Rating:** 69.5
- **Math Skill Rating:** 72.3

Other Details About the Related Jobs

Total Annual Job Openings: 16,000

Interest Area: 02 Architecture and Construction; 15 Scientific Research, Engineering, and Mathematics

Skills—Technology design; operations analysis; science; management of financial resources; installation; mathematics. **Values**—Authority; compensation; creativity; autonomy; ability utilization; working conditions. **Work Conditions**—Hazardous equipment; common protective or safety equipment.

Related Jobs

1. Engineering Managers

Personality Type:
Enterprising–Investigative–Realistic

Earnings: $105,430
Growth: 13.0%
Annual Openings: 15,000

Enterprising

Most Common Education/Training Level:
Work experience plus degree

Plan, direct, or coordinate activities in such fields as architecture and engineering or research and development in these fields. Confer with management, production, and marketing staff to discuss project specifications and procedures. Coordinate and direct projects, making detailed plans to accomplish goals and directing the integration of technical activities. Analyze technology, resource needs, and market demand to plan and assess the feasibility of projects. Plan and direct the installation, testing, operation, maintenance, and repair of facilities and equipment. Direct, review, and approve product design and changes. Recruit employees; assign, direct, and evaluate their work; and oversee the development and maintenance of staff competence. Prepare budgets, bids, and contracts and direct the negotiation of research contracts. Develop and implement policies, standards, and procedures for the engineering and technical work performed in the department, service, laboratory, or firm. Review and recommend or approve contracts and cost estimates. Perform administrative functions such as reviewing and writing reports, approving expenditures, enforcing rules, and making decisions about the purchase of materials or services. Present and explain proposals, reports, and findings to clients. Consult or negotiate with clients to prepare project specifications. Set scientific and technical goals within broad outlines provided by top management. Administer highway planning, construction, and maintenance. Direct the engineering of water control, treatment, and distribution projects. Plan, direct, and coordinate survey work with other staff activities, certifying survey work and writing land legal descriptions. Confer with and report to officials and the public to provide information and solicit support for projects.

2. Landscape Architects

Personality Type:
Artistic–Realistic–Investigative

Earnings: $55,140
Growth: 19.4%
Annual Openings: 1,000

Most Common Education/Training Level:
Bachelor's degree

Plan and design land areas for such projects as parks and other recreational facilities; airports; highways; hospitals; schools; land subdivisions; and commercial, industrial, and residential sites. Prepare site plans, specifications, and cost estimates for land development, coordinating arrangement of existing and proposed land features and structures. Confer with clients, engineering personnel, and architects on overall program. Compile and analyze data on conditions such as location, drainage, and location of structures for environmental reports and landscaping plans. Inspect landscape work to ensure compliance with specifications, approve quality of materials and work, and advise client and construction personnel.

Marketing

Personality Type: Enterprising–Conventional

Useful Facts About the Major

Prepares individuals to undertake and manage the process of developing consumer audiences and moving products from producers to consumers.

Related CIP Program: 52.1401 Marketing/Marketing Management, General

Specializations in the Major: Marketing management; marketing research.

Typical Sequence of College Courses: English composition, business writing, introduction to psychology, principles of microeconomics, principles of macroeconomics, calculus for business and social sciences, statistics for business and social sciences, introduction to management information systems, introduction to accounting, legal environment of business, principles of management and organization, operations management, strategic management, business finance, introduction to marketing, marketing research, buyer behavior, decision support systems for management, marketing strategy.

Typical Sequence of High School Courses: English, algebra, geometry, trigonometry, science, foreign language, computer science.

Career Snapshot

Marketing is the study of how buyers and sellers of goods and services find one another, how businesses can tailor their offerings to meet demand, and how businesses can anticipate and influence demand. It uses the findings of economics, psychology, and sociology in a business context. A bachelor's degree is good preparation for a job in marketing research. Usually some experience in this field is required before a person can move into a marketing management position. Job outlook varies, with some industries looking more favorable than others.

Useful Averages for the Related Jobs

- **Annual Earnings:** $92,429
- **Growth:** 20.1%
- **Self-Employed:** 3.9%
- **Part-Time:** 9.4%
- **Verbal Skill Rating:** 67.9
- **Math Skill Rating:** 56.7

Other Details About the Related Jobs

Total Annual Job Openings: 72,000

Interest Area: 14 Retail and Wholesale Sales and Service

Skills—Management of personnel resources; negotiation; management of financial resources; persuasion; operations analysis; service orientation. **Values**—Authority; creativity; compensation; working conditions; recognition; autonomy. **Work Conditions**—Indoors, environmentally controlled; sitting.

Related Jobs

1. Advertising and Promotions Managers

Personality Type: Artistic–Enterprising–Social

Earnings: $73,060
Growth: 20.3%
Annual Openings: 9,000

Enterprising

Most Common Education/Training Level:
Work experience plus degree

Plan and direct advertising policies and programs or produce collateral materials, such as posters, contests, coupons, or giveaways, to create extra interest in the purchase of a product or service for a department, for an entire organization, or on an account basis. Prepare budgets and submit estimates for program costs as part of campaign plan development. Plan and prepare advertising and promotional material to increase sales of products or services, working with customers, company officials, sales departments, and advertising agencies. Assist with annual budget development. Inspect layouts and advertising copy and edit scripts, audiotapes and videotapes, and other promotional material for adherence to specifications. Coordinate activities of departments, such as sales, graphic arts, media, finance, and research. Prepare and negotiate advertising and sales contracts. Identify and develop contacts for promotional campaigns and industry programs that meet identified buyer targets, such as dealers, distributors, or consumers. Gather and organize information to plan advertising campaigns. Confer with department heads or staff to discuss topics such as contracts, selection of advertising media, or product to be advertised. Confer with clients to provide marketing or technical advice. Monitor and analyze sales promotion results to determine cost-effectiveness of promotion campaigns. Read trade journals and professional literature to stay informed on trends, innovations, and changes that affect media planning. Formulate plans to extend business with established accounts and to transact business as agent for advertising accounts. Provide presentation and product demonstration support during the introduction of new products and services to field staff and customers. Direct, motivate, and monitor the mobilization of a campaign team to advance campaign goals. Plan and execute advertising policies and strategies for organizations. Track program budgets and expenses and campaign response rates to evaluate each campaign based on program objectives and industry norms. Assemble and communicate with a strong, diverse coalition of organizations or public figures, securing their cooperation, support, and action to further campaign goals. Train and direct workers engaged in developing and producing advertisements. Coordinate with the media to disseminate advertising.

2. Marketing Managers

Personality Type:
Enterprising–Conventional–Social

Earnings: $98,720
Growth: 20.8%
Annual Openings: 23,000

Most Common Education/Training Level:
Work experience plus degree

Determine the demand for products and services offered by a firm and its competitors and identify potential customers. Develop pricing strategies with the goal of maximizing the firm's profits or share of the market while ensuring that the firm's customers are satisfied. Oversee product development or monitor trends that indicate the need for new products and services. Develop pricing strategies, balancing firm objectives and customer satisfaction. Identify, develop, and evaluate marketing strategy, based on knowledge of establishment objectives, market characteristics, and cost and markup factors. Evaluate the financial aspects of product development, such as budgets, expenditures, research and development appropriations, and return-on-investment and profit-loss projections. Formulate, direct, and coordinate marketing activities and policies to promote products and services, working with advertising and promotion managers. Direct the hiring, training, and performance evaluations of marketing and sales staff and oversee their daily activities. Negotiate contracts with vendors and distributors to manage product distribution, establishing distribution networks and developing distribution strategies. Consult with product development personnel on product specifications such as design, color, and packaging. Compile lists describing product or service offerings. Use sales forecasting and strategic planning to ensure the sale and profitability of products, lines, or services, analyzing business developments and monitoring market trends. Select products and accessories to be displayed at trade or special production shows. Confer with legal staff to resolve problems such as copyright infringement and royalty sharing with outside producers and distributors. Coordinate and participate in promotional activities and trade shows, working with developers, advertisers, and production managers to market products and services. Advise business and other groups on local, national, and international factors affecting the buying and selling of products and services. Initiate market research studies and analyze their findings. Consult with buying personnel to gain advice regarding the types of products or services expected to be in demand. Conduct economic and commercial surveys to identify potential markets for products and services.

3. Sales Managers

Personality Type:
Enterprising–Conventional–Social

Earnings: $91,560
Growth: 19.7%
Annual Openings: 40,000

Most Common Education/Training Level:
Work experience plus degree

Direct the actual distribution or movement of a product or service to the customer. Coordinate sales distribution by establishing sales territories, quotas, and goals and establish training programs for sales representatives. Analyze sales statistics gathered by staff to determine sales potential and inventory requirements and monitor the preferences of customers. Resolve customer complaints regarding sales and service. Monitor customer preferences to determine focus of sales efforts. Direct and coordinate activities involving sales of manufactured products, services, commodities, real estate, or other subjects of sale. Determine price schedules and discount rates. Review operational records and reports to project sales and determine profitability. Direct, coordinate, and review activities in sales and service accounting and recordkeeping and in receiving and shipping operations. Confer or consult with department heads to plan advertising services and to secure information on equipment and customer specifications. Advise dealers and distributors on policies and operating procedures to ensure functional effectiveness of business. Prepare budgets and approve budget expenditures. Represent company at trade association meetings to promote products. Plan and direct staffing, training, and performance evaluations to develop and control sales and service programs. Visit franchised dealers to stimulate interest in establishment or expansion of leasing programs. Confer with potential customers regarding equipment needs and advise cus-

Enterprising

tomers on types of equipment to purchase. Oversee regional and local sales managers and their staffs. Direct clerical staff to keep records of export correspondence, bid requests, and credit collections and to maintain current information on tariffs, licenses, and restrictions. Direct foreign sales and service outlets of an organization. Assess marketing potential of new and existing store locations, considering statistics and expenditures.

Petroleum Engineering

Personality Type:
Enterprising–Realistic–Investigative

Useful Facts About the Major

Prepares individuals to apply mathematical and scientific principles to the design, development, and operational evaluation of systems for locating, extracting, processing, and refining crude petroleum and natural gas.

Related CIP Program: 14.2501 Petroleum Engineering

Specializations in the Major: Distribution; drilling/extraction; exploration; refining.

Typical Sequence of College Courses: English composition, introduction to computer science, technical writing, calculus, differential equations, general chemistry, general physics, physical geology, introduction to engineering, statics, dynamics, fluid mechanics, thermodynamics, numerical analysis, materials engineering, engineering economics, heat transfer, sedimentary rocks and processes, petroleum geology, petroleum development, petroleum production methods, petroleum property management, formation evaluation, natural gas engineering, reservoir fluids, reservoir engineering, well testing and analysis, drilling engineering, reservoir stimulation, senior design project.

Typical Sequence of High School Courses: English, algebra, geometry, trigonometry, precalculus, calculus, chemistry, physics, computer science.

Career Snapshot

Petroleum engineers devise technically effective and economically justifiable ways of locating, extracting, transporting, refining, and storing petroleum and natural gas. They apply basic principles of science to oil wells deep in the ground or high-towering refineries. Usually they begin with a bachelor's degree. Management is sometimes an option later in their careers. The job outlook is favorable in the United States and even better in foreign countries, where many American-trained petroleum engineers work.

Useful Averages for the Related Jobs

- **Annual Earnings:** $104,897
- **Growth:** 12.0%
- **Self-Employed:** 1.0%
- **Part-Time:** 3.0%
- **Verbal Skill Rating:** 74.7
- **Math Skill Rating:** 79.2

Other Details About the Related Jobs

Total Annual Job Openings: 16,000

Interest Area: 01 Agriculture and Natural Resources; 15 Scientific Research, Engineering, and Mathematics

Skills—Science; technology design; operations analysis; management of financial resources; mathematics; installation. **Values**—Authority; creativity; autonomy; compensation; ability utilization; working conditions. **Work Conditions**—Indoors, environmentally controlled; sitting.

Related Jobs

1. Engineering Managers
Personality Type:
Enterprising–Investigative–Realistic

Enterprising

Earnings: $105,430
Growth: 13.0%
Annual Openings: 15,000

Most Common Education/Training Level:
Work experience plus degree

Plan, direct, or coordinate activities in such fields as architecture and engineering or research and development in these fields. Confer with management, production, and marketing staff to discuss project specifications and procedures. Coordinate and direct projects, making detailed plans to accomplish goals and directing the integration of technical activities. Analyze technology, resource needs, and market demand to plan and assess the feasibility of projects. Plan and direct the installation, testing, operation, maintenance, and repair of facilities and equipment. Direct, review, and approve product design and changes. Recruit employees; assign, direct, and evaluate their work; and oversee the development and maintenance of staff competence. Prepare budgets, bids, and contracts and direct the negotiation of research contracts. Develop and implement policies, standards, and procedures for the engineering and technical work performed in the department, service, laboratory, or firm. Review and recommend or approve contracts and cost estimates. Perform administrative functions such as reviewing and writing reports, approving expenditures, enforcing rules, and making decisions about the purchase of materials or services. Present and explain proposals, reports, and findings to clients. Consult or negotiate with clients to prepare project specifications. Set scientific and technical goals within broad outlines provided by top management. Administer highway planning, construction, and maintenance. Direct the engineering of water control, treatment, and distribution projects. Plan, direct, and coordinate survey work with other staff

activities, certifying survey work and writing land legal descriptions. Confer with and report to officials and the public to provide information and solicit support for projects.

2. Petroleum Engineers

Personality Type:
Realistic–Investigative–Conventional

Earnings: $98,380
Growth: –0.1%
Annual Openings: 1,000

Most Common Education/Training Level:
Bachelor's degree

Devise methods to improve oil and gas well production and determine the need for new or modified tool designs. Oversee drilling and offer technical advice to achieve economical and satisfactory progress. Assess costs and estimate the production capabilities and economic value of oil and gas wells to evaluate the economic viability of potential drilling sites. Monitor production rates and plan rework processes to improve production. Analyze data to recommend placement of wells and supplementary processes to enhance production. Specify and supervise well modification and stimulation programs to maximize oil and gas recovery. Direct and monitor the completion and evaluation of wells, well testing, or well surveys. Assist engineering and other personnel to solve operating problems. Develop plans for oil and gas field drilling and for product recovery and treatment. Maintain records of drilling and production operations. Confer with scientific, engineering, and technical personnel to resolve design, research, and testing problems. Write technical reports for engineering and management personnel. Evaluate findings to develop, design, or test equipment or processes. Assign work to staff to obtain maximum utilization of personnel. Interpret drilling and testing information for personnel. Design and implement environmental controls on oil and gas operations. Coordinate the installation, maintenance, and operation of mining and oilfield equipment. Supervise the removal of drilling equipment, the removal of any waste, and the safe return of land to structural stability when wells or pockets are exhausted. Inspect oil and gas wells to determine that installations are completed. Simulate reservoir performance for different recovery techniques, using computer models. Take samples to assess the amount and quality of oil, the depth at which resources lie, and the equipment needed to properly extract them. Coordinate activities of workers engaged in research, planning, and development. Design or modify mining and oilfield machinery and tools, applying engineering principles. Test machinery and equipment to ensure that it is safe and conforms to performance specifications. Conduct engineering research experiments to improve or modify mining and oil machinery and operations.

Enterprising

Public Administration

Personality Type: Enterprising–Conventional

Useful Facts About the Major

Prepares individuals to serve as managers in the executive arm of local, state, and federal government; focuses on the systematic study of executive organization and management.

Related CIP Program: 44.0401 Public Administration

Specializations in the Major: Economic development; finance and budgeting; personnel and labor relations; policy analysis; program management.

Typical Sequence of College Courses: English composition, oral communication, accounting, introduction to business management, American government, state and local government, college algebra, introduction to economics, organizational behavior, statistics for business and social sciences, organizational theory, introduction to psychology, urban politics, public policy making process, public finance and budgeting, political science research methods, planning and change in public organizations, seminar (reporting on research).

Typical Sequence of High School Courses: Algebra, English, foreign language, social science, trigonometry, history, public speaking, computer science.

Career Snapshot

The public sector includes many kinds of agencies working in the fields of health, law enforcement, environmental protection, transportation, and taxation, to name just a few. Because of this variety of fields, graduates who have been trained in administrative skills (perhaps at the master's level) often find it helpful to combine that background with specific training in another field, such as health, science, engineering, or accounting. Public administration programs usually include internships that give students actual experience working in a public agency.

Useful Averages for the Related Jobs

- **Annual Earnings:** $86,701
- **Growth:** 16.5%
- **Self-Employed:** 3.1%
- **Part-Time:** 7.2%
- **Verbal Skill Rating:** 65.5
- **Math Skill Rating:** 55.0

Other Details About the Related Jobs

Total Annual Job Openings: 310,000

Interest Area: 04 Business and Administration; 07 Government and Public Administration; 12 Law and Public Safety; 16 Transportation, Distribution, and Logistics

Skills—Management of financial resources; management of personnel resources; management of material resources; monitoring; negotiation; coordination. **Values**—Authority; autonomy; creativity; responsibility; working conditions; social status. **Work Conditions**—Indoors, environmentally controlled.

Related Jobs

1. Administrative Services Managers

Personality Type:
Enterprising–Conventional–Social

Earnings: $67,690
Growth: 16.9%
Annual Openings: 25,000

Most Common Education/Training Level: Work experience plus degree

Plan, direct, or coordinate supportive services of an organization, such as recordkeeping, mail distribution, telephone operator/receptionist, and other office support services. May oversee facilities planning and maintenance and custodial operations. Monitor the facility to ensure that it remains safe, secure, and well-maintained. Direct or coordinate the supportive services department of a business, agency, or organization. Set goals and deadlines for the department. Prepare and review operational reports and schedules to ensure accuracy and efficiency. Analyze internal processes and recommend and implement procedural or policy changes to improve operations such as supply changes or the disposal of records. Acquire, distribute, and store supplies. Plan, administer, and control budgets for contracts, equipment, and supplies. Oversee construction and renovation projects to improve efficiency and to ensure that facilities meet environmental, health, and security standards and comply with government regulations. Hire and terminate clerical and administrative personnel. Oversee the maintenance and repair of machinery, equipment, and electrical and mechanical systems. Manage leasing of facility space. Participate in architectural and engineering planning and design, including space and installation management. Conduct classes to teach procedures to staff. Dispose of, or oversee the disposal of, surplus or unclaimed property.

2. Chief Executives

Personality Type:
Enterprising–Conventional–Social

Earnings: More than $145,600
Growth: 14.9%
Annual Openings: 38,000

Most Common Education/Training Level: Work experience plus degree

Determine and formulate policies and provide the overall direction of companies or private- and public-sector organizations within the guidelines set up by a board of directors or similar governing body. Plan, direct, or coordinate operational activities at the highest level of management with the help of subordinate executives and staff managers. Direct and coordinate an organization's financial and budget activities in order to fund operations, maximize investments, and increase efficiency. Confer with board members, organization officials, and staff members to discuss issues, coordinate activities, and resolve problems. Analyze operations to evaluate performance of a company and its staff in meeting objectives and to determine areas of potential cost reduction, program improvement, or policy change. Direct, plan, and implement policies, objectives, and activities of organizations or businesses in order to ensure continuing operations, to maximize returns on investments, and to increase productivity. Prepare budgets for approval, including those for funding and implementation of programs. Direct and coordinate activities of businesses or departments concerned with production, pricing, sales, and/or distribution of products. Negotiate or approve contracts and agreements with suppliers, distributors, federal and state agencies, and other organizational entities. Review reports submitted by staff members in order to recommend approval or to suggest changes. Appoint department heads or managers and assign or delegate responsibilities to them. Direct human resources activities, including the approval of human resource plans and activities,

Enterprising

the selection of directors and other high-level staff, and establishment and organization of major departments. Preside over or serve on boards of directors, management committees, or other governing boards. Prepare and present reports concerning activities, expenses, budgets, government statutes and rulings, and other items affecting businesses or program services. Establish departmental responsibilities and coordinate functions among departments and sites. Implement corrective action plans to solve organizational or departmental problems. Coordinate the development and implementation of budgetary control systems, recordkeeping systems, and other administrative control processes. Direct non-merchandising departments such as advertising, purchasing, credit, and accounting. Deliver speeches, write articles, and present information at meetings or conventions in order to promote services, exchange ideas, and accomplish objectives.

3. Emergency Management Specialists

Personality Type: No data available

Earnings: $47,410
Growth: 22.8%
Annual Openings: 2,000

Most Common Education/Training Level:
Work experience in a related occupation

Coordinate disaster response or crisis management activities, provide disaster-preparedness training, and prepare emergency plans and procedures for natural (e.g., hurricanes, floods, earthquakes), wartime, or technological (e.g., nuclear power plant emergencies, hazardous materials spills) disasters or hostage situations. Keep informed of activities or changes that could affect the likelihood of an emergency, as well as those that could affect response efforts and details of plan implementation. Prepare plans that outline operating procedures to be used in response to disasters or emergencies such as hurricanes, nuclear accidents, and terrorist attacks and in recovery from these events. Propose alteration of emergency response procedures based on regulatory changes, technological changes, or knowledge gained from outcomes of previous emergency situations. Maintain and update all resource materials associated with emergency-preparedness plans. Coordinate disaster response or crisis management activities such as ordering evacuations, opening public shelters, and implementing special needs plans and programs. Develop and maintain liaisons with municipalities, county departments, and similar entities in order to facilitate plan development, response effort coordination, and exchanges of personnel and equipment. Keep informed of federal, state, and local regulations affecting emergency plans and ensure that plans adhere to these regulations. Design and administer emergency and disaster-preparedness training courses that teach people how to effectively respond to major emergencies and disasters. Prepare emergency situation status reports that describe response and recovery efforts, needs, and preliminary damage assessments. Inspect facilities and equipment such as emergency management centers and communications equipment to determine their operational and functional capabilities in emergency situations. Consult with officials of local and area governments, schools, hospitals, and other institutions in order to determine their needs and capabilities in the event of a natural disaster or other emergency. Develop and perform tests and evaluations of emergency management plans in accordance with state and federal regulations. Attend meetings, conferences, and workshops related to emergency management to learn new information and to develop working relationships with other emergency management specialists.

4. General and Operations Managers

Personality Type: No data available

Earnings: $85,230
Growth: 17.0%
Annual Openings: 208,000

Most Common Education/Training Level:
Work experience plus degree

Plan, direct, or coordinate the operations of companies or public- and private-sector organizations. Duties and responsibilities include formulating policies, managing daily operations, and planning the use of materials and human resources, but are too diverse and general in nature to be classified in any one functional area of management or administration, such as personnel, purchasing, or administrative services. Includes owners and managers who head small business establishments whose duties are primarily managerial. Direct and coordinate activities of businesses or departments concerned with the production, pricing, sales, or distribution of products. Manage staff, preparing work schedules and assigning specific duties. Review financial statements, sales and activity reports, and other performance data to measure productivity and goal achievement and to determine areas needing cost reduction and program improvement. Establish and implement departmental policies, goals, objectives, and procedures, conferring with board members, organization officials, and staff members as necessary. Determine staffing requirements and interview, hire, and train new employees or oversee those personnel processes. Monitor businesses and agencies to ensure that they efficiently and effectively provide needed services while staying within budgetary limits. Oversee activities directly related to making products or providing services. Direct and coordinate organization's financial and budget activities to fund operations, maximize investments, and increase efficiency. Determine goods and services to be sold and set prices and credit terms based on forecasts of customer demand. Manage the movement of goods into and out of production facilities. Locate, select, and procure merchandise for resale, representing management in purchase negotiations. Perform sales floor work such as greeting and assisting customers, stocking shelves, and taking inventory. Develop and implement product marketing strategies, including advertising campaigns and sales promotions. Plan and direct activities such as sales promotions, coordinating with other department heads as required. Direct non-merchandising departments of businesses, such as advertising and purchasing. Recommend locations for new facilities or oversee the remodeling of current facilities. Plan store layouts and design displays.

5. Legislators

Personality Type: No data available

Earnings: $15,660
Growth: 2.0%
Annual Openings: 3,000

Most Common Education/Training Level:
Work experience plus degree

Develop laws and statutes at the federal, state, or local level. Attend receptions, dinners, and conferences to meet people, exchange views and information, and develop working relationships. Analyze and understand the local and national implications of proposed legislation. Represent their government at local, national, and international meetings and conferences. Promote the industries and products of their electoral

Enterprising

districts. Oversee expense allowances, ensuring that accounts are balanced at the end of each fiscal year. Organize and maintain campaign organizations and fundraisers in order to raise money for election or re-election. Evaluate the structure, efficiency, activities, and performance of government agencies. Establish personal offices in local districts or states and manage office staff. Encourage and support party candidates for political office. Conduct "head counts" to help predict the outcome of upcoming votes. Speak to students to encourage and support the development of future political leaders. Alert constituents of government actions and programs by way of newsletters, personal appearances at town meetings, phone calls, and individual meetings. Write, prepare, and deliver statements for the Congressional Record. Vote on motions, amendments, and decisions on whether or not to report a bill out from committee to the assembly floor. Serve on commissions, investigative panels, study groups, and committees in order to examine specialized areas and recommend action. Develop expertise in subject matters related to committee assignments. Appoint nominees to leadership posts or approve such appointments. Determine campaign strategies for media advertising, positions on issues, and public appearances. Debate the merits of proposals and bill amendments during floor sessions, following the appropriate rules of procedure. Seek federal funding for local projects and programs. Hear testimony from constituents, representatives of interest groups, board and commission members, and others with an interest in bills or issues under consideration. Keep abreast of the issues affecting constituents by making personal visits and phone calls, reading local newspapers, and viewing or listening to local broadcasts.

6. Postmasters and Mail Superintendents

Personality Type:
Enterprising–Conventional–Social

Earnings: $55,790
Growth: 0.0%
Annual Openings: 2,000

Most Common Education/Training Level:
Work experience in a related occupation

Direct and coordinate operational, administrative, management, and supportive services of a U.S. post office or coordinate activities of workers engaged in postal and related work in assigned post office. Organize and supervise activities such as the processing of incoming and outgoing mail. Direct and coordinate operational, management, and supportive services of one or a number of postal facilities. Resolve customer complaints. Hire and train employees and evaluate their performance. Prepare employee work schedules. Negotiate labor disputes. Prepare and submit detailed and summary reports of post office activities to designated supervisors. Collect rents for post office boxes. Issue and cash money orders. Inform the public of available services and of postal laws and regulations. Select and train postmasters and managers of associate postal units. Confer with suppliers to obtain bids for proposed purchases and to requisition supplies; disburse funds according to federal regulations.

7. Social and Community Service Managers

Personality Type: Social–Enterprising–Artistic

Earnings: $52,070
Growth: 25.5%
Annual Openings: 17,000

Most Common Education/Training Level: Bachelor's degree

Plan, organize, or coordinate the activities of a social service program or community outreach organization. Oversee the program or organization's budget and policies regarding participant involvement, program requirements, and benefits. Work may involve directing social workers, counselors, or probation officers. Establish and maintain relationships with other agencies and organizations in community to meet community needs and to ensure that services are not duplicated. Prepare and maintain records and reports, such as budgets, personnel records, or training manuals. Direct activities of professional and technical staff members and volunteers. Evaluate the work of staff and volunteers to ensure that programs are of appropriate quality and that resources are used effectively. Establish and oversee administrative procedures to meet objectives set by boards of directors or senior management. Participate in the determination of organizational policies regarding such issues as participant eligibility, program requirements, and program benefits. Research and analyze member or community needs to determine program directions and goals. Speak to community groups to explain and interpret agency purposes, programs, and policies. Recruit, interview, and hire or sign up volunteers and staff. Represent organizations in relations with governmental and media institutions. Plan and administer budgets for programs, equipment, and support services. Analyze proposed legislation, regulations, or rule changes to determine how agency services could be impacted. Act as consultants to agency staff and other community programs regarding the interpretation of program-related federal, state, and county regulations and policies. Implement and evaluate staff training programs. Direct fundraising activities and the preparation of public relations materials.

8. Transportation, Storage, and Distribution Managers

Personality Type: Enterprising–Conventional–Realistic

Earnings: $73,080
Growth: 12.7%
Annual Openings: 15,000

Most Common Education/Training Level: Work experience in a related occupation

Job Specializations

Storage and Distribution Managers. Plan, direct, and coordinate the storage and distribution operations within an organization or the activities of organizations that are engaged in storing and distributing materials and products. Supervise the activities of workers engaged in receiving, storing, testing, and shipping products or materials. Plan, develop, and implement warehouse safety and security programs and activities. Review invoices, work orders, consumption reports, and demand forecasts to estimate peak delivery periods and to issue work assignments. Schedule and monitor air or surface pickup, delivery, or distribution of products or materials. Interview, select, and train warehouse and supervisory personnel. Confer with department heads to coordinate warehouse activities, such as production, sales, records control, and purchasing. Respond to customers' or shippers' questions and complaints regarding storage and distribution services. Inspect physical conditions of warehouses, vehicle fleets, and equipment and order testing, maintenance, repair, or replacement as necessary. Develop and document standard and emergency operating procedures for receiving, handling, storing, shipping, or salvaging products or materials. Examine products or materials to estimate quantities or weight and type of container required for storage or transport. Negotiate with carriers,

Enterprising

warehouse operators, and insurance company representatives for services and preferential rates. Issue shipping instructions and provide routing information to ensure that delivery times and locations are coordinated. Examine invoices and shipping manifests for conformity to tariff and customs regulations. Prepare and manage departmental budgets. Prepare or direct preparation of correspondence; reports; and operations, maintenance, and safety manuals. Arrange for necessary shipping documentation and contact customs officials to effect release of shipments. Advise sales and billing departments of transportation charges for customers' accounts. Evaluate freight costs and the inventory costs associated with transit times to ensure that costs are appropriate. Participate in setting transportation and service rates. Track and trace goods while they are en route to their destinations, expediting orders when necessary. Arrange for storage facilities when required.

Transportation Managers. Plan, direct, and coordinate the transportation operations within an organization or the activities of organizations that provide transportation services. Direct activities related to dispatching, routing, and tracking transportation vehicles such as aircraft and railroad cars. Plan, organize, and manage the work of subordinate staff to ensure that the work is accomplished in a manner consistent with organizational requirements. Direct investigations to verify and resolve customer or shipper complaints. Serve as contact persons for all workers within assigned territories. Implement schedule and policy changes. Collaborate with other managers and staff members to formulate and implement policies, procedures, goals, and objectives. Monitor operations to ensure that staff members comply with administrative policies and procedures, safety rules, union contracts, and government regulations. Promote safe work activities by conducting safety audits, attending company safety meetings, and meeting with individual staff members. Develop criteria, application instructions, procedural manuals, and contracts for federal and state public transportation programs. Monitor spending to ensure that expenses are consistent with approved budgets. Direct and coordinate, through subordinates, activities of operations department to obtain use of equipment, facilities, and human resources. Direct activities of staff performing repairs and maintenance to equipment, vehicles, and facilities. Conduct investigations in cooperation with government agencies to determine causes of transportation accidents and to improve safety procedures. Analyze expenditures and other financial information to develop plans, policies, and budgets for increasing profits and improving services. Negotiate and authorize contracts with equipment and materials suppliers and monitor contract fulfillment. Supervise workers assigning tariff classifications and preparing billing. Set operations policies and standards, including determination of safety procedures for the handling of dangerous goods. Recommend or authorize capital expenditures for acquisition of new equipment or property to increase efficiency and services of operations department. Prepare management recommendations, such as proposed fee and tariff increases or schedule changes.

Public Relations

Personality Type: Enterprising–Artistic–Social

Useful Facts About the Major

Focuses on the theories and methods for managing the media image of a business, organization, or individual and the communication process with stakeholders, constituencies, audiences, and the general public; prepares individuals to function as public relations assistants, technicians, and managers.

Related CIP Program: 09.0902 Public Relations/Image Management

Specializations in the Major: Creative process; management; new media.

Typical Sequence of College Courses: English composition, oral communication, introduction to marketing, introduction to economics, principles of public relations, communications theory, public relations message strategy, communication ethics, public relations media, public relations writing, public relations techniques and campaigns, organizational communications, mass communication law, introduction to communication research, visual design for media.

Typical Sequence of High School Courses: English, algebra, foreign language, art, literature, public speaking, social science.

Career Snapshot

Public relations specialists work for business, government, and nonprofit organizations and encourage public support for the employer's policies and practices. Often several "publics" with differing interests and needs have to be targeted with different messages. The work requires an understanding of psychology, the business and social environments, effective writing, and techniques used in various media for persuasive communications. A bachelor's degree is good preparation for an entry-level job in this competitive field, and an internship or work experience is an important advantage. On-the-job experience may lead to a job managing public relations campaigns; a master's degree can speed up the process of advancement.

Useful Averages for the Related Jobs

- **Annual Earnings:** $55,966
- **Growth:** 22.4%
- **Self-Employed:** 3.3%
- **Part-Time:** 18.7%
- **Verbal Skill Rating:** 69.4
- **Math Skill Rating:** 42.8

Other Details About the Related Jobs

Total Annual Job Openings: 52,000

Interest Area: 03 Arts and Communication; 14 Retail and Wholesale Sales and Service

Skills—Management of financial resources; service orientation; persuasion; negotiation; writing; monitoring. **Values**—Creativity; recognition; ability utilization; achievement; authority; variety. **Work Conditions**—Sitting.

Related Jobs

1. Advertising and Promotions Managers

Personality Type: Artistic–Enterprising–Social

Earnings: $73,060
Growth: 20.3%
Annual Openings: 9,000

Enterprising

Most Common Education/Training Level:
Work experience plus degree

Plan and direct advertising policies and programs or produce collateral materials, such as posters, contests, coupons, or giveaways, to create extra interest in the purchase of a product or service for a department, for an entire organization, or on an account basis. Prepare budgets and submit estimates for program costs as part of campaign plan development. Plan and prepare advertising and promotional material to increase sales of products or services, working with customers, company officials, sales departments, and advertising agencies. Assist with annual budget development. Inspect layouts and advertising copy and edit scripts, audiotapes and videotapes, and other promotional material for adherence to specifications. Coordinate activities of departments, such as sales, graphic arts, media, finance, and research. Prepare and negotiate advertising and sales contracts. Identify and develop contacts for promotional campaigns and industry programs that meet identified buyer targets, such as dealers, distributors, or consumers. Gather and organize information to plan advertising campaigns. Confer with department heads or staff to discuss topics such as contracts, selection of advertising media, or product to be advertised. Confer with clients to provide marketing or technical advice. Monitor and analyze sales promotion results to determine cost-effectiveness of promotion campaigns. Read trade journals and professional literature to stay informed on trends, innovations, and changes that affect media planning. Formulate plans to extend business with established accounts and to transact business as agent for advertising accounts. Provide presentation and product demonstration support during the introduction of new products and services to field staff and customers. Direct, motivate, and monitor the mobilization of a campaign team to advance campaign goals. Plan and execute advertising policies and strategies for organizations. Track program budgets and expenses and campaign response rates to evaluate each campaign based on program objectives and industry norms. Assemble and communicate with a strong, diverse coalition of organizations or public figures, securing their cooperation, support, and action to further campaign goals. Train and direct workers engaged in developing and producing advertisements. Coordinate with the media to disseminate advertising.

2. Public Relations Managers

Personality Type: No data available

Earnings: $82,180
Growth: 21.7%
Annual Openings: 5,000

Most Common Education/Training Level:
Work experience plus degree

Plan and direct public relations programs designed to create and maintain a favorable public image for employer or client or, if engaged in fundraising, plan and direct activities to solicit and maintain funds for special projects and nonprofit organizations. Identify main client groups and audiences and determine the best way to communicate publicity information to them. Write interesting and effective press releases, prepare information for media kits, and develop and maintain company Internet or intranet Web pages. Develop and maintain the company's corporate image and identity, which includes the use of logos and signage. Manage communications budgets. Manage special events such as sponsorship of races, parties introducing new products, or other activities the firm supports to gain public attention through the media without advertising directly. Draft speeches for company executives and arrange interviews and other forms of contact for them. Assign, supervise, and review the activities of public relations staff. Evaluate advertising and promotion programs for compatibility with public relations efforts. Establish and maintain effective working relationships with local and municipal government officials and media representatives. Confer with labor relations managers to develop internal communications that keep employees informed of company activities. Direct activities of external agencies, establishments, and departments that develop and implement communication strategies and information programs. Formulate policies and procedures related to public information programs, working with public relations executives. Respond to requests for information about employers' activities or status. Establish goals for soliciting funds, develop policies for collection and safeguarding of contributions, and coordinate disbursement of funds. Facilitate consumer relations or the relationship between parts of the company such as the managers and employees or different branch offices. Maintain company archives. Manage in-house communication courses. Produce films and other video products, regulate their distribution, and operate film library. Observe and report on social, economic, and political trends that might affect employers.

3. Public Relations Specialists

Personality Type: Enterprising–Artistic–Social

Earnings: $47,350
Growth: 22.9%
Annual Openings: 38,000

Most Common Education/Training Level: Bachelor's degree

Engage in promoting or creating good will for individuals, groups, or organizations by writing or selecting favorable publicity material and releasing it through various communications media. May prepare and arrange displays and make speeches. Prepare or edit organizational publications for internal and external audiences, including employee newsletters and stockholders' reports. Respond to requests for information from the media or designate another appropriate spokesperson or information source. Establish and maintain cooperative relationships with representatives of community, consumer, employee, and public interest groups. Plan and direct development and communication of informational programs to maintain favorable public and stockholder perceptions of an organization's accomplishments and agenda. Confer with production and support personnel to produce or coordinate production of advertisements and promotions. Arrange public appearances, lectures, contests, or exhibits for clients to increase product and service awareness and to promote goodwill. Study the objectives, promotional policies, and needs of organizations to develop public relations strategies that will influence public opinion or promote ideas, products, and services. Consult with advertising agencies or staff to arrange promotional campaigns in all types of media for products, organizations, or individuals. Confer with other managers to identify trends and key group interests and concerns or to provide advice on business decisions. Coach client representatives in effective communication with the public and with employees. Prepare and deliver speeches to further public relations objectives. Purchase advertising space and time as required to promote client's product or agenda. Plan and conduct market and public opinion research to test products or determine potential for product success, communicating results to client or management.

Enterprising

Transportation and Logistics Management

Personality Type: Enterprising–Conventional

Useful Facts About the Major

Prepares individuals to plan, administer, and coordinate physical transportation operations, networks, and systems or to manage and coordinate all logistical functions in an enterprise.

Related CIP Programs: 52.0203 Logistics and Materials Management; 52.0209 Transportation/Transportation Management

Specializations in the Major: Inventory control; location analysis; management information systems; materials handling; order fulfillment; planning and forecasting; traffic and transportation management; warehouse operations.

Typical Sequence of College Courses: English composition, business writing, introduction to psychology, principles of microeconomics, principles of macroeconomics, calculus for business and social sciences, statistics for business and social sciences, introduction to management information systems, introduction to accounting, legal environment of business, business finance, introduction to marketing, human resource management, introduction to logistics, transportation management, inventory management, analysis and design of logistics systems.

Typical Sequence of High School Courses: English, algebra, geometry, trigonometry, foreign language, computer science, public speaking, pre-calculus.

Career Snapshot

Transportation and logistics managers find the fastest and most cost-effective ways to keep materials flowing through our economy. Any business that produces goods or uses supplies—and that means practically every business—faces problems that these specialists are trained to solve. Some enter the field with a bachelor's in transportation and logistics management. On-the-job experience is important for advancement. Those interested in a technical specialization such as inventory control, packaging, or forecasting may major in (or get a master's degree in) management information systems, operations research, or industrial engineering.

Useful Averages for the Related Jobs

- **Annual Earnings:** $101,203
- **Growth:** 15.1%
- **Self-Employed:** 8.8%
- **Part-Time:** 11.4%
- **Verbal Skill Rating:** 64.2
- **Math Skill Rating:** 56.5

Other Details About the Related Jobs

Total Annual Job Openings: 85,000

Interest Area: 04 Business and Administration; 16 Transportation, Distribution, and Logistics

Skills—Management of financial resources; management of personnel resources; management of material resources; monitoring; coordination; negotiation. **Values**—Authority; autonomy; responsibility; creativity; working conditions; social status. **Work Conditions**—Indoors, environmentally controlled; sitting.

Related Jobs

1. Administrative Services Managers

Personality Type:
Enterprising–Conventional–Social

Earnings: $67,690
Growth: 16.9%
Annual Openings: 25,000

Most Common Education/Training Level:
Work experience plus degree

Plan, direct, or coordinate supportive services of an organization, such as recordkeeping, mail distribution, telephone operator/receptionist, and other office support services. May oversee facilities planning and maintenance and custodial operations. Monitor the facility to ensure that it remains safe, secure, and well-maintained. Direct or coordinate the supportive services department of a business, agency, or organization. Set goals and deadlines for the department. Prepare and review operational reports and schedules to ensure accuracy and efficiency. Analyze internal processes and recommend and implement procedural or policy changes to improve operations such as supply changes or the disposal of records. Acquire, distribute, and store supplies. Plan, administer, and control budgets for contracts, equipment, and supplies. Oversee construction and renovation projects to improve efficiency and to ensure that facilities meet environmental, health, and security standards and comply with government regulations. Hire and terminate clerical and administrative personnel. Oversee the maintenance and repair of machinery, equipment, and electrical and mechanical systems. Manage leasing of facility space. Participate in architectural and engineering planning and design, including space and installation management. Conduct classes to teach procedures to staff. Dispose of, or oversee the disposal of, surplus or unclaimed property.

2. Chief Executives

Personality Type:
Enterprising–Conventional–Social

Earnings: More than $145,600
Growth: 14.9%
Annual Openings: 38,000

Most Common Education/Training Level:
Work experience plus degree

Determine and formulate policies and provide the overall direction of companies or private and public sector organizations within the guidelines set up by a board of directors or similar governing body. Plan, direct, or coordinate operational activities at the highest level of management with the help of subordinate executives and staff managers. Direct and coordinate an organization's financial and budget activities in order to fund operations, maximize investments, and increase efficiency. Confer with board members, organization officials, and staff members to discuss issues, coordinate activities, and resolve problems. Analyze operations to evaluate performance of a company and its staff in meeting objectives and to determine areas of potential cost reduction, program improvement, or policy change. Direct, plan, and implement policies, objectives, and activities of organizations or businesses in order to ensure continuing operations, to maximize returns on investments, and to increase productivity. Prepare budgets for approval, including those for funding and implementation of programs. Direct and coordinate activities of businesses or departments concerned with production, pricing, sales, and/or distribution of products. Negotiate or approve contracts and

Enterprising

agreements with suppliers, distributors, federal and state agencies, and other organizational entities. Review reports submitted by staff members in order to recommend approval or to suggest changes. Appoint department heads or managers and assign or delegate responsibilities to them. Direct human resources activities, including the approval of human resource plans and activities, the selection of directors and other high-level staff, and establishment and organization of major departments. Preside over or serve on boards of directors, management committees, or other governing boards. Prepare and present reports concerning activities, expenses, budgets, government statutes and rulings, and other items affecting businesses or program services. Establish departmental responsibilities and coordinate functions among departments and sites. Implement corrective action plans to solve organizational or departmental problems. Coordinate the development and implementation of budgetary control systems, recordkeeping systems, and other administrative control processes. Direct non-merchandising departments such as advertising, purchasing, credit, and accounting. Deliver speeches, write articles, and present information at meetings or conventions in order to promote services, exchange ideas, and accomplish objectives.

3. Logisticians

Personality Type: No data available

Earnings: $63,430
Growth: 13.2%
Annual Openings: 7,000

Most Common Education/Training Level: Bachelor's degree

Analyze and coordinate the logistical functions of a firm or organization. Responsible for the **entire life cycle of a product, including acquisition, distribution, internal allocation, delivery, and final disposal of resources.** Maintain and develop positive business relationships with a customer's key personnel involved in or directly relevant to a logistics activity. Develop an understanding of customers' needs and take actions to ensure that such needs are met. Direct availability and allocation of materials, supplies, and finished products. Collaborate with other departments as necessary to meet customer requirements, to take advantage of sales opportunities, or, in the case of shortages, to minimize negative impacts on a business. Protect and control proprietary materials. Review logistics performance with customers against targets, benchmarks, and service agreements. Develop and implement technical project management tools such as plans, schedules, and responsibility and compliance matrices. Direct team activities, establishing task priorities, scheduling and tracking work assignments, providing guidance, and ensuring the availability of resources. Report project plans, progress, and results. Direct and support the compilation and analysis of technical source data necessary for product development. Explain proposed solutions to customers, management, or other interested parties through written proposals and oral presentations. Provide project management services, including the provision and analysis of technical data. Develop proposals that include documentation for estimates. Plan, organize, and execute logistics support activities such as maintenance planning, repair analysis, and test equipment recommendations. Participate in the assessment and review of design alternatives and design change proposal impacts. Support the development of training materials and technical manuals. Stay informed of logistics technology advances and apply appropriate technology in order to improve logistics processes. Redesign the movement of goods in order to maximize value and minimize costs. Manage subcontractor activities, reviewing proposals, developing performance specifications, and serving as liaisons between subcontractors and organizations. Manage the logistical aspects of product life cycles, including coordination or provisioning of samples and the minimization of obsolescence.

4. Transportation, Storage, and Distribution Managers

Personality Type:
Enterprising–Conventional–Realistic

Earnings: $73,080
Growth: 12.7%
Annual Openings: 15,000

Most Common Education/Training Level:
Work experience in a related occupation

Job Specializations

Storage and Distribution Managers. Plan, direct, and coordinate the storage and distribution operations within an organization or the activities of organizations that are engaged in storing and distributing materials and products. Supervise the activities of workers engaged in receiving, storing, testing, and shipping products or materials. Plan, develop, and implement warehouse safety and security programs and activities. Review invoices, work orders, consumption reports, and demand forecasts to estimate peak delivery periods and to issue work assignments. Schedule and monitor air or surface pickup, delivery, or distribution of products or materials. Interview, select, and train warehouse and supervisory personnel. Confer with department heads to coordinate warehouse activities, such as production, sales, records control, and purchasing. Respond to customers' or shippers' questions and complaints regarding storage and distribution services. Inspect physical conditions of warehouses, vehicle fleets, and equipment and order testing, maintenance, repair, or replacement as necessary. Develop and document standard and emergency operating procedures for receiving, handling, storing, shipping, or salvaging products or materials. Examine products or materials to estimate quantities or weight and type of container required for storage or transport. Negotiate with carriers, warehouse operators, and insurance company representatives for services and preferential rates. Issue shipping instructions and provide routing information to ensure that delivery times and locations are coordinated. Examine invoices and shipping manifests for conformity to tariff and customs regulations. Prepare and manage departmental budgets. Prepare or direct preparation of correspondence; reports; and operations, maintenance, and safety manuals. Arrange for necessary shipping documentation and contact customs officials to effect release of shipments. Advise sales and billing departments of transportation charges for customers' accounts. Evaluate freight costs and the inventory costs associated with transit times to ensure that costs are appropriate. Participate in setting transportation and service rates. Track and trace goods while they are en route to their destinations, expediting orders when necessary. Arrange for storage facilities when required.

Transportation Managers. Plan, direct, and coordinate the transportation operations within an organization or the activities of organizations that provide transportation services. Direct activities related to dispatching, routing, and tracking transportation vehicles such as aircraft and railroad cars. Plan, organize, and manage the work of subordinate staff to ensure that the work is accomplished in a manner consistent with organizational requirements. Direct

Enterprising

investigations to verify and resolve customer or shipper complaints. Serve as contact persons for all workers within assigned territories. Implement schedule and policy changes. Collaborate with other managers and staff members to formulate and implement policies, procedures, goals, and objectives. Monitor operations to ensure that staff members comply with administrative policies and procedures, safety rules, union contracts, and government regulations. Promote safe work activities by conducting safety audits, attending company safety meetings, and meeting with individual staff members. Develop criteria, application instructions, procedural manuals, and contracts for federal and state public transportation programs. Monitor spending to ensure that expenses are consistent with approved budgets. Direct and coordinate, through subordinates, activities of operations department to obtain use of equipment, facilities, and human resources. Direct activities of staff performing repairs and maintenance to equipment, vehicles, and facilities. Conduct investigations in cooperation with government agencies to determine causes of transportation accidents and to improve safety procedures. Analyze expenditures and other financial information to develop plans, policies, and budgets for increasing profits and improving services. Negotiate and authorize contracts with equipment and materials suppliers and monitor contract fulfillment. Supervise workers assigning tariff classifications and preparing billing. Set operations policies and standards, including determination of safety procedures for the handling of dangerous goods. Recommend or authorize capital expenditures for acquisition of new equipment or property to increase efficiency and services of operations department. Prepare management recommendations, such as proposed fee and tariff increases or schedule changes.

Conventional Majors

Accounting

Personality Type: Conventional–Enterprising

Useful Facts About the Major

Prepares individuals to practice the profession of accounting and to perform related business functions.

Related CIP Program: 52.0301 Accounting

Specializations in the Major: Accounting computer systems; auditing; cost accounting; financial reporting; forensic accounting; taxation.

Typical Sequence of College Courses: English composition, business writing, introduction to psychology, principles of microeconomics, principles of macroeconomics, calculus for business and social sciences, statistics for business and social sciences, introduction to management information systems, introduction to accounting, legal environment of business, principles of management and organization, operations management, strategic management, business finance, introduction to marketing, cost accounting, auditing, taxation of individuals, taxation of corporations, partnerships and estates.

Typical Sequence of High School Courses: English, algebra, geometry, trigonometry, science, foreign language, computer science.

Career Snapshot

Accountants maintain the financial records of an organization and supervise the recording of transactions. They provide information about the fiscal condition and trends of the organization, and they devise the figures for tax forms and financial reports. They advise management and therefore need good communication skills. A bachelor's degree is sufficient preparation for many entry-level jobs, but some employers prefer a master's degree. Accountants with diverse skills may advance to management after a few years. The job outlook is generally good.

Useful Averages for the Related Jobs

- **Annual Earnings:** $54,500
- **Growth:** 19.9%
- **Self-Employed:** 9.3%
- **Part-Time:** 22.0%
- **Verbal Skill Rating:** 64.1
- **Math Skill Rating:** 62.3

Other Details About the Related Jobs

Total Annual Job Openings: 173,000

Interest Area: 04 Business and Administration; 06 Finance and Insurance; 07 Government and Public Administration

Skills—Management of financial resources; mathematics; systems analysis; judgment and decision making; operations analysis; time management. **Values**—Working conditions; compensation; advancement; authority; responsibility; ability utilization. **Work Conditions**—Indoors, environmentally controlled; sitting.

Related Jobs

1. Accountants and Auditors

Personality Type:
Conventional–Enterprising–Investigative

Earnings: $54,630
Growth: 22.4%
Annual Openings: 157,000

Most Common Education/Training Level:
Bachelor's degree

Job Specializations

Accountants. Analyze financial information and prepare financial reports to determine or maintain record of assets, liabilities, profit and loss, tax liability, or other financial activities within an organization. Prepare, examine, or analyze accounting records, financial statements, or other financial reports to assess accuracy, completeness, and conformance to reporting and procedural standards. Compute taxes owed and prepare tax returns, ensuring compliance with payment, reporting, or other tax requirements. Analyze business operations, trends, costs, revenues, financial commitments, and obligations to project future revenues and expenses or to provide advice. Report to management regarding the finances of establishment. Establish tables of accounts and assign entries to proper accounts. Develop, maintain, and analyze budgets, preparing periodic reports that compare budgeted costs to actual costs. Develop, implement, modify, and document recordkeeping and accounting systems, making use of current computer technology. Prepare forms and manuals for accounting and book-keeping personnel and direct their work activities. Survey operations to ascertain accounting needs and to recommend, develop, or maintain solutions to business and financial problems. Work as Internal Revenue Service (IRS) agents.

Advise management about issues such as resource utilization, tax strategies, and the assumptions underlying budget forecasts. Provide internal and external auditing services for businesses or individuals. Advise clients in areas such as compensation, employee health-care benefits, the design of accounting or data processing systems, or long-range tax or estate plans. Investigate bankruptcies and other complex financial transactions and prepare reports summarizing the findings. Represent clients before taxing authorities and provide support during litigation involving financial issues. Appraise, evaluate, and inventory real property and equipment, recording information such as the description, value, and location of property. Maintain or examine the records of government agencies. Serve as bankruptcy trustees or business valuators.

Auditors. Examine and analyze accounting records to determine financial status of establishment and prepare financial reports concerning operating procedures. Collect and analyze data to detect deficient controls; duplicated effort; extravagance; fraud; or non-compliance with laws, regulations, and management policies. Report to management about asset utilization and audit results and recommend changes in operations and financial activities. Prepare detailed reports on audit findings. Review data about material assets, net worth, liabilities, capital stock, surplus, income, and expenditures. Inspect account books and accounting systems for efficiency, effectiveness, and use of accepted accounting procedures to record transactions. Examine and evaluate financial and information systems, recommending controls to ensure system reliability and data integrity. Supervise auditing of establishments and determine scope of investigation required. Prepare, analyze, and verify annual reports, financial statements, and other records, using accepted accounting and statistical procedures to assess financial condition and facilitate financial planning. Confer with company officials about financial and regulatory matters. Inspect cash on hand, notes receivable and payable, negotiable securities, and canceled checks to confirm that records are accurate. Examine inventory to verify journal and ledger entries. Examine whether the organization's objectives are reflected in its management activities and whether employees understand the objectives. Examine records and interview workers to ensure recording of transactions and compliance with laws and regulations. Direct activities of personnel engaged in filing, recording, compiling, and transmitting financial records. Produce up-to-the-minute information, using internal computer systems, to allow management to base decisions on actual, not historical, data. Conduct pre-implementation audits to determine if systems and programs under development will work as planned. Review taxpayer accounts and conduct audits on site, by correspondence, or by summoning taxpayer to office. Evaluate taxpayer finances to determine tax liability, using knowledge of interest and discount rates, annuities, valuation of stocks and bonds, and amortization valuation of depletable assets.

2. Budget Analysts

Personality Type:
Conventional–Enterprising–Realistic

Earnings: $61,430
Growth: 13.5%
Annual Openings: 6,000

Most Common Education/Training Level:
Bachelor's degree

Examine budget estimates for completeness, accuracy, and conformance with procedures and regulations. Analyze budgeting and accounting reports for the purpose of maintaining expenditure controls. Direct the preparation of regular and special budget reports. Consult with managers to ensure that budget adjustments are made in accordance with program changes. Match appropriations for specific programs with appropriations for broader programs, including items for emergency funds. Provide advice and technical assistance with cost analysis, fiscal allocation, and budget preparation. Summarize budgets and submit recommendations for the approval or disapproval of funds requests. Seek new ways to improve efficiency and increase profits. Review operating budgets to analyze trends affecting budget needs. Perform cost-benefit analyses to compare operating programs, review financial requests, or explore alternative financing methods. Interpret budget directives and establish policies for carrying out directives. Compile and analyze accounting records and other data to determine the financial resources required to implement a program. Testify before examining and fund-granting authorities, clarifying and promoting the proposed budgets.

3. Credit Analysts

Personality Type:
Conventional–Enterprising–Investigative

Earnings: $52,350
Growth: 3.6%
Annual Openings: 3,000

Most Common Education/Training Level:
Bachelor's degree

Analyze current credit data and financial statements of individuals or firms to determine the degree of risk involved in extending credit or lending money. Prepare reports with this credit information for use in decision-making.

Evaluate customer records and recommend payment plans based on earnings, savings data, payment history, and purchase activity. Confer with credit association and other business representatives to exchange credit information. Complete loan applications, including credit analyses and summaries of loan requests, and submit to loan committees for approval. Generate financial ratios, using computer programs, to evaluate customers' financial status. Review individual or commercial customer files to identify and select delinquent accounts for collection. Compare liquidity, profitability, and credit histories of establishments being evaluated with those of similar establishments in the same industries and geographic locations. Consult with customers to resolve complaints and verify financial and credit transactions. Analyze financial data such as income growth, quality of management, and market share to determine expected profitability of loans.

4. Financial Examiners

Personality Type:
Enterprising–Social–Conventional

Earnings: $65,370
Growth: 9.5%
Annual Openings: 3,000

Most Common Education/Training Level:
Bachelor's degree

Enforce or ensure compliance with laws and regulations governing financial and securities institutions and financial and real estate transactions. May examine, verify correctness of, or establish authenticity of records. Investigate activities of institutions in order to enforce laws and regulations and to ensure legality of transactions and operations or financial solvency. Review and analyze new, proposed, or revised laws, regulations, policies, and procedures in order to interpret their meaning and determine their impact. Plan, supervise, and review work of assigned subordinates. Recommend actions to ensure compliance with laws and regulations or to protect solvency of institutions. Examine the minutes of meetings of directors, stockholders, and committees in order to investigate the specific authority extended at various levels of management. Prepare reports, exhibits, and other supporting schedules that detail an institution's safety and soundness, compliance with laws and regulations, and recommended solutions to questionable financial conditions. Review balance sheets, operating income and expense accounts, and loan documentation in order to confirm institution assets and liabilities. Review audit reports of internal and external auditors in order to monitor adequacy of scope of reports or to discover specific weaknesses in internal routines. Train other examiners in the financial examination process. Establish guidelines for procedures and policies that comply with new and revised regulations and direct their implementation. Direct and participate in formal and informal meetings with bank directors, trustees, senior management, counsels, outside accountants, and consultants in order to gather information and discuss findings. Verify and inspect cash reserves, assigned collateral, and bank-owned securities in order to check internal control procedures. Review applications for mergers, acquisitions, establishment of new institutions, acceptance in Federal Reserve System, or registration of securities sales in order to determine their public interest value and conformance to regulations and recommend acceptance or rejection. Resolve problems concerning the overall financial integrity of banking institutions, including loan investment portfolios, capital, earnings, and specific or large troubled accounts.

5. Tax Examiners, Collectors, and Revenue Agents

Personality Type:
Conventional–Enterprising–Investigative

Earnings: $45,620
Growth: 5.1%
Annual Openings: 4,000

Most Common Education/Training Level:
Bachelor's degree

Determine tax liability or collect taxes from individuals or business firms according to prescribed laws and regulations. Collect taxes from individuals or businesses according to prescribed laws and regulations. Maintain knowledge of tax code changes and of accounting procedures and theory to properly evaluate financial information. Maintain records for each case, including contacts, telephone numbers, and actions taken. Confer with taxpayers or their representatives to discuss the issues, laws, and regulations involved in returns and to resolve problems with returns. Contact taxpayers by mail or telephone to address discrepancies and to request supporting documentation. Send notices to taxpayers when accounts are delinquent. Notify taxpayers of any overpayment or underpayment and either issue a refund or request further payment. Conduct independent field audits and investigations of income tax returns to verify information or to amend tax liabilities. Review filed tax returns to determine whether claimed tax credits and deductions are allowed by law. Review selected tax returns to determine the nature and extent of audits to be performed on them. Enter tax return information into computers for processing. Examine accounting systems and records to determine whether accounting methods used were appropriate and in compliance with statutory provisions. Process individual and corporate income tax returns and sales and excise tax returns. Impose payment deadlines on delinquent taxpayers and monitor payments to ensure that deadlines are met. Check tax forms to verify that names and taxpayer identification numbers are correct, that computations have been performed correctly, or that amounts match those on supporting documentation. Examine and analyze tax assets and liabilities to determine resolution of delinquent tax problems. Recommend criminal prosecutions or civil penalties. Determine appropriate methods of debt settlement, such as offers of compromise, wage garnishment, or seizure and sale of property. Secure a taxpayer's agreement to discharge a tax assessment or submit contested determinations to other administrative or judicial conferees for appeals hearings. Prepare briefs and assist in searching and seizing records to prepare charges and documentation for court cases.

Actuarial Science

Personality Type: Conventional–Investigative

Useful Facts About the Major

Focuses on the mathematical and statistical analysis of risk and their applications to insurance and other business management problems.

Related CIP Program: 52.1304 Actuarial Science

Specializations in the Major: Insurance; investment.

Typical Sequence of College Courses: Calculus, linear algebra, advanced calculus, introduction to computer science, introduction to probability, introduction to actuarial mathematics, mathematical statistics, applied regression, actuarial models, introduction to accounting, principles of microeconomics, principles of macroeconomics, financial management, programming in C, investment analysis, price theory, income and employment theory.

Typical Sequence of High School Courses: English, algebra, geometry, trigonometry, science, pre-calculus, calculus, computer science.

Career Snapshot

Actuarial science is the analysis of mathematical data to predict the likelihood of certain events, such as death, accident, or disability. Insurance companies are the main employers of actuaries; actuaries determine how much the insurers charge for policies. The usual entry route is a bachelor's degree, but actuaries continue to study and sit for exams to upgrade their professional standing over the course of 5 to 10 years.

The occupation is expected to grow at a good pace, and there will probably be many openings for those who are able to pass the series of exams.

Useful Averages for the Related Job

- **Annual Earnings:** $82,800
- **Growth:** 23.2%
- **Self-Employed:** 0.0%
- **Part-Time:** 2.3%
- **Verbal Skill Rating:** 71.5
- **Math Skill Rating:** 89.0

Other Details About the Related Job

Total Annual Job Openings: 3,000

Interest Area: 15 Scientific Research, Engineering, and Mathematics

Skills—Instructing; monitoring; writing; mathematics; learning strategies; active learning. **Values**—Autonomy; working conditions; advancement; independence; supervision, human relations; recognition. **Work Conditions**—Indoors, environmentally controlled; sitting.

Related Job

Actuaries

Personality Type:
Conventional–Investigative–Realistic

Earnings: $82,800
Growth: 23.2%
Annual Openings: 3,000

Most Common Education/Training Level: Work experience plus degree

Analyze statistical data, such as mortality, accident, sickness, disability, and retirement rates, and construct probability tables to forecast risk and liability for payment of future benefits. May ascertain premium rates required and cash reserves necessary to ensure payment of future benefits. Ascertain premium rates required and cash reserves and liabilities necessary to ensure payment of future benefits. Analyze statistical information to estimate mortality, accident, sickness, disability, and retirement rates. Design, review, and help administer insurance, annuity, and pension plans, determining financial soundness and calculating premiums. Collaborate with programmers, underwriters, accounts, claims experts, and senior management to help companies develop plans for new lines of business or improving existing business. Determine or help determine company policy and explain complex technical matters to company executives, government officials, shareholders, policy-holders, or the public. Testify before public agencies on proposed legislation affecting businesses. Provide advice to clients on a contract basis, working as a consultant. Testify in court as expert witness or to provide legal evidence on matters such as the value of potential lifetime earnings of a person who is disabled or killed in an accident. Construct probability tables for events such as fires, natural disasters, and unemployment, based on analysis of statistical data and other pertinent information. Determine policy contract provisions for each type of insurance. Manage credit and help price corporate security offerings. Provide expertise to help financial institutions manage risks and maximize returns associated with investment products or credit offerings. Determine equitable basis for distributing surplus earnings under participating insurance and annuity contracts in mutual companies. Explain changes in contract provisions to customers.

APPENDIX A

Resources for Further Exploration

The facts and pointers in this book provide a good beginning to the subject of college majors and related jobs that may suit your personality. If you want additional details, we suggest you consult some of the resources listed here.

Facts About Majors and Careers

College Majors Handbook with Real Career Paths and Payoffs, by Neeta P. Fogg, Ph.D.; Paul E. Harrington, Ed.D.; and Thomas F. Harrington, Ph.D. (JIST): This book, based on a U.S. Census Bureau study of 150,000 college graduates, describes 60 majors and the courses they require; discusses jobs that graduates actually obtain; and gives information on employers, tasks, and salaries.

The College Entrance Examination Board describes college majors and the careers related to them at http://www.collegeboard.com/csearch/majors_careers/profiles.

Occupational Outlook Handbook (or the *OOH*) (JIST): Updated every two years by the U.S. Department of Labor, this book provides descriptions for 270 major jobs covering more than 85 percent of the workforce.

O*NET Dictionary of Occupational Titles (JIST): The only printed source of the more than 900 jobs described in the U.S. Department of Labor's Occupational Information Network database. It covers all the jobs in the book you're now reading, but it offers more topics than we were able to fit here.

New Guide for Occupational Exploration (JIST): An important career reference that allows you to explore all major O*NET jobs based on your interests. The information in this book is based on the 16 Department of Education clusters that relate your interests to careers. (An outline of the Interest Areas and Work Groups included appears in Appendix C.)

Educational and Career Decision Making and Planning

90-Minute College Major Matcher, by Laurence Shatkin, Ph.D. (JIST): This book can help you identify majors that are consistent with your skills and your favorite high school courses.

College Majors Scorecard, by Neeta P. Fogg, Ph.D.; Paul E. Harrington, Ed.D.; and Thomas F. Harrington, Ph.D. (JIST): This 147-item assessment leads directly to the 49 most common college majors. Based on the kinds of work activities that each major is most likely to lead to, it helps you pick a major by making a connection between your knowledge and abilities, your choice of major, and your future career options.

50 Best Jobs for Your Personality, by Michael Farr and Laurence Shatkin, Ph.D. (JIST): This book is built around the same Holland personality types as the book you're now reading and includes lists and descriptions of high-paying and high-growth jobs linked to those personality types.

Best Resumes for College Students and New Grads, by Louise M. Kursmark (JIST): Containing sample resumes and more, this book describes the skills and attributes that employers find valuable in the workplace and shows how to demonstrate them in writing.

One-Hour College Application Essay, by Jan Melnik (JIST): This book helps students quickly craft an effective application essay with targeted questions, worksheets, quick-start strategies, advice from admissions directors, and many examples.

200 Best Jobs for College Graduates, by Michael Farr with database work by Laurence Shatkin, Ph.D. (JIST): Identify jobs that may be right for you with more than 60 "best jobs" lists, based on earnings, growth, openings, education, interests, and more, and then browse more than 200 information-packed job descriptions.

APPENDIX B

Majors Sorted by Three-Letter Personality Code

This list can identify the best college majors in this book that may appeal to you. It is organized by the one-, two-, and three-letter RIASEC personality codes assigned to majors. (Learn about these codes in Part I).

If you are aware of your dominant personality type (see Part II), you may find it helpful to make a note of all majors that have RIASEC codes beginning with the letter for your dominant type. If you are aware of one or more additional personality types that you resemble, you may want to pay special attention to the majors that share their second or third RIASEC codes (either or both) with you. You may also find it useful to consider majors that have your dominant personality type as their second or third RIASEC code. For example, if you describe yourself as IR, you may want to look not only at majors coded IR (such as Biochemistry) or IR_ (such as Computer Engineering, coded IRC), but also at the major that has R as its first code, Civil Engineering (coded RIE).

This listing is based on the coding used by the O*NET database of the U.S. Department of Labor to classify the occupations related to the majors. Other publishers may not create the exact same set of linkages between RIASEC codes and majors or occupations. For example, some sales jobs that are coded as Social by Psychological Assessment Resources, Inc., the publisher of the *Self-Directed Search,* are coded as Enterprising by O*NET.

Here is a reminder of the personality type that each code letter represents:

R = Realistic

I = Investigative

A = Artistic

S = Social

E = Enterprising

C = Conventional

RIASEC Code	College Major	RIASEC Code	College Major
RIE	Civil Engineering	SIA	Women's Studies
I	Medicine	SA	Early Childhood Education
IR	Biochemistry	ERI	Architecture
IR	Microbiology	ERI	Landscape Architecture
IRE	Aeronautical/Aerospace Engineering	ERI	Petroleum Engineering
IRE	Electrical Engineering	EIR	Industrial Engineering
IRC	Computer Engineering	EA	Advertising
IRC	Computer Science	EAS	Public Relations
IS	Physician Assisting	ES	Health Information Systems Administration
ICR	Pharmacy	ES	Hospital/Health Facilities Administration
A	Art	ESC	Human Resources Management
A	English		
A	Industrial Design	ESC	Industrial and Labor Relations
A	Journalism and Mass Communications	EC	Business Management
AE	Communications Studies/Speech	EC	Finance
AES	Drama/Theater Arts	EC	International Business
AES	Film/Cinema Studies	EC	International Relations
SR	Occupational Therapy	EC	Marketing
SRI	Physical Therapy	EC	Public Administration
SI	Graduate Study for College Teaching	EC	Transportation and Logistics Management
SI	Nursing (R.N. Training)	CI	Actuarial Science
SIA	African-American Studies	CE	Accounting
SIA	American Studies		
SIA	Area Studies		
SIA	Humanities		

APPENDIX C

The GOE Interest Areas and Work Groups

As the introduction explains, the GOE is a way of organizing the world of work into large Interest Areas. Within each Interest Area it also identifies more specific Work Groups containing jobs that have a lot in common. In the descriptions of majors in Part IV, you'll find the Interest Areas for the jobs related to each major. We thought you would want to see the complete GOE taxonomy so you would have a sense of the detailed Work Groups belonging to these Interest Areas. In some cases, the Work Groups titles resemble titles of college majors or specializations within majors, so the Work Groups may suggest areas of employment related to a major that interests you.

In the GOE Taxonomy the Interest Areas have two-digit code numbers; the Work Groups have four-digit code numbers beginning with the code number for the Interest Area in which they are classified. These are the 16 GOE Interest Areas and 117 Work Groups:

01 Agriculture and Natural Resources

     01.01 Managerial Work in Agriculture and Natural Resources

     01.02 Resource Science/Engineering for Plants, Animals, and the Environment

     01.03 Resource Technologies for Plants, Animals, and the Environment

     01.04 General Farming

     01.05 Nursery, Groundskeeping, and Pest Control

     01.06 Forestry and Logging

     01.07 Hunting and Fishing

     01.08 Mining and Drilling

02 Architecture and Construction

     02.01 Managerial Work in Architecture and Construction

     02.02 Architectural Design

     02.03 Architecture/Construction Engineering Technologies

     02.04 Construction Crafts

     02.05 Systems and Equipment Installation, Maintenance, and Repair

     02.06 Construction Support/Labor

03 Arts and Communication

        03.01 Managerial Work in Arts and Communication

        03.02 Writing and Editing

        03.03 News, Broadcasting, and Public Relations

        03.04 Studio Art

        03.05 Design

        03.06 Drama

        03.07 Music

        03.08 Dance

        03.09 Media Technology

        03.10 Communications Technology

        03.11 Musical Instrument Repair

04 Business and Administration

        04.01 Managerial Work in General Business

        04.02 Managerial Work in Business Detail

        04.03 Human Resources Support

        04.04 Secretarial Support

        04.05 Accounting, Auditing, and Analytical Support

        04.06 Mathematical Clerical Support

        04.07 Records and Materials Processing

        04.08 Clerical Machine Operation

05 Education and Training

        05.01 Managerial Work in Education

        05.02 Preschool, Elementary, and Secondary Teaching and Instructing

        05.03 Postsecondary and Adult Teaching and Instructing

        05.04 Library Services

        05.05 Archival and Museum Services

        05.06 Counseling, Health, and Fitness Education

06 Finance and Insurance

        06.01 Managerial Work in Finance and Insurance

        06.02 Finance/Insurance Investigation and Analysis

        06.03 Finance/Insurance Records Processing

        06.04 Finance/Insurance Customer Service

        06.05 Finance/Insurance Sales and Support

07 Government and Public Administration

      07.01 Managerial Work in Government and Public Administration

      07.02 Public Planning

      07.03 Regulations Enforcement

      07.04 Public Administration Clerical Support

08 Health Science

      08.01 Managerial Work in Medical and Health Services

      08.02 Medicine and Surgery

      08.03 Dentistry

      08.04 Health Specialties

      08.05 Animal Care

      08.06 Medical Technology

      08.07 Medical Therapy

      08.08 Patient Care and Assistance

      08.09 Health Protection and Promotion

09 Hospitality, Tourism, and Recreation

      09.01 Managerial Work in Hospitality and Tourism

      09.02 Recreational Services

      09.03 Hospitality and Travel Services

      09.04 Food and Beverage Preparation

      09.05 Food and Beverage Service

      09.06 Sports

      09.07 Barber and Beauty Services

10 Human Service

      10.01 Counseling and Social Work

      10.02 Religious Work

      10.03 Child/Personal Care and Services

      10.04 Client Interviewing

11 Information Technology

      11.01 Managerial Work in Information Technology

      11.02 Information Technology Specialties

      11.03 Digital Equipment Repair

12 Law and Public Safety

    12.01 Managerial Work in Law and Public Safety

    12.02 Legal Practice and Justice Administration

    12.03 Legal Support

    12.04 Law Enforcement and Public Safety

    12.05 Safety and Security

    12.06 Emergency Responding

    12.07 Military

13 Manufacturing

    13.01 Managerial Work in Manufacturing

    13.02 Machine Setup and Operation

    13.03 Production Work, Assorted Materials Processing

    13.04 Welding, Brazing, and Soldering

    13.05 Production Machining Technology

    13.06 Production Precision Work

    13.07 Production Quality Control

    13.08 Graphic Arts Production

    13.09 Hands-On Work, Assorted Materials

    13.10 Woodworking Technology

    13.11 Apparel, Shoes, Leather, and Fabric Care

    13.12 Electrical and Electronic Repair

    13.13 Machinery Repair

    13.14 Vehicle and Facility Mechanical Work

    13.15 Medical and Technical Equipment Repair

    13.16 Utility Operation and Energy Distribution

    13.17 Loading, Moving, Hoisting, and Conveying

14 Retail and Wholesale Sales and Service

    14.01 Managerial Work in Retail/Wholesale Sales and Service

    14.02 Technical Sales

    14.03 General Sales

    14.04 Personal Soliciting

    14.05 Purchasing

    14.06 Customer Service

15 Scientific Research, Engineering, and Mathematics

    15.01 Managerial Work in Scientific Research, Engineering, and Mathematics

    15.02 Physical Sciences

15.03 Life Sciences

15.04 Social Sciences

15.05 Physical Science Laboratory Technology

15.06 Mathematics and Data Analysis

15.07 Research and Design Engineering

15.08 Industrial and Safety Engineering

15.09 Engineering Technology

16 Transportation, Distribution, and Logistics

16.01 Managerial Work in Transportation

16.02 Air Vehicle Operation

16.03 Truck Driving

16.04 Rail Vehicle Operation

16.05 Water Vehicle Operation

16.06 Other Services Requiring Driving

16.07 Transportation Support Work

APPENDIX D

Definitions of Skills Used in Descriptions of Majors

In the Part IV descriptions of majors, you can see the top skills required by the jobs related to each major. Because some of the skill names may not be completely familiar to you, we present here the definitions of all the skills referred to in this book. Note that not every skill included in the O*NET database is included in this book; among college-level jobs, certain skills tend to dominate.

Skill Name	Definition
Active Learning	Understanding the implications of new information for both current and future problem-solving and decision-making.
Active Listening	Giving full attention to what other people are saying, taking time to understand the points being made, asking questions as appropriate, and not interrupting at inappropriate times.
Complex Problem Solving	Identifying complex problems and reviewing related information to develop and evaluate options and implement solutions.
Coordination	Adjusting actions in relation to others' actions.
Critical Thinking	Using logic and reasoning to identify the strengths and weaknesses of alternative solutions, conclusions, or approaches to problems.
Installation	Installing equipment, machines, wiring, or programs to meet specifications.
Instructing	Teaching others how to do something.
Judgment and Decision Making	Considering the relative costs and benefits of potential actions to choose the most appropriate one.
Learning Strategies	Selecting and using training/instructional methods and procedures appropriate for the situation when learning or teaching new things.

(continued)

(continued)

Skill Name	Definition
Management of Financial Resources	Determining how money will be spent to get the work done and accounting for these expenditures.
Management of Material Resources	Obtaining and seeing to the appropriate use of equipment, facilities, and materials needed to do certain work.
Management of Personnel Resources	Motivating, developing, and directing people as they work; identifying the best people for the job.
Mathematics	Using mathematics to solve problems.
Mathematics	Knowledge of arithmetic, algebra, geometry, calculus, and statistics and their applications.
Monitoring	Monitoring/assessing your performance or that of other individuals or organizations to make improvements or take corrective action.
Negotiation	Bringing others together and trying to reconcile differences.
Operations Analysis	Analyzing needs and product requirements to create a design.
Persuasion	Persuading others to change their minds or behavior.
Programming	Writing computer programs for various purposes.
Quality Control Analysis	Conducting tests and inspections of products, services, or processes to evaluate quality or performance.
Reading Comprehension	Understanding written sentences and paragraphs in work related documents.
Science	Using scientific rules and methods to solve problems.
Service Orientation	Actively looking for ways to help people.
Social Perceptiveness	Being aware of others' reactions and understanding why they react as they do.
Speaking	Talking to others to convey information effectively.
Systems Analysis	Determining how a system should work and how changes in conditions, operations, and the environment will affect outcomes.
Systems Evaluation	Identifying measures or indicators of system performance and the actions needed to improve or correct performance relative to the goals of the system.
Technology Design	Generating or adapting equipment and technology to serve user needs.

Skill Name	Definition
Time Management	Managing one's own time and the time of others.
Troubleshooting	Determining causes of operating errors and deciding what to do about them.
Writing	Communicating effectively in writing as appropriate for the needs of the audience.

APPENDIX E

Definitions of Values Used in Descriptions of Majors

Each description of a major in Part IV includes a list of the most important work-related values associated with the jobs that are linked to the major, according to O*NET. To help you understand these values, we present here the O*NET definition of each value referred to in this book.

Value Name	Definition
Ability Utilization	Workers on this job make use of their individual abilities.
Achievement	Workers on this job get a feeling of accomplishment.
Activity	Workers on this job are busy all the time.
Advancement	Workers on this job have opportunities for advancement.
Authority	Workers on this job give directions and instructions to others.
Autonomy	Workers on this job plan their work with little supervision.
Compensation	Workers on this job are paid well in comparison with other workers.
Co-workers	Workers on this job have co-workers who are easy to get along with.
Creativity	Workers on this job try out their own ideas.
Independence	Workers on this job do their work alone.
Recognition	Workers on this job receive recognition for the work they do.
Responsibility	Workers on this job make decisions on their own.
Social Service	Workers on this job have work where they do things for other people.
Social Status	Workers on this job are looked up to by others in their company and their community.
Supervision, Human Relations	Workers on this job have supervisors who back up their workers with management.
Variety	Workers on this job have something different to do every day.
Working Conditions	Workers on this job have good working conditions.

Index

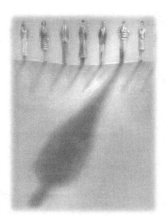

D

E